THE NAMES OF COMEDY

ANNE BARTON

The Names of Comedy

UNIVERSITY OF TORONTO PRESS
Toronto Buffalo

© University of Toronto Press 1990
Toronto Buffalo
Printed in Canada
ISBN 0–8020–5657–1

Printed on acid-free paper

Canadian Cataloguing in Publication Data

Barton, Anne
The names of comedy

(The Alexander lectures)
Expanded version of four lectures entitled Comedy
and the naming of parts presented as the Alexander
memorial lectures at University College, Toronto in
Nov. 1983.
ISBN 0–8020–5657–1

1. Names, Personal, in literature. 2. Characters
and characteristics in literature. 3. English
drama (Comedy) – History and criticism. 4. English
drama – To 1500 – History and criticism. 5. English
drama – Early modern and Elizabethan, 1500–1600 –
History and criticism. 6. English drama – 17th
century – History and criticism. I. Title.
II. Series.

PR635.N35B37 1990   822'.0523'09   C89–095366–X

To John Kerrigan

Si (como el griego afirma en el Cratilo)
El nombre es arquetipo de la cosa,
En las letras de *rosa* está la rosa,
Y todo el Nilo en la palabra *Nilo*.

Jorge Luis Borges   'El Golem'

CONTENTS

ACKNOWLEDGMENTS

This book springs directly out of earlier work on Ben Jonson and is in some ways complementary to my *Ben Jonson, Dramatist* (1984), in particular chapter 8 ('Names: The Chapter Interloping'). For the stimulus to begin it, however, I am indebted to University College, University of Toronto, and the great privilege of giving the Alexander Memorial Lectures there in November 1983. *The Names of Comedy* is a much expanded version of those four lectures, originally called 'Comedy and the Naming of Parts,' and concentrating on classical comedy, Shakespeare, and Jonson. The focus of the present book remains English comedy, and its classical antecedents, from the beginnings to 1642. I should like to thank everyone at the University of Toronto involved with my stay there for making it such a rewarding and happy occasion, in particular the then Principal of University College, Professor G.P. Richardson, Ann Hutchison, and James Carley, who quickly became friends, and Ron Bryden, an old friend felicitously re-encountered.

I should also like to thank the Folger Shakespeare Library, which generously provided me with an apartment in Washington DC during my tenure of a visiting fellowship at the Folger in the autumn of 1983, and the typewriter on which much of the Alexander Lectures was written. I am particularly grateful to John Andrews for all his help.

A number of people have read *The Names of Comedy* either in part or as a whole before publication, and I have benefited greatly from their comments and suggestions. The criticism and advice of Peter Holland and Jeremy Maule was especially valuable. I am also deeply indebted to Neil Hopkinson, who read the entire typescript from a classicist's point of view, and rescued me from a number of blunders and misapprehensions. Any that remain are to be attributed to my own stubbornness, not to any want of vigilance on his part. I should also like to thank John Barton, Richard Beadle, Warren Boutcher, Michael Cordner, Peter Dronke, George Forrest, Nicholas Grene, Eric Handley, Alison Hennegan, Roger Holdsworth, John Marenbon, Ruth Padel, Sheila Stern, and the Museum of the Theatre, London, for material, suggestions, and advice. Also (although for none of these things) Tarlton.

Prudence Tracy at the University of Toronto Press befriended this book from the start, and kept me working at it despite other intervening commitments. At a later stage, Fred Unwalla was an acute and careful copy-editor. I should like to thank Simon Alderson for taking time out from his own research to prepare the indexes.

Unless otherwise indicated, dates given for English plays before 1700 are those suggested in *Annals of English Drama 975–1700*, by Alfred Harbage, revised by S. Schoenbaum (London 1964). Quotations from Shakespeare in the text refer to the Riverside Edition, edited by G. Blakemore Evans et al (Boston 1974). For ease of reference, those from Greek and classical Latin authors (with the exception of Aristophanes and Herodotus) are based upon the editions in the Loeb Classical Library. It has been my policy with respect to other plays to quote from the best available text in each instance, despite inevitable variations in the degree of modernization. The lines from *Old Possum's Book of Practical Cats*, by T.S. Eliot, are reprinted by permission of Faber and Faber Ltd and of Harcourt Brace Jovanovich.

As with *Ben Jonson, Dramatist*, by far my greatest obligation is to John Kerrigan, who has discussed and also read *The Names of Comedy* more times than I like to think, at all the different stages of its life. He has provided more acute criticism over a longer period, and saved me from more mistakes than anyone else. This book is (once again) dedicated to him.

Trinity College
Cambridge

April 1989

THE NAMES OF COMEDY

INTRODUCTION

According to 'Old Possum,' also known by the names of Thomas Stearns, T.S., and 'Tom' Eliot, 'the naming of Cats is a difficult matter.'[1] Cats, or at least sociable cats, as opposed to anonymous and solitary strays, require no fewer than 'THREE DIFFERENT NAMES':

> First of all, there's the name that the family use daily,
>   Such as Peter, Augustus, Alonzo or James,
> Such as Victor or Jonathan, George or Bill Bailey –
>   All of them sensible everyday names.
> There are fancier names if you think they sound sweeter,
>   Some for the gentlemen, some for the dames:
> Such as Plato, Admetus, Electra, Demeter –
>   But all of them sensible everyday names.

'Old Possum' scorns to notice such well-worn feline designations as 'Fluffy,' 'Snowball,' 'Pussy,' 'Gyb,' or (indeed) 'Tom.' What he calls 'sensible everyday names,' are either orthodox human baptismal names, most of them common, a few inclining towards the rare, or else, in the 'fancier' subdivision, ancient Greek. But none (Eliot, to his credit, resisted the pun) can fully categorize its bearer. So, he claims, a cat also

>   needs a name that's particular,
>   A name that's peculiar, and more dignified,
> Else how can he keep up his tail perpendicular,
>   Or spread out his whiskers, or cherish his pride?
> Of names of this kind, I can give you a quorum,
>   Such as Munkustrap, Quaxo, or Coricopat,

Such as Bombalurina, or else Jellylorum –
Names that never belong to more than one cat.

It might be thought that a cat with the title (say) of 'Augustus Coricopat' would consider itself quite adequately designated: endowed both with a name unique to itself and an ordinary one shared with other individuals.

But above and beyond there's still one name left over
And that is the name that you never will guess;
The name that no human research can discover –
But THE CAT HIMSELF KNOWS, and will never confess.
When you notice a cat in profound meditation,
The reason, I tell you, is always the same:
His mind is engaged in a rapt contemplation
Of the thought, of the thought, of the thought of his name:
His ineffable effable
Effanineffable
Deep and inscrutable singular Name.

This non-human name which both can and cannot be pronounced, effable and ineffable, is an allusion to the Tetragrammaton, or mystical name of God, a word regarded by the Jews as so potent that by the time of Christ it was spoken aloud only once a year, on the Day of Atonement, by the High Priest, as he entered the Holy of Holies. Eliot is also remembering what anthropologists have said about certain primitive societies which believe that a person's essential self is contained within his or her name, a name that ought never to be revealed to strangers, because if it is, its owner's very existence is placed in jeopardy.

In the most extreme manifestation of this belief, an individual is given two names.

One is for ordinary, everyday use and the other, his real name, is kept secret. It may be so secret that the man himself does not know it – it was whispered into his ear by his mother when he was a baby. If a sorcerer discovers the real name he can destroy the man, for instance

4

by magically enticing the name into leaves or straw which he burns or scatters. As the name is turned to ashes in the fire or blown away on the wind, the victim weakens and dies. His real name is his identity and as it disintegrates so does he.[2]

The idea behind this, that one's personality and very self are inextricably linked with one's name, can be traced in almost all ages and parts of the world, not just in primitive societies nor, necessarily, in association with magic and malediction. People still feel oddly protective about the official names that identify them on birth certificates and passports, marriage-licences and, finally, on the death certificate they do not see. They are likely to be even more sensitive about soubriquets: those other, more informal and intimate, names that we give, and accept, to express roles in a particular relationship or small social group.

Children bestow nicknames (usually unflattering) on each other in the playground: 'Carrot-top,' 'Big-Ears,' or 'Piggy.' Although most now are transient, they tend to be remembered by the bearer for life. There are also the pet names exchanged by lovers and close friends: 'Old Possum,' indeed, bestowed on Eliot by Ezra Pound, 'Malculus,' or 'Pippin' and 'Duck' which, astonishingly, is what Byron and Annabella Milbanke called each other in the early days of their marriage. In a letter of January 1787, Mozart addressed his friend Gottfried von Jacquin as

dearest Hikkiti Horky! That is your name, as you must know. We all invented names for ourselves on the journey. Here they are: I am Punkatiti. My wife is Schabla Pumfa. Hofer is Rozka Pumpa, Stadler is Notschibikitschibi. My servant Joseph is Sagadarata. My dog Goukerl is Schomanntzky. Madame Quallenberg is Runzifunzi. Mlle Crux is Rambo Schurimuri. Freistadtler is Gaulimauli. Be so kind as to tell him his name.[3]

Elizabeth I invented a whole series of such private names for her courtiers, animal for the most part. Alençon was 'Frog,' Christopher Hatton 'Sheep,' Lady Norris 'Crow,' and Burghley 'Sprite.'[4] When Helena, in Shakespeare's *All's Well That Ends Well*, imagines a 'world / Of pretty, fond, adoptious christen-

5

doms' (I.1.173–4) which Bertram will enter at court, she is thinking of names of this kind, names shutting her out from a glamorous coterie. Generated by a unique, unrepeatable phase of an individual life, they are, in a sense, the equivalents of Eliot's 'Munkustrap,' 'Quaxo,' and 'Coricopat.' Although few people would lay claim to the secret possession of an 'ineffable ... / Deep and inscrutable singular Name,' they continue to conceal behind their public names others more personal, and to feel, often, that in the latter they are both more vulnerable and more deeply 'there.' The use, sometimes even the knowledge, of such names by persons outside a particular relationship or group is prohibited, a feature that links them, at however great a distance, with those of primitive tribes governed by a name-taboo.

The Nambikwara Indians, as Claude Lévi-Strauss discovered when he went to live among them in the 1940s, had two names. The unimportant, public ones had been conferred on them from outside, by telegraph workers or anthropologists, as an agreed upon means of communication. Lévi-Strauss learned the names they used among themselves only because a little girl who had been struck by one of her play-mates took her revenge by whispering the culprit's 'real' name in the anthropologist's ear. The other little girl then betrayed the first one's name and, before long, Lévi-Strauss had triumphantly learned not only what all the children were called, but most of the adults as well.[5] This is the passage from *Tristes Tropiques* to which Derrida, in *De la Grammatologie*, takes particular exception, maintaining that Lévi-Strauss was led astray by his interest in the Nambikwara as individuals. The anthropologist deluded himself, according to Derrida, by thinking that he could understand these people by gaining a knowledge of their names, when really all he had done was insensitively to violate a tribal preserve, emerging with a code different from the one he (and the telegraph workers) already possessed, but no more important or revelatory. Names are discursive, not magical, to be construed externally as part of a system of discourse, not as though they were bound up with, or might help to explain, the people they designate. To believe otherwise is to impose upon life the conventions of the stage, or at least so his imagery implies.

6

Persistently, in describing the actions of Lévi-Strauss and of the people he was observing, Derrida employs the language of theatre. The children's play group is almost always a 'scène,' one at which Lévi-Strauss, 'un étranger silencieux assiste, immobile.'[6] The anthropologist is established as spectator, even as he is in that later 'mise en scène' where the illiterate Nambikwara chief, as Derrida puts it, is 'jouant la comédie de l'écriture.' The little girl who initially betrays her friend's name to the anthropologist is said to do so 'l'à part' (in an aside) and she herself is labelled 'la tricheuse' (the trickster) – a comic type at least as old as Aristophanes. Whether accidental or intended, this recourse to dramatic terminology is revealing. It points to, and can illuminate, the extent to which theatre audiences are like spectator/anthropologists: concerned, as was Lévi-Strauss, with the discovery of proper names as a means of access to other selves. This is particularly true in comedy, for reasons fundamental to the form.

❋   ❋   ❋

The argument between Derrida and Lévi-Strauss over the status of proper names is, in essence, a very old one. It goes back, in fact, almost to the beginning of Western philosophy, and Plato's dialogue *Cratylus* has for long been recognized as its central text. The *Cratylus* has for its subject the truthful or accidental nature of language. It begins when Hermogenes and Cratylus himself appeal to Socrates to settle their argument about whether names are purely arbitrary and conventional labels for people – initially the view of Hermogenes – or whether, as Cratylus maintains, they express the person named. Before the dialogue begins, Cratylus has already informed his companion, somewhat unkindly, that Hermogenes is not his correct name and that the fact that everyone calls him this is of no importance whatever. Hermogenes finds it both puzzling and a little unsettling to be summarily deprived of his name. He returns to the issue, unprompted, later in the dialogue. Socrates, however, guesses what Cratylus is implying. The name 'Hermogenes' means 'son of Hermes.' Hermogenes was apparently always trying to make

7

money and never succeeding. Therefore, according to Cratylus, his name is nonsense. It cannot, in fact, be his. (Cratylus' own name means something like 'man of power,' and he appears to be rather smugly convinced of its truth.)

Socrates' engagement, through most of the dialogue, is with Hermogenes. By the time he has finished with him, Hermogenes has conceded that names can indeed embody the truth of the thing named. The gods call people and things by the names that are naturally right. Great poets, who are divinely inspired, are particularly sensitive to these designations. The abilities, however, of human name-makers are unequal, and even the most skilled *onomatourgos*, like any other artisan, makes mistakes. Initially correct names, moreover, may become corrupted with time and use, often to the point where their original meaning is lost, or can be recovered only with difficulty. As Socrates goes on explaining to Hermogenes how, nonetheless, the true nature of gods and heroes is often to be deduced from their names, his etymologies become more and more fanciful and far-fetched: that the gods are called *theous*, for instance, from the word for a 'runner,' because sun, moon, earth, stars, and sky, the first deities to be worshipped in Greece, were observed to be always shifting about, or that Poseidon's name means 'foot-bond' (*posi-desmon*) because the original name-giver went out for a walk and found further progress impossible when he got to the sea.[7] Socrates begins, in fact, to play games. At intervals, this archetypal Old Possum interrupts his improvisation with mocking, or falsely ingenuous, asides. He claims to have stumbled upon 'a swarm of wisdom,' simultaneously probable and absurd, changes course upon the sudden descent of a 'fine intuition,' confesses that what he is saying is quite outrageous and nonsensical but that it is impossible to believe anything different, or confides that 'if I am not careful, before the day is over I am likely to be wiser than I ought to be.'[8] Slyly, he admits the ludic nature of his discourse, the extent to which he is making it all up as he goes along. His two interlocutors, however, are entirely persuaded. Not only does Hermogenes solemnly assure Socrates that he seems to him 'to be uttering oracles, exactly like an inspired prophet,' he even seeks enlightenment about 'Hermes, since Cratylus says I am not Hermogenes (son of Hermes),' accepts a wildly improbable etymology based on *hermeneus* and *eirein*, the words for interpreter and speech, and admits on the basis of it that his own name must be false: 'Cratylus was right in saying I was not Hermogenes; I certainly am no good contriver of speech.'[9]

Even when Socrates abruptly turns away from etymologies and proper names to investigate individual letters of the alphabet as imitative either of motion or of rest, creating a series of primary nouns and verbs from which the others are compounded, Hermogenes remains docile. It is at this point, almost three-quarters of the way through the dialogue, that Socrates engages for the first time with Cratylus, a man who has been silently congratulating himself that Socrates endorses his own opinion about names. Until comparatively recently, most commentators have agreed. That Socrates wants to modify the position of Cratylus has always been clear. More difficult is the question of how radically, and why. The last section of the dialogue is complex, and often obscure. Socrates, although he has now dropped his ludic role, sometimes seems to be presenting a bias more than an argument, and to be grappling with weaknesses in his position apparent to him although not to Cratylus and Hermogenes. Certainly his attempt to analyse sounds, and to establish a class of *prota onomata*, irreducible names from which all others are derived, is not only problematic in itself but uneasily related to his earlier way of proceeding. Basically, however, he departs from Cratylus in believing that, because of mistakes made by the first name-givers, the relation between *verba* and *res* is often irreparably flawed. Even more important, fascinating though names are, they should not be allowed to rival universals. For Cratylus, words are paramount. The nature of things is to be deduced from *them*, rather than from an attempt to understand the ideal forms that lie behind them, and this Socrates cannot accept.

Cratylus was a disciple of Heraclitus, who believed that everything in the world was in flux. It is difficult now to tell whether the teaching of Heraclitus himself lies behind Cratylus' contention that only names are fixed and stable, in a world otherwise impossible to define and know, or whether it represents a kind of neo-Heracliteanism developed independently by his pupil. In any case, the position is one against which Socrates revolts. By asking Cratylus to imagine a situation that was about to become important in Western comedy, that of a man who confronts his double, someone who looks exactly like him, has the same psychological organization, life, and name, he gets him to make a significant concession. Names, no matter how expertly given, cannot be exactly the same as the things they represent because, if they were, just as if there were two completely identical Cratyluses, no one would be able to tell one from the other, distinguish between the word and the thing. The door is now open to admit names that are approximations, more or less like the things they signify, but still useful representations of reality. In effect, Hermogenes can again be Hermogenes. Even if he is financially unlucky and also, as his performance with Socrates has demonstrated, not very good at 'speeches,' the name may be valid on other counts.

Cratylus, however, is stubborn. He is still refusing, at the end of the dialogue, to admit that an imperfect name can be a name at all, and he comes close to suggesting that further thought on the matter ought to bring Socrates closer to his own view. Socrates, for his part, remains entrenched in a position somewhere between and beyond those of Cratylus and Hermogenes. The names bestowed by inspired or gifted name-givers are obviously preferable to inaccurate or corrupted names. Ideas, however, are what really matter, entities that can be apprehended – most recent philosophers would not agree – independently of words. It is to these that attention should be directed. Names are sometimes revelatory, sometimes opaque or lamentably inapposite, but fundamentally both they and the things they designate repay investigation only as shadows of real forms.

＊   ＊   ＊

In late antiquity and during the Middle Ages and the Renaissance, an intense and sustained rivalry developed between what might be called the cratylic view of naming and the one Hermogenes tries and fails to uphold. No one seems to have questioned the idea that, essentially, Plato's allegiance lay with Cratylus. Yet once the works of Aristotle began to circulate, in particular his treatise *On Interpretation*, the anti-cratylic view acquired a spokesman far more powerful than Hermogenes. Aristotle was unequivocal in his claim that there is no natural language. Like Hermogenes, he maintained that words signify only according to arbitrary imposition and convention. Although the *Cratylus* itself disappeared in the West between late classical times and the fifteenth century, it continued to be known through paraphrase and commentary. Surprisingly, perhaps, many of these texts attempted to reconcile the cratylic view of language with that of Aristotle.[10] The desire to bring about so improbable a harmony constitutes a tribute, not just to Plato's reputation, but to the importance of the debate this particular work had helped to polarize, a debate quickened by the spread of Christianity.

Aristotle's authority was formidable. And yet, both the Old Testament and the New often seemed to support the rival, cratylic view. Adam's first act in Eden is to bestow true names upon the animals, under God's direction, names either obscured as a result of the Fall, or scattered when the confusion of languages overtook the human race after Babel. Many medieval and Renaissance scholars believed that, with the help of philology, these lost names might be pieced together and recovered. In pursuit of this Ur-language, they took comfort from the knowledge that both John the Baptist and Christ were named by divine mandate, before their birth, and that Christ himself in renaming his disciple 'Peter' (Matthew 16:18) had seemed to sanction both etymologies and the idea of *nomen omen*. The giving of names, whether in the sacrament of baptism, or to mark an individual's entry into the religious life, was weighted with Christian significance from early times. In the Book of Revelation alone believers found ample evidence of the Bible, God's Word, identifying names with intrinsic being, not only mystically, but in such apparently casual but tantalizing statements as 'Thou hast a few names even in Sardis which have not defiled their garments; and they shall walk with me in white' (3:4).

11

Both Jerome and Augustine believed in and defended the mysticism of proper names, as did Origen. In the seventh century, Isidore of Seville constructed what Ernst Curtius has called 'the basic book of the entire Middle Ages,'[11] the enormous *Etymologiarum libri*, upon the premise that the nature of everything in the world could be known through a proper understanding of its name. To clear away misconceptions about the meanings of words, revealing their logical and original sense, is to restore both them and the things they signify to their rightful place in the great scheme of God's truth. Isidore can have had only the vaguest knowledge of Plato's *Cratylus*, if indeed he was aware of it at all, yet he plays delightedly with etymologies in a fashion that often seems to outdo Socrates at his ludic best. The cat, for instance, he declares in Book XII (*De Animalibus*), is rightly called *musio* as being the enemy of mice (*mus*).[12] There is also, however, virtue to be found in the more vulgar name *cattus*, possibly deriving from *captura*, because it captures mice, or perhaps from *cattat* ('keen') because this animal can pierce the darkest night with the brilliance of its eyes. But then, Isidore reflects, the Greek word *kaiesthai* (literally, 'to throw a flame') could be even more relevant, because cats are so clever (*ingeniosus*) – by which point, he has begun to sound less like a man attempting to recover what Adam said in Eden when the first cat paraded past, or even like Socrates, than some Old Possum seeking the ineffable name of a household pet.

As an imaginative response to experience, the product of an instinctive need to find correspondences between words and things, cratylism is deeply rooted in human nature. It was not really surprising that, despite the veneration of Aristotle, the alternative view of language should remain powerful, or that when the *Cratylus* itself was recovered from Byzantium, in the Renaissance, it should be seized upon avidly by christianizing commentators. Few of these readers can have thought of the work as ludic at all, or regarded Socrates as being anything but entirely serious throughout. Yet however earnest their own religious purpose when building on the dialogue, they were often no better than Isidore at preventing onomastic games from becoming something suspiciously like an end in themselves.

The *Cratylus* is not only a complicated but, at present, a controversial dialogue.[13] Among philosophers, there has been for some time a tendency to try and separate Socrates decisively from the viewpoint of Cratylus and, correspondingly, to bring him more into line with the nominalist approach proposed, however feebly, by Hermogenes. Given the general direction of post-Wittgensteinian philosophy – even in such revisionary works as Saul Kripke's *Naming and Necessity* – this is scarcely surprising. As A.J. Ayer writes in *The Concept of a Person and Other Essays*,

There are not many philosophers nowadays who would wish to identify the meaning of a name with its bearer. They have been taught by Wittgenstein that it is a mistake to suppose that the meaning of a proper name, or indeed of any linguistic expression, is a special type of object: instead of looking for meanings, in this sense, we should ask how the expression is used.[14]

Hermogenes may be triumphant in the field of linguistic philosophy. The voice of Cratylus, however, cannot be silenced. 'Devenu "poète," ' as he has in *Mimologiques: Voyage en Cratylie*, Gérard Genette's brilliant account of Plato's dialogue and some of the works, both theoretical and fictional, descended from it, he still confronts his ancient adversary on equal terms.[15]

In *Mimologiques*, Genette affirms that Socrates, although obviously needing to separate himself from the simplistic positions of both his interlocutors, nevertheless does side essentially, just as tradition would have it, with Cratylus. His consciously fanciful etymologies (or *éponymies*, as Genette prefers to call these particular examples of mimological play) not only constitute an enduring form of imaginative activity. By speculating freely in particular instances as to why the original name-giver might have been led to choose the word he did, Socrates illuminates the nature of the object or person named and, in a sense, of the name-giver too. He also reveals, as in the notorious *sôma-sèma* association, in which the Greek word for the body is validated through its supposed resemblance to the one for a tomb (the body being the tomb of the soul), a whole world of hidden correspondences and relationships faithfully mirrored in words. Names often gesture towards other names, adjacent or hidden within them, which explain and help to develop their own significance. Although Socrates never actually says this, the aura of names, that tangential field of (often phonic) suggestiveness upon which many of his 'etymologies' draw, does not necessarily depend upon linguistic roots. Nor, where they are adduced, Genette argues, does it matter – any more than it does with the meditations on certain place-names in Proust – whether they are philologically false or true.

It is hard to disagree with Genette that the position of Cratylus has always been far more attractive and interesting than that of Hermogenes:

En vingt siècles de 'théorie raissonable,' Hermogène n'a rien produit qui puisse séduire, et son corpus, de Démocrite à Saussure, se réduit presque à quelques négations laconiques. Cratyle, au contraire, nous laisse une série d'œuvres pittoresques, amusantes, parfois troublantes ... [16]

In his 'voyage' among these diverse works, Genette never as it happens pauses to consider comic drama. And yet, from the time of Aristophanes' *Acharnians* onwards, this is the principal arena in which the debate between Cratylus and Hermogenes has been played out. Comedy is the one form which (even more strikingly than that later phenomenon, the novel) forces the writer to give names. He rarely inherits them, in the manner of his tragic counterpart. Indeed, even where this is possible, as when adapting the work of an earlier writer, he usually refuses to take up the option. Unlike the novel, moreover, comedy asks its audience not only to interpret, but actually to discover, as the play unfolds, what particular characters are called. Its fundamental bias, over the centuries, has always been cratylic. It is, however, a cratylism perpetually being encroached upon and modified by the dissenting voice of Hermogenes. More congenial to some dramatists than others, traditionally associated with certain kinds of play, comedic cratylism is endlessly self-questioning, and it has assumed a variety of forms. Like

Adam in paradise, comic dramatists confront naming as both a privilege, and a responsibility of a special and exacting kind. The onomastic decisions they make, whether essentially cratylic, hermogenean, or (more usually) a compound of the two, will say a great deal about them as artists and about the quality and structure of the imaginary worlds they create.

Chapter One

Perhaps because Aristophanes in the *Clouds* had poked a good deal of fun at Socrates and his 'Thinkery,' Plato was careful in the *Symposium* to present the relationship between the great comic writer and the great philosopher as entirely amicable. As usual, Socrates dominates the dialogue. And yet, Aristophanes' own contribution to the discussion of Love, his bizarre but oddly touching myth of human sexuality, sounds so like something he would joyously have staged, if only it had been technically feasible, that one likes to believe it really was what he said on this or some similar occasion. Near the end of the *Symposium* everyone, except Socrates, the tragic dramatist Agathon (in whose house the party was taking place), and Aristophanes, has either gone home or passed out. When Aristodemus, on whose memory of the occasion the dialogue purports to rely, recovered consciousness at dawn, he found Socrates 'driving them to the admission that the same man could have the knowledge required for writing comedy and tragedy, that the fully skilled tragedian could be a comedian as well.'[1] According to Aristodemus, Agathon and Aristophanes were forced to assent to this, being drowsy, and not quite following the argument. Then, both of them dropped off to sleep, while the indefatigable Socrates went off into the early-morning streets of Athens to button-hole somebody else.

It is difficult now, conditioned as we are by Shakespeare and other ambidextrous sixteenth- and seventeenth-century English dramatists, to do justice to the enormity of Socrates' contention. Although Greek tragic writers were certainly not without a sense of humour – indeed they were officially required to demonstrate it in the satyr play – as dramatic forms, comedy and tragedy seem to have been kept rigorously distinct. A man might be a comic dramatist or a tragic dramatist, but not both. Comedy and tragedy exploited different subject matter and poetic metres, different leading actors, costumes, kinds of chorus, and they presupposed a different relationship with the audience. In a fragment that survives from his lost comedy *Poesis*, Antiphanes, a dramatist who won his first victory at Athens in 385 BC, claims that the art of the comic writer is more exacting and difficult than that of his tragic counterpart. The comic dramatist does not rely on traditional material. He must, as Antiphanes says, invent everything: 'new names, new plots, new speeches, and then the antecedent circumstances, the present situation, the outcome, the prologue.'[2] Let Oedipus present himself, Antiphanes asserts, and the audience knows all about him even before he says a word: 'his father was Laius, his mother Iocasta; they know who his daughters were, his sons, what he will suffer, what he has done.' This is not true with a character in comedy. He must be named and built up from scratch.

Mythological comedy, as written by Cratinus and others, including Aristophanes himself in the *Frogs*, clearly presented a special case. In the main, however, Antiphanes' distinction seems to have been just. Although the titles of plays, together with authors' and actors' names, were probably communicated to Greek audiences in a *proagon*, those of characters were not. (Even in manuscripts, end-lists of dramatis personae, where they appear at all, are late scholarly additions.) Tragedies were commonly named after their protagonists, or at least in ways suggesting a particular myth. When, on the other hand, at the beginning of Aristophanes' comedy called the *Acharnians*, a solitary figure walked onto the stage and began to complain pungently about all the things recently annoying him – including the fact that no one else has arrived on time for the Assembly – the spectators in the Theatre of Dionysus could not have had the faintest idea who he was, or what he should be called.

Many of the gods and heroes whose names Socrates etymologizes in the *Cratylus* appear as characters in tragedy: Apollo,

Athena, Dionysus, Agamemnon, Orestes, Hector, and others. All these names mean something, although exactly what has in some cases long been a matter of dispute. Yet in the plays by Aeschylus, Sophocles, and Euripides that have survived, puns or allusions to such meanings tend to be glancing and few. A significant amount of word-play on the name Oedipus as both 'Swell-foot' and 'Know-foot' has been shown to exist in the *Tyrannos*.[3] Euripides' *Ion* (see chapter seven) is exceptional: a play specifically about naming, which is also, significantly, a New Comedy prototype. Elsewhere, the meaning of names is either passed over quickly, or ignored. When Dionysus in the *Bacchae* of Euripides tells Pentheus that he is about to understand the meaning of his own name ('grief'), the reminder is like a lightning flash, but scarcely much longer in duration. The same is true when Sophocles' Ajax suddenly apprehends that his name ('Aias,' or 'agony') corresponds to his fate, when Polyneices is accused of being, as his name implies, 'quarrelsome,' when Prometheus, or 'Forethought,' is mocked for not anticipating his punishment, or Cassandra, in the *Agamemnon* of Aeschylus, puns on the latent meaning 'Destroyer' in the god Apollo's name. All are passing gestures of recognition. The one real exception occurs in the *Agamemnon* of Aeschylus. As Simon Goldhill has observed, Helen is never referred to by name – only as 'woman' – in this play, until after the herald brings news to Argos of the fall of Troy. Now that the adultery which placed her outside the bounds of society, thus rendering her nameless, has been avenged, she can again be 'Helen,' and the Chorus meditates darkly on the fatality implicit in the name, speculating on the nature of the power that guided the *onomatourgos* in making his choice:

Who can have given a name so altogether true – was it some power invisible guiding his tongue aright by forecasting of destiny? – who named that bride of the spear and source of strife with the name of Helen? For, true to her name, a Hell she proved to ships, Hell to men, Hell to city ...[4]

Helen, however, does not appear as a character in the *Oresteia*.

Games played with proper names usually have little appeal for tragic writers. Greek tragedy, in particular, has all the determinism it needs already embedded in the stories of Oedipus and Agamemnon, Ajax, or Antigone. It is wary of additional determinism of the wrong kind, emanating from a cratylic view of proper names. To suggest that the name a tragic character bears will program his or her actions and responses, and that its meaning cannot be contradicted or changed, is to imperil the freedom of such characters to make an unavoidable destiny – something callously visited upon them by fate, or a family past – inalienably their own. The way Orestes, Agamemnon, Electra, and Hecuba respond to their situations must remain unpredictable. It cannot be controlled or explained by their names. As for lesser characters for whom there were no traditional names – the Farmer in Euripides' *Electra* or the Old Shepherd in Sophocles' *Oedipus Tyrannos* – they remain, in tragedy, anonymous. No attempt is made to provide them with names. Indeed, certain subsidiary figures who do have names in Homer lose them in tragedy, as in the case of Talthybius, reduced in the *Agamemnon* to a nameless herald.

Old Comedy, by contrast, revels in etymologies and invented names. Names, generally, constitute one of the most striking features of Aristophanes' plays. Although not all of his speaking characters have individual designations (one major figure and a host of minor ones remain anonymous throughout), almost every page is crowded, not only with the names of gods and heroes, the nomenclature of tragedy, but with those of contemporary Athenian politicians, demogogues, and generals, together with the names of their fathers and sons, names of notorious Athenian eccentrics, scoundrels, fops, pederasts, and drunks, of philosophers, rival dramatists, and poets, and also names recorded as those of ordinary, contemporary Athenians, Attic farmers, and slaves. There are personifications too, like Diallage, Opōra, and Theoria, as well as joke names that Aristophanes has made up from adjectives or common nouns. Some of these titles are attached to speaking parts, some to mute figures, but the greater number of them belong to people who are present only through reference and allusion – who exist, in fact, only because they are named.

Even the Aristophanic Chorus, although it speaks in unison, tends to individuate itself through naming, as tragic Choruses never do. A particular Chorus will rebuke one of its supposed members by the name 'Comias' for lagging behind the rest of them, inquire of Strymodorus of Conthyle whether or not old Euergides and Chabes from Phyla have turned up yet, encourage Draces, or worry about Lacrateides, whose name means 'the son of strength,' but who moves now, alas, on feeble legs. Where the literal meaning of a name is apparent, or can be imaginatively teased out, Aristophanes is likely to pounce on it. That slippery distinction between proper name and common noun which, in the *Cratylus*, Socrates so cunningly avoids addressing is for him a major source of comic invention. 'Carcinus,' for instance, the name of a contemporary dramatist, means 'crab.' Accordingly, at the end of the *Wasps*, three undersized and spindly crustaceans emerge from the sea, execute a grotesque parody of a tragic dance, and are at once identified as his sons. *Peace* begins by teasing its audience as to whether the *kantharos* described as voraciously swallowing shit off-stage is a contemporary of Aristophanes who happened to bear that name or (as it turns out) an actual dung-beetle.[5]

In the *Birds*, Aristophanes briefly pretends that he is about to clarify the troublesome relationship between proper names and ordinary nouns – only to leave it murkier than before. The hoopoe was once human, a king named 'Tereus.' Peisetaerus tries to summon it out of its house with an imitation of the hoopoe's cry, 'Epopoi,' clearly the source of the bird's generic name, *epopa*. Accused by the hoopoe's feathered servant, who comes to the door, of being human bird-catchers, Peisetaerus and Euelpides each claim membership of a hastily invented ornithological species: 'I'm a Fearfowl, a Libyan bird.' 'I'm a Shitterling, from the land of Phasis.'[6] Yet when Euelpides, later, sees a second hoopoe, he expresses astonishment: 'So you're not the only hoopoe – there's also this other one?'[7] He has been regarding the former Tereus as unique, the only representative of a species. The hoopoe, however, misunderstanding the question, thinks Euelpides is asking if any other bird answers to 'Hoopoe' as a personal name. The second bird, it assures him, is a grandson and therefore (as was frequently the case in Athens) a namesake: 'He's the son of Philocles' hoopoe, and I'm his grandfather.' Philocles, as it happens, was a contemporary dramatist who had written a tragedy about Tereus. Proper names and generic nouns, not to mention the human and non-human worlds, have become wonderfully confused.

In the kaleidoscopic, vital world of Aristophanes, horses row boats, birds mass together to build a brick-walled city in the midst of the air and (when necessary) speak impeccable Greek, while even coal-scuttles or vine-poles can be activated by powerful emotions. We still christen ships, and customarily think of them as feminine, but Aristophanes goes so far as to imagine a number of lady triremes holding a public meeting, at which one of them, announcing herself proudly as 'Nauphante, daughter of Nauson,' categorically refuses to sail to Carthage on the orders of the present government. A play with the unfortunate title of the *Mice*, which failed at its first performance in the Theatre of Dionysus, is said to have been strangled by the cat at nightfall.

In Aristophanic comedy, a man or woman's name can be the most important thing about them, especially if its meaning is readily decipherable. Aristophanes often drags his contemporaries into a play simply because of their names, which he treats in a strictly cratylic fashion. History exonerates the Athenian general Lamachus of being either grasping or particularly bellicose. Indeed, in 421 BC, he was one of the peacemakers in Athens, and he seems never to have been wealthy. It was purely because his name contained the root of the Greek word for 'battle' that Aristophanes caricatured him in the *Acharnians* as a man horribly stuffed with epithets of war, the son of Gorgasus, or 'the fierce' (actually, Lamachus' father was called 'Xenophanes,' as Aristophanes was well aware), to be pilloried in such punning invocations as 'O toils and battles and Lamachus!'[8] Aristophanes went on taking swipes at Lamachus until he was killed in battle in 414, at which point, as though the name had suddenly altered its significance for him, he calmly transformed it into a title of praise.

21

A man so alert to the meanings of proper names might be expected to name his own protagonists with great care. These are the characters whose business it is, in the majority of Aristophanes' plays, to concoct some apparently impossible scheme, put it into operation and, against appalling odds, sweep everything before them. In the *Clouds*, Aristophanes playfully makes one of these self-centred, but energetic and highly imaginative heroes reflect on how important it is to give good and appropriate names. Strepsiades is a countryman, from simple, hardworking, rustic stock, who married a city girl from a family both wealthy and pretentious. When their first son was born, so Strepsiades tells the audience, he wanted to call him 'Pheidonides,' after his own father. The name means 'son of thrift.' His wife, however, had fixed her heart on something more elegant and upper class, preferably suggestive of expensive horses rather than goats: 'Xanthippus,' perhaps, or 'Chaerippus,' or 'Callipides,' all of them names actually recorded in Athens. Eventually, the parents compromised, and called the child 'Pheidippides,' a name that (although traditionally assigned to the Marathon runner) is etymologically nonsensical, meaning something like 'son of thrift-horse.' The consequences of such incompetent name-giving were dire. Although the father kept telling the boy, as he was growing up, that he must learn to be content with a leather smock and a flock of goats, the equine side of the name waged war against the thrift side and eventually won. Strepsiades is in the predicament he is at the beginning of the *Clouds* because his son has bankrupted him on purebred horses.

Parents make mistakes. Poets, on the other hand, as Socrates claimed, are or should be gifted name-givers. Certainly Aristophanes' fictional children, including Strepsiades himself, are brilliantly named. Among the eleven comedies that survive, one, the *Frogs*, has the god Dionysus as its protagonist. Another the *Thesmophoriazusae*, or *Women at the Thesmophoria*, rather surprisingly gives its central character no name at all, while in the *Plutus*, Aristophanes' last surviving play, the name 'Chremylus' is uncharacteristically arbitrary and opaque. All the other comedies bestow upon the comic hero or heroine an ostentatiously fictional, made-up name. This designation, like Eliot's

22

'Munkustrap' or 'Coricopat,' is usually the sole property of the individual it identifies, although there may be one or more recorded names that shadow it, as 'Lysimache,' borne by the priestess of Athena Polias at the time of Aristophanes' *Lysistrata*, shadows that of his eponymous heroine. The name 'Dicaeopolis' has been traced to one of Aristophanes' fellow demes-men. It was, however, extremely rare. In every case, the meaning of this centrally placed name is important to the audience's understanding both of the character concerned and of the play. This is true of 'Dicaeopolis' in the *Acharnians*, 'Agoracritus' in the *Knights*, 'Strepsiades' in the *Clouds*, 'Trygaeus' in the *Peace*, 'Peisetaerus' in the *Birds*, 'Lysistrata,' 'Praxagora' in the *Ecclesiazusae*, and (up to a point) 'Philocleon' in the *Wasps*.

Greek tragic dramatists were accustomed to name their protagonists in the dialogue as soon as possible after their first appearance, even if they would have been identified without difficulty by the audience. This is not the practice of Aristophanes. It is normal for him to withhold the name of his central character, sometimes for a third, or even three-quarters of a play that this character has effectively dominated from the start. In seven of his comedies, the name of the comic protagonist is kept back in this way, while in the eighth, it is never spoken at all. Modern editions of the *Thesmophoriazusae* do often name Euripides' relative, that very distinctive and long-suffering citizen who allows himself to be dressed up as a woman and pushed into an all-female gathering. There is, however, no warrant in Aristophanes for calling him 'Mnesilochus,' after Euripides' historical father-in-law. The practice originates in late Roman times, when the play was being studied but not performed. Commentators found the anonymity of its protagonist so embarrassing that they insisted upon identifying him with a relative of Euripides whose name they happened to know. They were too scrupulous, however, to introduce this name into the body of the play.

It is important to remember that speech prefixes in dramatic texts are a comparatively modern innovation. The first surviving text of a comedy in which prefixes of this kind are used dates from the first or second century AD, hundreds of years after Aristophanes' plays had begun to circulate in manuscript. It is, moreover, an isolated example. Even in the tenth century, many scribes continued, both with comedy and tragedy, to indicate changes of speaker only by way of a particular pen-stroke, or paragraphus, sometimes by a di-colon. A dramatic text of this kind was certainly calculated to keep the reader alert, as well as providing a few puzzles for editors. It is, however, closer to the play as it was meant to be experienced in the theatre. Modern texts of Aristophanes, like texts of Shakespeare and other Renaissance dramatists, continually name parts prematurely. In doing so, they are often guilty of providing readers with information that the dramatist, thinking of his play primarily as something for the stage, did not intend to divulge at this point in the action.

Even in nondramatic works, delayed naming can be obscured by the conventions of a written text. Those tiny (often inaccurate) summaries, for instance, that head each canto of Spenser's *Faerie Queene*, are modelled on the ones Caxton supplied in the printed text of Malory's *Morte d'Arthur*. Their presence in *The Faerie Queene*, however, disrupts an otherwise clear policy about the release of certain names. When Spenser, for instance, finally reveals in Book I that the giant is called 'Orgoglio,' that the 'goodly Lady clad in scarlet red' is 'Duessa,' or that 'Lucifera' is the mistress of the sad house of Pride, readers are plainly meant to find in those names a confirmation of their own independent assessment of what these characters intrinsically are. The telltale cratylic names, when released, merely ratify a judgment arrived at earlier by way of an essentially moral interpretation of their actions and words. Delayed naming in Aristophanes is not quite like this. His comic protagonists are usually far less interesting for what they are than for what they do, a fact clearly reflected in both the composition and the handling of their names. Again and again, the protagonist's name is something that must be earned not, as in Spenser, by the vigilance of the reader, but by the character itself. The Aristophanic name identifies the hero or heroine with the action on which he or she has embarked, the particular thing to be accomplished, and it is not morally exemplary.

That solitary citizen at the beginning of the *Acharnians* becomes 'Dicaeopolis' ('Just-City') only after he has stopped complaining, embarked on his apparently lunatic course of making a private peace treaty with Sparta for himself and his family, and begun to demonstrate why such a policy of enlightened self-interest, if enough people pursued it, might be the salvation of Athens. The sausage-seller of the *Knights* becomes 'Agoracritus' ('the man chosen through debate in the market-place') at the very end of the comedy, when he is crowned by Demos, otherwise 'the People.' Trygaeus, in the *Peace*, gets his name ('the vintager,' or 'gathering the fruit of the vine') and his appropriate bride, Opōra, or 'harvest-home,' only after he has stormed Olympus on the back of a giant beetle and begun negotiations to bring Peace herself, the goddess 'most loving of the vine' as the very symbol of peace in its sacral aspect, back to earth.[9] In the *Birds*, Peisetaerus, 'the persuader of companions,' remains anonymous for two-thirds of the play, until the audience, by watching him in action, can almost guess what the name ought to be, while Praxagora, in the *Ecclesiazusae*, becomes 'she who does things in the market-place' only as a result of actually doing them. Strepsiades, or 'Twistson,' in the *Clouds*, could not possess his name at the start of the play. That frugal and honest countryman who wanted to call his son 'Pheidonides' becomes devious only when he finally determines to knock on Socrates' door, with the aim of learning how to defraud his creditors. It is from that decision that he is named.

Once uncovered, the protagonist's name is usually reiterated, and its cratylic significance driven home. So, the 'twistiness' of Strepsiades suddenly becomes endemic in the verse. In the *Acharnians*, after Dicaeopolis' name has been released at line 406, everybody all at once knows and uses it: odd members of a wedding party, a messenger, slaves, Lamachus, even total strangers like the man with pigs from Megara, although nobody seems to have wanted to call him anything before. As for the three comedies that name the protagonist at once (*Lysistrata*, the *Wasps*, and the *Frogs*), and the *Thesmophoriazusae*, where he is never named at all, they help to explain Aristophanes' more usual delay. The *Frogs* stands apart by virtue of having Dionysus himself, a god whose name cannot be treated like the others, as its central character. Lysistrata, on the other hand, 'the looser of armies,' is named at line 6 (and in the title) because her scheme is already in operation when the play opens: thanks to her, the Acropolis has been occupied by women. It is only a matter of time before the men of Athens and of Sparta will be forced to recognize that they either do without sex, or put an end to a stupid war. The *Wasps*, where the protagonist is named before he appears, and the *Thesmophoriazusae*, where he remains anonymous, are slightly different cases. Although Philocleon and Euripides' kinsman are, purely as individuals, the most vivid and memorable of all Aristophanes' protagonists, neither of them ever manages to *do* anything. Philocleon spends the first part of the play in abortive efforts to escape from his son, a sober young man trying to cure his father of an unseemly passion for jury-duty. After being forced to adjudicate in a mock-trial, where he is tricked into acquitting the canine defendant, Philocleon collapses, allows himself to be led off to a respectable Athenian social evening, and ends up scandalously drunk and facing charges for disorderly conduct. He is both awful and endearing. His name, however, 'he who loves [the demogogue] Cleon,' says remarkably little about the person he has slowly revealed himself to be. It is equally applicable, in fact, to the Chorus, a waspish collection of elderly jury-men who, like Philocleon, support a politician Aristophanes detested. As for Euripides' kinsman, he is an extremely funny, but even more passive sufferer, victimized first by his relative, whose idea it is that he should insinuate himself into the Thesmophoria, and then by the outraged women themselves. The protagonist of the *Thesmophoriazusae* is unforgettable simply for himself, but that, in an Aristophanic scheme of things where the identity of such characters is associated with achievement, does not entitle him to a personal name.

Towards the end of his life, Aristophanes began to experiment with a different kind of comedy. The *Plutus*, his last surviving play, sets itself apart in a number of respects from his earlier work. Apolitical and domestic, it is sparing of contemporary allusion. Moreover, its protagonist Chremylus has what Eliot

26

might call a 'sensible everyday name.' It is, in fact, a variant of 'Chremes,' one of the two names that Antiphanes singles out in the *Poesis* as typical for characters in Greek Middle and New Comedy. 'Chremylus' means very little (some slight suggestion, perhaps, of 'a grumbler'), and although Aristophanes chooses not to release it for 335 lines, the delay here seems like the mere product of dramatic habit. This protagonist has certainly done something – restored the eyesight of the blind god of Wealth – but the social results of his action are dubious, and quite unrelated to his own neutral, uncommunicative name. The truly important name in this comedy, reiterated more frequently than that of any other character in Aristophanes, is the one in the title. Plutus, Wealth personified, equivocates and tries to evade identification when Chremylus follows him away from Apollo's shrine. And indeed, once he has been forced to name himself, he is effectively mastered. Chremylus is no sorcerer, but he comes to possess Wealth in the archetypal way: through discovering what he is called. Once spoken, the name 'Plutus' is on everyone's lips. This, however, is not the old kind of Aristophanic broadcasting. Like Spenser's 'Duessa' or 'Orgoglio,' 'Plutus' is a name that gives local habitation to an idea, not to a particular thing done. It is, in fact, like the names in English morality drama. The *Plutus* seems, today, to suffer by comparison with the *Birds* or the *Acharnians*. Its allegorizing treatment of Wealth, on the other hand, was at least partly responsible for the fact that, during the Renaissance, it became overwhelmingly the most popular of Aristophanes' plays.

※   ※   ※

Not all ancient Greek comedy was cratylic, even in the modified form of the *Plutus*. The New Comedy of Menander and his contemporaries reflected life in an Athens ruled now from Macedonia and, beyond that, the vicissitudes of Fortune in an unsettled, Hellenistic world. Issues of identity, what might be called the recovery of the missing birth certificate, a theme entirely foreign to Aristophanes, lay at its heart. As early as the third century BC, the indebtedness of this comedy to certain experimental tragedies of Euripides – among them, his *Ion*, *Helen*, and *Iphigenia in Tauris* – had already been remarked. Satyrus, in his biography of Euripides, asserted that *'peripeteiai*, violations of maidens, substitution of children, recognition by means of rings and necklaces ... are the very stuff of New Comedy, and it was Euripides who developed them.'[10]

Aristophanes never reused the name of a comic protagonist, because he never repeated a comic plot. Even counting the smallest parts, only four names given to speaking characters appear twice in eleven comedies. In Menander, by contrast, in a corpus consisting of one complete play (*Discolos*) and fragments, some of them very minimal, of some sixteen others, the same names turn up over and over again: 'Smicrines,' 'Moschion,' 'Charisius,' 'Getas,' 'Parmenon,' 'Sostratus,' 'Demeas,' or 'Laches.' He gives the name 'Daos' to no fewer than ten speaking characters. Almost all these names, with the exception of a few for which real-life owners have yet to be found, were common in Athens at the time. Many appear in other New Comedy fragments. The meanings of some lie close to the surface. 'Daos,' for instance, indicates derivation from the Daoi, a northern tribe. 'Onesimus,' a name St Paul was later to play on in his epistle to Philemon, in a context very different from that of the *Epitrepontes*, means 'helpful' (Philemon 11). Menander was also given to calling country boys 'Gorgias,' and soldiers by names formed out of the words for violence, boldness, or war: 'Polemon' or 'Thrasonides.' Again, these are attested names in the Athens of his day. Yet cratylism of the Aristophanic kind seems understated in Menander, or even accidental. The probable northern origin of the various 'Daos' characters is a factor of no importance in their various plays. The slave Onesimus is neither helpful nor sufficiently the opposite so that his name might register ironically. Menander never calls attention to its meaning, any more than he subjects his soldiers' names to commentary and puns of the kind Aristophanes continually meted out to Lamachus. His men of war, indeed, are by no means uniformly belligerent.

The significance of the great majority of Menander's names was probably about as noticeable to his original audience as the anvil behind 'Smith' or the farm building behind 'Barton' are today. Like other writers of New Comedy, his onomastic attitude seems to have been broadly hermogenean. Yet Menandrian naming is anything but unconsidered, or devoid of significance. It develops, indeed, its own very special kind of cratylism. Apart from a few minor figures, all Menander's characters are named in the dialogue as early as possible, usually, as in tragedy, within a few lines of their first appearance. The stock names of New Comedy, moreover, constituted a code, helping the audience to find its way quickly into the situation and circumstances of the play.[11] Some, whatever the variety of their use in real life, seem always to have been the fictive property of courtesans, others of respectable young women, or of slaves. 'Smicrines' is usually a tight-fisted old man; the various 'Moschion' characters are young, weak, and inclined towards sexual misconduct. A girl named 'Plangon' can be relied upon to turn out free-born, even if she begins the comedy as a slave. Specific comic masks may well have been associated with these names, but more important is the suggestion that as soon as the Hellenistic audience heard 'Plangon' or 'Parmenon' pronounced, it must have nourished particular expectations, as it did with 'Oedipus' or 'Agamemnon.' Although it could not know how a particular comedy plot would work out, it was entitled to feel that the behaviour and fortunes of characters endowed with these names would be contained within certain limits, even as in the much later but associated form of Italian *commedia dell'arte* 'Pantalone' in a given scenario will sometimes be married, sometimes not, sometimes on good terms with the Dottore next door, at others his enemy, sometimes impotent, sometimes a patron of courtesans, but never young, generous with money, or successful in his pursuit of the heroine.

New Comedy naming, then, is hermogenean in a special and qualified sense. As the plays accumulated, repeated names gravitated increasingly towards the expressive and speaking, not by way of etymologies and puns, but through continued theatrical association: the audience's awareness of the range and implications of their previous use. It seems clear that Menander himself found conventional names indispensable, not only as a

29

practical dramatic shorthand, but because they enabled him to define individuality, picking out a character's particular ways of feeling and reacting, against the stable background of a type. 'Polemon,' for instance, in the *Periceiromene*, prepares the audience for a soldier. A character with this name can be expected, when he returns from military service and finds his mistress embracing another man, to fly into a jealous fury and, without asking any questions, humiliate her by brutally shearing off all her hair. What the name does not anticipate is his subsequent grief and self-reproach when she walks out on him, the impulse that makes him drag an embarrassed next-door neighbour up to Glycera's empty room to look at the clothes she has scrupulously left behind, mute reminders of the bird that has flown. Glycera herself has a name that, whatever the variety of its use in real life, always belongs in comedy to a courtesan. It defines her age and position, usefully, at the start of the play, but not the sensitivity and dignity she subsequently reveals, or her conflicting emotions when she recovers her father Pataecus and true social status, while realizing that this father, once, abandoned her to die.

❊ ❊ ❊

Although T.S. Eliot did manage to write a play about Orestes and call the protagonist 'Harry,' the names of tragic characters are almost always inseparable from their stories. 'Real' or 'existing' names (*onomata genomena*), as Aristotle called them, they are unlike the 'random' (*tuchonta*) designations of comedy in not being easily or profitably changed.[12] Writers of comedy, however, unlike their tragic counterparts, usually feel impelled when drawing upon a pre-existing narrative or dramatic source to alter the names they find there. This onomastic independence can be traced back as far as Roman comedy. Although both Plautus and Terence regularly based their plays upon Greek originals, their otherwise close relationship with their models breaks down significantly when it comes to the question of names.

It has been estimated that, among a stage population of some one hundred and fifty named characters in Plautus, only thirteen, five of them present in two plays, have names traceable in Greek New Comedy. When he does employ them at all, Plautus likes to relegate the names preferred by Menander and his contemporaries to characters who remain unseen, 'down the street, in the house, in the past, in imaginary lists.'[13] So, he makes the slave Chrysalus in the *Bacchides* differentiate himself scornfully from 'your Parmenos and Syruses who take two or three minas from their masters.' Not only were 'Parmenon' and 'Syrus' stock names for slaves in Greek New Comedy, the original of Chrysalus himself, in the *Dis Exapaton* had been a 'Syrus.'[14] Presumably, few members of Plautus' audience were equipped to pick up this particular joke. All of them, however, must have responded to the typically Plautine word-play on 'Chrysalus' and *chrysos* (gold) in a plot much concerned with his machinations in connection with that metal, or to its sinister perversion into 'Crucisalus' as the possibility of his punishment by crucifixion increased. Name-play of this kind, alien to Greek New Comedy, seems to reach back to the work of Aristophanes.

Plautus, writing for Roman audiences in the early second century BC, may not have known the work of Aristophanes. Temperamentally, however, he seems to have been inclined when adapting plays by Menander, Diphilus, or Philemon to wrest their essentially hermogenean nomenclature back in the direction of the sportively cratylic. He delighted in puns, etymologies, and what one of the characters in the *Persa* calls 'longa nomina contortiplicata.'[15] Like Aristophanes, Plautus loves to make up names, many of them – 'Pyrgpolinices,' 'Thereapontigonus Platigorus,' or 'Polymachaeroplagides' – calculatedly absurd. Most of these names, like the cities in which the comedies are supposed to be taking place, are Greek. A few, however, are Roman, and some a preposterous mixture of the two. Characters regularly elaborate and pun on their meanings, usually of a physically descriptive or amorally behavioural kind. Plautus is also fond, as was Aristophanes, of using names to blur the distinction between humans and animals, or even the animate and inanimate worlds, as he does with the pimp Lycus in the *Poenulus*, often spoken of as though he were literally a wolf, or when Peniculus, the 'little brush' of the *Menaechmi*, so

31

nicknamed because his appetite always sweeps the table clean, is more than once confused with the article itself.

Peniculus is a parasite, tormented by the insatiable and obsessive hunger of his kind. In the end, after a confused attempt to revenge himself on the local Menaechmus for a gastronomic disappointment occasioned by his twin, he loses not only the promised dinner, but his comfortable position as hanger-on in the family. There is no place for Peniculus in the happy ending: he has already taken himself off to the Forum in search of another patron. Yet, like other parasites in Plautus, he is treated leniently on the whole, straightforward gluttony being a forgivable weakness in this as in most comedy, whereas the pimp's professional desire to coin money out of other people's lovemaking is not. Plautus' kindness to Peniculus and his kin, like his indulgence of clever slaves, usually involves allowing them a particularly keen awareness of the meaning of names, their own and those of other people. Pimps, on the other hand, tend to be onomastically obtuse – like the one in the *Persa* who, after asking suspiciously for the name of a supposed foreigner, accepts a fifty-five-syllable enormity containing a clear announcement of its bearer's treacherous intent, without registering anything but the fact that such a title must be very troublesome to write out. Dordalus' failure here is not moral, as it would become in English medieval drama. He is merely stupid, in a Plautine world which (again like that of Aristophanes) tends to place a premium on intelligence, however oddly employed.

Characters in Plautus often go by titles that Plato's Cratylus would describe as spurious, so patently inappropriate that, as in the case of Hermogenes, he could not countenance them as being their names at all. Pyrgopolinices ('taker of towers') is an egregious blusterer who clearly never took a tower in his life; Demaenetus ('praised by the people') succeeds only in becoming an object of public ridicule, and Theopropides ('son of prophecy') is quite unable to see through the deceptions practised on him by his slave. Designations of this kind, however, really represent a form of cratylism: they point so unerringly to what individuals might like to be but are not as to function as a definition by opposites. As such, they are transparent not only

32

to the theatre audience but to the tricksters and schemers, people whose perceptiveness about names is one reason why they are able to handle other characters as effectively as they do.

Terence, writing a generation after Plautus, was temperamentally far less attracted than his predecessor either to name-play or to those clever rogues whose specialty it tended to be. 'The Roman Menander,' as he has been called, can claim that title on a number of grounds, not least among them his marked preference for neutral, essentially hermogenean names drawn from the traditional Greek New Comedy list. Although Terence too regularly changes the names provided in his source plays, he does so far more conservatively than Plautus, preferring to rearrange the established repertoire, rather than invent designations of his own. In six surviving plays, he contrives to use more Menandrian names than Plautus had in twenty-one.[16] Like Menander too, and unlike Plautus, he tends to repeat a limited number of names, including those of major characters, from play to play. Some appear to have possessed particular associations for him, were likely to attach themselves to certain kinds of role. Only rarely, however, does he display any interest in etymologies, in teasing out the meaning of a name and using it (whether straightforwardly or in reverse) to characterize its owner.

Aristophanic cratylism, as opposed to the fundamentally hermogenean nature of Menandrian naming, had helped to articulate two distinct kinds of Greek comedy. Terence's bias towards neutral, subtly associative nomenclature accords with, and in some measure dictates, his particular brand of Roman comedy: a comedy concerned with ordinary, decent people in situations often more painful than funny. It is very difficult to engage with a man called Thereapontigonus Platigorus, no matter how roughly he is treated by his fellow human beings. Because, in general, Terence means to exact more sympathy for his characters than Plautus, he avoids giving even his dupes preposterous and distancing names of this kind. His stock of Hellenistic proper names at most gently suggests, without limiting, the nature of individual men and women. More reflective and troubled than those of Plautus, his characters seem psycho-

33

logically more complex. It is less important to them to interpret names correctly than to escape from literary and social stereotypes as obvious to them as to the theatre audience. So, Terence produces courtesans concerned to prove that they are not, in fact, mercenary; a mother-in-law brooding over the fact that people will regard her apparently unsympathetic treatment of her son's wife as entirely predictable; an uncle determined not to behave like the typical, repressive *senex* in the way he brings up his brother's son.

Significantly less popular with contemporary Romans than the fast-moving, eminently theatrical work of Plautus, Terence's thoughtful, sententious, and illusionist comedy managed to a surprising extent to surmount the antitheatrical prejudice of the Middle Ages. The object then of an admiration largely denied him in his own lifetime, he was quoted, even imitated, and respectfully read. Plautus, however, was the dramatist whose influence was paramount when secular comedy looking back to classical models began to be written and staged in sixteenth century England. There were a number of reasons why this should have been so. Among them, however, almost certainly was the ease with which Plautine naming could be grafted onto the native morality play tradition.

Chapter Two

It is one of the anomalies of Shakespeare's *Measure for Measure* that its prison seems to be the nicest place in Vienna. The Provost, as the Duke discovers, conducts himself less like a 'steeled jailor' than a 'friend of men' (IV.2.87). When Pompey, Mistress Overdone's tapster and bawd, finally arrives there in Act IV, he finds that the place is just like home. 'I am as well acquainted here,' he announces, 'as I was in our house of profession. One would think it were Mistress Overdone's own house, for here be many of her old customers.' And he begins to list them: Master Rash, in for a commodity of brown paper and old ginger, Master Caper, imprisoned at the suit of Master Three-pile the mercer, young Dizzy, and young Master Deep-vow, Master Copper-spur, 'and Master Starve-lackey the rapier and dagger man, and young Drop-heir that kill'd lusty Pudding, and Master Forthlight the tilter, and brave Master Shoe-tie the great traveller, and wild Half-can that stabb'd Pots, and I think forty more ...' (IV.3.1–18).

We never see any of these prisoners, never know any more about them than what their surnames, together with Pompey's few scraps of biography, suggest. Yet the effect of this list of invisible characters is potent. Suddenly, a formerly quiet, almost vacant jail becomes populous. It teems – like a drop of pond water upon which a microscope has just been focused – with the vigorous, darting life of individuals for whom the plight of Isabella and Claudio is not of the slightest concern. In a sense, Barnardine functions as their spokesman. When, a few lines later, he comes rustling up out of his straw, he seems to carry with him not only his own, untidy individuality (that

35

of a man who 'will not consent to die this day, that's certain' [IV.3.55–6]), but also that of all those other prisoners – and there is at least one murderer among them too – whose wayward lives defy the strict statutes and most biting laws of Vienna, not to mention the reforming strategies of her Duke. As is usual in Shakespearean comedy, most of the speaking characters in *Measure for Measure* (Vincentio, Escalus, Claudio, Juliet, Angelo, Isabella, Lucio, Mariana, Barnardine) possess vaguely Italianate Christian names and, so far as one can tell, no surnames at all. The ten invisible prisoners in Pompey's list, on the other hand, exist only by way of their surnames. As a bawd, despised socially even by the executioner Abhorson, Pompey does not pretend to familiarity with the Christian names of Mistress Overdone's former clients. That is why, although he himself acknowledges two names – he is 'Pompey Bum,' as Escalus discovers – Caper, Rash, Starve-lackey, and the rest have to be conjured up by a single designation. These naked surnames are uniformly cratylic, indicative of the habits and dispositions of their off-stage owners as 'Lucio' or 'Claudio' are not. And yet, unequivocally English though they are, as firmly rooted in the Jacobean London of Shakespeare's audience as are the dubious social and financial activities of their bearers, no one in 1604 could possibly have mistaken this for a list of actual, contemporary family names. Then, as now, they would have registered, taken together, as exaggerations, powerfully communicative comic inventions of the kind Aristophanes liked to deploy.

Aristophanes was by no means unknown in Renaissance England. There was a performance of the *Plutus*, in Greek, at St John's College, Cambridge in 1536. Ten years later, John Dee seems to have celebrated his election to a fellowship at Trinity, down the road, by staging a performance of the *Peace* that was almost too successful. (Dark mutterings about necromancy and devilish assistance clustered about what was obviously a spectacular ascent to heaven in the college hall by Trygaeus on his dung beetle.) Later in the century, Ben Jonson owned several copies of the works of Aristophanes, and could refer to the *vetus comoedia* of the ancient world in terms that assumed at least a measure of familiarity on the part of his readers. Shakespeare, however, did not need any first hand knowledge of Greek Old Comedy in order to name Pompey's former clients: Rash and Caper, Dizzy, Deep-vow, Forthlight, Shoe-tie, and the rest. Their origins are as native as their names, part of a legacy Shakespeare inherited from medieval English drama, not directly from Greece or Rome.

Although the Virgin Mary and Joseph found themselves confronting a number of difficulties as a result of the Immaculate Conception, one problem they did not have was the normal parental one of 'what shall we call the baby?' Adam, in Paradise, had named the entire earthly creation:

> both ffysche and foulys þat swymmyn and gon
> to everych of hem a name þou take
> Bothe tre and frute and bestys echon
> red and qwyte bothe blew and blake
> þou ȝeve hem name be þi self alon
> Erbys and gresse both beetys and brake
> þi wyff þou ȝeve name Also[1]

as God is made to say, elaborating somewhat on Genesis, in the N-Town Creation play. Whether he was giving generic names to birds and beasts, flowers and trees, or (somewhat later) a personal proper name to his wife, Adam had been an inspired name-giver: divining and giving linguistic form to the essence of the thing designated. In the New Testament, however, Mary and Joseph have to be told by the angel (he speaks to Joseph in the Gospel According to St Matthew, to Mary in St Luke), that of all the contemporary names available to Joseph and herself, they are to select 'Jesus' (derived from the Hebrew word meaning 'Saviour') for the infant Son of God, 'for he shall save his people from their sins' (Matthew 1:21). Similarly, the aged parents of the Baptist, Elizabeth and Zacharias, need divine instruction in order to arrive at the correct name of 'John.'

Like Elizabeth and Zacharias, Mary and Joseph, those minor clerics who were responsible in the main for the texts of the great fourteenth and fifteenth-century craft cycles, received the majority of the names they bestowed from God, as transmitted through the Holy Scriptures. They were, if anything, even less free to tamper with the names of Adam and Eve, Cain and Abel, Noah, Mary and Joseph, Herod, Caiaphas and Judas than Greek tragic dramatists had been with Oedipus and Electra, Agamemnon, Helen, and Orestes. Nor, as it seems, did they often feel impelled to exploit the meanings of these inherited names. Despite the strength of the Christian cratylic tradition, the authors of the guild plays made surprisingly little use of those numerous passages in both the Old and New Testaments in which names are said to reveal something important about the nature and function of their bearers, or were divinely changed in order to express a new direction imposed upon individual lives. It is possible, of course, that these dramatists were inhibited by their recognition that English equivalents to Old Testament Hebrew (and even New Testament Greek) names could be only approximate, at a significant remove from the sacred originals. Nevertheless, it seems remarkable that, across the cycles, only Lucifer, the 'light-bearer,' in the various accounts of the rebellion in Heaven, has his name consistently – and ironically – played upon.[2] He himself knows, and is forever being reminded, that he is 'wounderous brighte, / amongest you all shininge full cleare,' or else, after his defeat, that name and appearance are now at odds: 'My bryghtnes es blakkeste and blo nowe.'[3] The N-Town Angel Gabriel, very exceptionally, is allowed some serious onomastic play: 'þis name Eva is turnyd Ave / þat is to say: with-owte sorwe ar ʒe now.'[4] When Pilate, however, in the York 'Dream of Pilate's Wife,' tries to expound his name to the audience –

> my modir hight Pila þat proude was o plight;
> O Pila þat prowde, Atus hir fadir he hight.
> This 'Pila' was hadde into 'Atus' –
> Nowe renkis, rede yhe it right?[5]

– he merely makes himself absurd.

Among the surviving Corpus Christi plays that deal with life in Eden, those from Chester and N-Town refer briefly to the passage in Genesis (2.19–20) in which Adam, under the direction of God, names the beasts of the field and fowls of the air. Only the Cornish 'Creation of the World,' however, makes any attempt to dramatize it – with loving and very Cornish attention to the fish: 'Shewyan, pengarnas, selyas' ('breams, gurnets, eels').[6] All these plays assume that Adam received his own name from his creator, but bypass the opportunity of pointing out that it means 'earth,' the substance from which Adam is explicitly said to have been made. Only Chester picks up the Biblical references to the two names Adam gave his wife: one before, the other after, the Fall, and explains their etymological significance.[7] In York and Towneley, God, not Adam, first refers to Eve by name, and without reference to its meaning. It looks very much as though, like Greek tragic dramatists, the authors of the craft cycles were wary of name-play, even where it was present in the Bible. York, Towneley, Chester, and N-Town, for instance, all tell the story of Abraham, but only in York does Isaac's father remember that, in promising them a son, God also bestowed meaningful new names upon his wife and himself:

> Abram first named was I
>   And sythen he sette a sylypp ma;
> And my wiffe hyght Sarae
>   And sythen was scho named Sara.[8]

The Digby 'Conversion of St Paul,' despite its title, retains the form 'Saul' throughout, making not the slightest effort to remind audiences that, as a result of his experience on the road to Damascus, this former scourge of the Christians was renamed 'Paul.'

English drama, however, unlike Greek, seems to have possessed almost from its beginnings a hankering towards mixed and impure forms. Once released from the liturgy, and the physical confines of the church, Biblical plays, even those dealing with the darkest episodes of the Old Testament, or the Passion of Christ, tended to reach out for the comic. With comedy there entered a different attitude towards names: one endowing dramatists with a measure of Adam's original freedom in

Paradise. This comedy may be grim. In the manuscript of the *Mystère d'Adam*, an Anglo-Norman play of the late twelfth century still deeply indebted to liturgical drama, God (addressed by the characters themselves as 'Sire') had been alluded to in speech prefixes and stage directions only as 'Figura.' Such earlier reverence, reflecting uneasiness about representing the Creator, as well as scruples about the Tetragrammaton, the inexpressible name of God, makes Cain's ribald address to the 'Deus' of the Towneley 'Killing of Abel' as 'Hob-over-the-Wall' seem doubly shocking. Equally outrageous is the nickname Caiaphas substitutes, again in Towneley, for the divinely bestowed 'Jesus': 'King Coppin,' or 'Empty Skein.'

Significantly, dramatists who felt no compulsion to invent names for anonymous angels, or for undesignated Biblical characters who happen to be serious and good, tended to react quite differently when it came to figures with comic potential. Thus, the Towneley 'First Shepherds' Play' identifies 'Gyb,' 'Jack Horne,' and (the last to appear) 'Slow-pace' in the dialogue. Mak, the rogue hero of 'The Second Shepherds' Play,' is not only given a name, but branded by it as an outsider (it happens to be Gaelic)[9] even before he makes off with the stolen sheep. All the cycles are punctuated with non-Biblical English names: 'Ribald,' 'Froward,' 'Spyll-pain,' 'Gobet,' 'Tud,' 'Daw,' 'Sir Waradrake,' 'Sibyll Slut,' 'Dame Parnell,' 'Jack Cope,' 'Watkin,' 'Pikeharness,' or 'Grymball Launcher.' Some of them are attached to speaking parts; others to individuals who, like those in Pompey's list, remain not only mute but invisible. The majority belong to humble people rather than grand, and they tend to be comically derogatory. Yet, however unlikely such names may seem now, after centuries during which the most unflattering or ominous surnames have generally been suppressed or else corrupted into more dignified forms, very few of them can have struck contemporaries as obviously 'fictitious.' There were, for instance, no fewer than six people answering, however reluctantly, to the name 'Ribald' in Norfolk in 1329/30,[10] while 'Froward,' the aptly named torturer of the Towneley 'Buffeting' – 'well had thou thi name / for thou was ever curst' – seems to have become a common Middle English surname.[11]

One play, the N-Town 'Trial of Joseph and Mary,' opens with a roll-call of invisible individuals even longer and more elaborate than the one in *Measure for Measure*. Mary, the virgin wife who has mysteriously become great with child, is about to appear in court along with her husband to answer charges of unchastity brought against her by two extremely energetic detractors, 'Reyse slawdyr' (who teases the audience to 'telle me what men me calle')[12] and his colleague 'Backbytere.' A third character, Sym Sumnore, has Mary and Joseph's names written down in his book, but as he turns to confront the theatre audience it becomes apparent that he also expects the presence in court of a great many other people:

> both Johan Jurdon and Geffrey Gyle
> Malkyn mylkedoke and fayr mabyle
> Stevyn sturdy and Jak at þe style
>   and sawdyr sadelere.
>
> Thom tynkere and betrys belle
> peyrs pottere and whatt at þe welle
> Symme Smalfeyth and kate kelle
>   and bertylmew þe bochere
> kytt cakelere and colett crane
> gylle fetyse and fayr jane
> powle pewterere and pernel prane
>   and phelypp þe good flecchere.
>
> Cok crane and davy drydust
> Luce lyere and letyce lytyl trust
> Miles þe myllere and colle Crake crust
>   bothe bette þe bakere and Robyn rede
> And loke ӡe rynge wele in ӡour purs
> Ffor ellys ӡour cawse may spede þe wurs
> þow þat ӡe slynge goddys curs
>
>   Evyn at myn hede Ffast com A-way
> Bothe boutyng þe browstere and sybyly slynge
> Megge mery wedyr and sabyn sprynge

Tyffany Twynkelere ffayle ffor no thynge
The courte xal be þis day.[13]

This litany, freely and sportively put together, may well have
been a way of collecting money from the spectators.[14] On another level, it intends to make them participants in the action,
haling them into court alongside Joseph and Mary. The per-
sistent alliteration fantasticates the list; it is unlikely that any
attempt was being made here to single out real individuals in
the crowd. Yet it could not have fulfilled its function in the play
had it not corresponded to a considerable extent to the contemporary audience's own practice and understanding of naming.

Hereditary surnames were virtually unknown in England
before the Norman Conquest. They came in gradually, and
perforce, because of the Norman legal system and (in particular) Norman methods of keeping records.[15] Predictably, it was
among landed people identified with particular buildings and
estates that they established themselves most rapidly. It took
centuries for ordinary folk everywhere to acquire single, fixed
surnames, as opposed to Christian names qualified by some descriptive epithet, a 'nickname' that might alter more than once
during the lifetime of a man or woman and was not necessarily
transmitted to the next generation. It has been estimated that, in
1300, at least one third of the entire male population of England
was called either 'William' or 'John.'[16] Some parents, moreover,
seem to have been content to produce three strapping sons and
christen all of them 'John,' with the result that even within the
family it became imperative to identify them by way of diminutives and pet-names: 'Jack,' 'Properjohn,' 'Jenkin,' 'Jenning,' or
'Fairjohn.' As late as 1520, John Heywood could write a play
containing only three characters and call both the men 'John,'
distinguishing Tib's husband as 'Johan Johan' from 'Syr Johan,'
the generically named priest. He did not do this to set up any
confusion of identities – as with the two 'Bacchises' in Plautus' *Bacchides*, or the two 'Luces' in *The Wise Woman of Hogs-
don* (1604) – let alone to enforce a thematic parallelism of the
kind Dekker and Middleton were to establish between the two
'Marys' of *The Roaring Girl* (?1607). Heywood's duplication,

42

occurring as it does in an early sixteenth-century domestic farce, is merely a form of realism.

Despite its alliterative contrivance, Sym Sumnore's roll-call in 'The Trial of Joseph and Mary' suggests a good deal about the formation and development of surnames in England. 'Fayre mabyle' and 'fayre jane,' for instance, are women apparently without surnames: merely an accepted designation ('fayre') used to single them out, at this period of their lives, from among other, less conspicuously blonde, or attractive, Mabels and Janes. 'Jak at þe style' and 'whatt at þe welle' are similarly at the mercy of changing circumstance, in this case, place of abode. Among the many occupational names in the list, some appear to be in a transitional state – 'Miles þe myllere,' 'bertylmew þe bochere,' and 'phelypp þe good flecchere' having yet to negotiate the movement already accomplished by 'Thom tynkere,' 'peyrs pottere,' or 'sawdyr sadelere.' (The early sixteenth-century satirical poem *Cocke Lorelles Bote*, in fact, includes a 'Phyllyp Fletcher,' as well as a 'Pers Potter.') In the medieval context of the N-Town play, it is impossible to tell whether such names as 'Sturdy,' 'Smalfeyth,' or 'Drydust' pretend to describe a characteristic of the present owner, or whether they are hereditary. Even 'Belle' might be transmitted in this way, surnames in the period not infrequently descending from the maternal side.

The situation here is far more fluid and complex than it was to be among the invisible prisoners in *Measure for Measure*. It is also more realistic in terms of contemporary practice. Of the thirty-four names mentioned in the prologue to 'The Trial of Joseph and Mary,' not one would have struck the audience for which the play was written as blatantly fictional. All of them, even the least flattering, are recorded in the period, either exactly, or in analogous forms. ('Mylkedoke,' for instance, being paralleled by 'Mylkegos,' 'gullible enough to expect milk from a duck/goose,' 'Lytyltrust' by 'Lytylworth,' 'Crakecrust' by 'Crakebone.')[17] They are different, in this respect, from Shakespeare's 'Dizzy,' 'Deep-vow,' 'Starve-lackey,' 'Copper-spur,' and the rest, nicknames uniformly presented by Pompey under the guise of surnames, but – apart from 'Pudding' and the ambiguously human 'Pots' – with little plausibility as such by the early seventeenth century. In accepting Pompey's names, Shakespeare's audience, unlike the one summoned into court in 'The Trial of Joseph and Mary,' must have connected them far less with their own experience than with another and still-surviving dramatic tradition: that of the moral play.

❧   ❧   ❧

Although both 'Pilate' and 'Caiaphas' are recorded as English surnames, probably through association with individuals who played those parts in the cycles, their life was understandably brief. It is also possible that a few names that survive to this day – 'Verity' or 'Peace' – derive from medieval drama.[18] Abstract names were by no means unheard of in the mysteries, but in morality drama they became central. From the beginning, cratylic designations – 'Good Deeds,' 'Pity,' 'Newguise,' 'Avarice,' 'Iniquity,' 'Contemplation,' or 'Pride' – lay at the heart of this form. Fifteenth-century popular moralities such as *Everyman*, *Mankind*, or *The Castle of Perseverance* are 'comedies' primarily in Dante's sense. Yet their authors, unlike the minor clerics chiefly responsible for the Biblical craft cycles, enjoyed something like the freedom of Aristophanes or Menander when it came to giving names. It was, moreover, in the nature of morality drama as a form that these authorial acts of naming should be absolutely central, controlling plot as well as character to a degree unheard of in ancient comedy. Plato's Cratylus, had he been able to see a morality play, would surely have found it, in most respects, incomprehensible. Yet its nomenclature represents the triumph of his point of view.

In morality drama, names sum up the true nature of their bearers. There are no exceptions to this rule. If a character behaves in ways incompatible with his name, then that name is false. He may call himself 'Policy' or 'Worship'; he is really 'Avarice' or 'Pride.' The later moral interludes often make very sophisticated use of this convention. In the anonymous *New Custom* (1571), the eponymous Protestant hero spends most of the play trying to teach Ignorance and various Catholic foes that

44

'I am not New Custom, as you have been misled, / But am Primitive Constitution, from the very head / Of the church, which is Christ and his disciples all.'[19] The entire plot of Ulpian Fulwell's *Like Will to Like*, first printed in 1568, when Shakespeare was a child, is a dramatization of the naming system characteristic of most moralities. What the title turns out to mean is that with only the slightest assistance from the Vice (one Nicholas Newfangle) characters with names like 'Tom Tosspot,' 'Rafe Roister,' 'Pierce Pickpurse,' and 'Cuthbert Cutpurse' will all tend to gravitate into the same society and, eventually, come to sticky ends. The tell-tale names which, for readers or members of a theatre audience, constitute a moral indictment, suggest to their owners only the likelihood of shared tastes, a common outlook and mutually congenial way of life. As Tosspot tells his new acquaintance Roister, 'And as our names be much of one accord, and much like, / So I think our condicions be not far unlike.'[20] At the same time, characters called 'God's Promise,' 'Honour,' and 'Good Fame' are inevitably drawn into the orbit of one 'Vertuous Life.' The play polarizes around the two antagonistic groups of names, groups as different as the behaviour and respective destinies of the two circles of friends.

Not only is the identity of name with nature a cardinal rule of morality play nomenclature, integral to its didactic purpose, selected nouns are continually shifting their status from common to proper and back again in a way that focuses attention sharply upon names. Important words like 'mankind,' 'idleness,' 'mercy,' or 'repentance' will continue to be used abstractly in the dialogue while, at the same time, some of them become incarnate: able to walk and speak, wear contemporary clothes, suffer, tempt, and persuade. Here again, printed texts often obscure the nature of the play as originally performed. A list of dramatis personae, especially when accompanied by suggestions for the doubling of roles, is invaluable to a group, whether amateur or professional, contemplating its own resources, and concerned to know whether or not 'five may easely play this enterlude.' For the theatre audience, on the other hand, uncertainty as to just which abstract words are going to become vocal and concrete – some of them, given the nature of this

45

drama, at a very late stage in the action – is part of the technique of these plays. By the time of *Hick Scorner* (?1514), the complaint of a virtuous character, 'now is lechery called love indeed, / And murder named manhood in every need,'[21] has to be seen as deliberately raising false expectations in an audience familiar with morality conventions. Are 'Lechery' and 'Murder,' characters passing themselves off as 'Love' and 'Manhood,' about to take shape on stage? As it happens, they are not, but the dramatist has slyly encouraged his audience to entertain the possibility. Ancient and universal ideas about the magical potency of naming often seem to govern such transformations. In *Mankind*, for instance, Mercy is appalled to find himself suddenly surrounded by three boisterous undesirables who maintain firmly that he has requested their presence: 'I harde yow call "New Gyse, Nowadays, Nought,"' one of them affirms.[22] Mercy is baffled by this claim: 'Say me yowr namys, I know yow not.' What has occurred is that several dismissive terms employed by Mercy in his harangue to the audience have turned into the things themselves. He did not mean this to happen; the summoning was quite inadvertent. But it can be risky, as the old adage has it, to 'speak of the devil ...'

Once in possession of their names, Mercy knows exactly what kind of rogues these are. Virtuous personifications always interpret names correctly as, for that matter, do the various personifications of vice. The audience too, privileged to overhear the painstaking self-introduction of characters often far less candid with each other, is rarely in doubt. For the protagonists of these plays, on the other hand, the men and women whose souls are actually at risk, the situation is usually far more cloudy. Sometimes, especially in early moralities, the representative of humanity allies himself with the agents of hell in full consciousness of their true names, if not always of everything those names signify. That is something he will painfully discover. More often, he is gulled into crediting a virtuous-sounding pseudonym, while failing to notice that the behaviour and proffered counsel of its owner are at odds with his self-declared title. Such onomastic obtuseness is a sin in morality drama, the uncanonical but crucial error that usually opens the door for Belyal, Iniquity, and all seven of the Deadlies.

To be persuaded to abandon a good and holy Christian name, a mistake made by the heroine of that early sixteenth-century Dutch play *Mariken van Nieumeghen*, when she reluctantly allows the Devil to restyle her 'Emmekyn,' is to set one's foot on the road to Hell. Not to establish the name of a new acquaintance, something Anima (for instance) neglects with the spruce gallant, Lucifer himself in disguise, in *Wisdom*, is equally unwise. Virtuous abstractions are never guilty of such omissions. Their clear-sightedness about names, assumed or real, is so predictable as sometimes to provoke a feigned loss of memory on the part of the disreputable character being questioned. This becomes particularly striking in several of the moral interludes of the Tudor period. In Fulwell's *Like Will to Like*, the Vice Nicholas Newfangle explains to his interrogator, 'Vertuous Life,' that 'Indeed, I was but little when I was first borne, / And my mother to tell me my name thought it scorne.'[23] Vertuous Life, however, will have none of this: 'I will never acquaint me with such in any place / As are ashamed of their names, by God's grace.' Forced to 'remember' his name ('now it is come to minde: / I have mused much before I could it find'), Newfangle and his offers of friendship are instantly repudiated by a scandalized Vertuous Life. Protagonists sometimes begin with a measure of this onomastic clairvoyance but, unlike their virtuous mentors, they almost always make the mistake of crediting aliases, largely because they lack any true understanding of the quality to which vice is pretending. So, in Francis Merbury's interlude *The Marriage between Wit and Wisdom* (printed 1579), Wit in his unfallen state behaves impeccably when he insists upon eliciting the name of a frisky newcomer, and in his subsequent rejection of Idleness as a companion, only to fall at the last hurdle:

WIT
I pray thee, what is thy name?
to me it declare
IDLENES
nay, I am no nigard of my name.

47

nay, for that I will not spare.
ha! by the masse! I could have told
you even now.
what a short-brained villian am I!
I am as wise as my mothers sowe.
I pray you, sur, what is my name?
cannot you tell?
is there any here that knowes where
my god-father doth dwell?
gentellmen, if you will tarry while I
goe luck,
I am sure my name is in the Churc[h]
booke.
WIT
I prethy come of, & tell me thy name wth redyni[s].
IDLENES
faith, if you will neades knowe, my name is Idelnes.
WIT
Marry, fie one thee, knave! I nead not
thy compony.
IDLENES
what, because I spoke in jest, will you take
it so angerly?
for my name is honest recreation,
I let you well to witt.
there is not in all the world
acompanion for you more fitt.
WIT
And if thy name be honest recreation
thou art as welcome as any in this
laund.
IDLENES
yea, mary is it!
WIT
why then give me thy hand.[24]

Wit ought, of course, to have recognized that the trivialities and
horse-play of an interlocutor who claims that 'I was never staind

but once, / faling out of my mothers plumtre' are incompatible with the name 'Honest Recreation.'

The audience runs no danger of making Wit's mistake. It has already been informed, five lines into the Vice's opening soliloquy, that 'if you list to knowe my name / – I wis I am toy well knownen to some men – / My name is Idlenes, the flower / of the frying pan!' The opponents of plays and playing might well expostulate (and probably did, given that Merbury's interlude was both popular and remarkably long-lived) that to watch *Wit and Wisdom* at all was, in fact, to mistake Idleness for Honest Recreation. That, however, was certainly not Merbury's aim. Dramatists, particularly in fifteenth-century moralities and early sixteenth-century moral interludes, did occasionally attempt to embarrass audiences by cajoling them into an unwary, and ultimately sobering, cooperation with vice wearing its comic mask – as when Nought in *Mankind* persuades 'all þe yemandry þat ys here / to synge wyth ws wyth a mery chere,'[25] the song itself being so foul as to indict the spectators, as soon as it is over, of a heedless countenancing of ribald comedy. By 1579, however, English drama had for some time accustomed itself both to a more respectful attitude towards the audience and to a relaxation of didactic intent that permitted some kinds of laughter, at least, to become ends in themselves.

'Honest mirthe and pastime,' as Nicholas Udall announced in the prologue to *Jacke Jugeler* (1555), 'is requisite and necessarie' for the well-being of the mind, even if the matter itself be 'not worthe an oyster shel.'[26] Not an attitude that would have recommended itself to the author of *The Castle of Perseverance* or *Mankind* – even Udall sounds a little defensive – it nonetheless gained ground rapidly throughout the sixteenth century. In John Heywood's *Play of the Wether* (1528), the usual delaying tactics employed by a fantastically dressed Vice reluctant to divulge his name have a novel outcome. Although Jupiter initially repudiates 'Mayster Mery Reporte' when he does elicit his title – 'Thou arte no mete man in our bysynes'[27] – he is soon won over by the Vice's spirited defence of himself as (in effect) the voice of comedy:

49

And syns your entent is but for the wethers,
What skyls our apparell to be fryse or fethers?
I thynke it wysdome, syns no man for bad it,
Wyth thys to spare a better, yf I had it.
And for my name, reportyng alwaye trewly,
What hurte to reporte a sad mater merely?

Although just as cheeky and irrepressible as his morality play
brethren, Mery Reporte turns out, in the context of Heywood's
interlude, to be harmless: Honest Recreation indeed, his feath-
ers and parti-coloured garb censurable only by killjoys as being
those of culpable Idleness. Neither Jupiter, into whose service
he enters, nor the theatre audience, will have any reason to re-
gret Mery Reporte's fellowship. Even his outrageous account of
that widow to whom he was obliged to bring news of a dearly
loved husband's death, but who became merrier and merrier as
she listened to his ludicrous account of the disaster, asks to be
seen as the triumph of Comedy's point of view: unsentimen-
tal, even somewhat brutal, but in its priorities, its privileging
of life over death, vigorous, and compelling. Heywood's play,
essentially secular, designed for a sophisticated and courtly audience, has to a large extent broken free of the native morality
tradition. And yet, even within that tradition, there were from
the beginning elements at odds with its didactic purpose.

❖   ❖   ❖

Far more concerned, as a form, with the world actually inhabited by the contemporary audience than the mysteries, morality
drama invited from the start a comparison between its own
transparent and instructive system of naming and actual practice in an England gravitating towards the inherited, and increasingly hermogenean, surname as something typical of all
classes. Even in the relatively early *Mankind*, the shock must
have been considerable when Titivillus (a devil's name bor-
rowed form the Towneley 'Judgement' and, before that, from
nondramatic accounts of a particular fiend whose business it
was to parcel up missed-out or mumbled words from the divine

50

offices and bear them to hell as evidence against the offenders) commands Nowadays, New Gyse, and Nought to 'go and espy where ye may do harm.'[28] Abruptly, the cratylic naming that otherwise governs the entire morality gives place to something else:

NEW GYSE
Fyrst I xall begyn at Master Huntyngton of Sauston,
Fro thens I xall go to Wylliam Thurlay of Hauston,
Ande so forth to Pycharde of Trumpyngton.
        I wyll kepe me to þes thre.
NOWADAYS
I xall goo to Wyllyham Baker of Waltom,
To Rycherde Bollman of Gayton;
I xall spare Master Woode of Fullburn,
        He ys a noli me tangere.
NOUGHT
I xall goo to Wyllyam Patryke of Massyngham,
I xall spare Master Alyngton of Botysam
And Hamonde of Soffeham,
        For drede of in manus tuas qweke.
Felous, cum forth, and go we hens togethyr.

This, unlike the fancifully alliterative list of names in the N-Town 'Trial of Joseph and Mary,' is a roll-call of real, local people. The individuals named by Nowadays, New Gyse, and Nought were actually living at the time in those Cambridgeshire villages from which *Mankind*, in the version that survives, hoped to draw a substantial part of its audience. The surnames themselves, a mixture of Norman, Saxon, and Latin, derive in the main from place. It is clear, however, that none of their present owners is to be found in the locality from which he takes his name: Master Huntingdon now lives in Sawston, Master Allington in Bottisham. Nor, apparently, did this late fifteenth-century William Baker make bread.[29] 'Patrick,' a praenomen transformed into a surname, has forgotten that it began life as a nickname (the Latin *patricius*, or 'patrician'), and Master Pycharde's East Anglian neighbours are unlikely to remember that this man's forebears came to England from Picardy. Once-descriptive designations, now become neutral and arbitrary, none of these names says anything about the life or nature of the man by whom it has almost certainly been inherited, not personally earned. The one thing that is clear about the group as a whole is that all its members are men of wealth and substance: otherwise they would not be worth the sinister attention of New Gyse and his cronies, nor would they be likely to possess fixed family names.

Mankind was written and performed around 1466. But even in Jacobean England, thousands of people still had no hereditary surnames, only descriptive nicknames that changed freely in the course of their lives. This instability, particularly marked among the lower classes, registers itself naturally in comedy. In Fulwell's interlude *Like Will to Like*, written a century after *Mankind*, Newfangle introduces two rogues named 'Cutpurse' and 'Pickpurse' to one another and finds nothing unusual about the fact that

> thou, Cuthbert Cutpurse, wast Cuthbert Cutthrotes sonne,
> And thou, Pierce Pickpurse, by that time thou hast doon,
> Canst derive thy pedigree from an ancient house:
> Thy father was Tom Theef, thy mother Tib Louce.[30]

This genealogy, in which a nickname does the duty of a surname for the lifetime of the individual, and Cuthbert Cutpurse inherits only his father's Christian name, while earning 'Cutpurse' as the result of his own activities, must have looked far more realistic to Fulwell's contemporaries than it does today. Although there is one listing, in 1275, for 'Cuttepurs' as a surname,[31] it failed, for obvious reasons, to maintain itself, the fate of many other recorded but similarly undesirable designations: 'Smallbehynd,' 'John de Halfnaked,' or 'Swete-in-Bedde.' As a nickname, however, it was still going strong in the seventeenth century. When Middleton and Dekker, around 1607, put the real-life Mary Frith into their comedy *The Roaring Girl*, they were perfectly aware that 'Frith,' a surname deriving from place of abode ('a wooded copse') was the legal name she had been born with, and 'Moll Cutpurse' a title she had acquired by her own efforts. They still found it natural to stress the nickname, not her official surname, even while insisting, paradoxically, upon the scrupulous honesty of their fictional Moll.

In the case of Fulwell's Cuthbert Cutpurse and his various disreputable friends, 'Tom Tosspot,' 'Rafe Roister,' and the rest, a Christian name and a nickname appear to be all they have. These nicknames are accurate in what they have to say about their owners, and uniformly unflattering. Yet they have a curious and subversive effect in the context of the play, especially when measured against the nomenclature associated with virtuous characters. They are, in the first place – or would have been for contemporaries – more realistic. Certainly, in the light of such legally recorded appellations as 'Drinkalup,' 'Aydrunken,' 'Potfulofale,' or 'Fillecuppe,' Fulwell's 'Tosspot' ceases to look purely like didactic self-indulgence. In the early sixteenth century, apprentices still often adopted their master's surname.[32] A public executioner might well be forced, like Hankin Hangman in this play, to personify his opprobrious trade, even if this meant jettisoning his family name. When Mistress Overdone, in *Measure for Measure*, insists upon addressing Pompey as 'Thomas Tapster' (I.2.112), both assimilating him to his primary function in the brothel and giving him an alliterative first name, she aligns herself with a tradition stretching back to the Middle Ages, and forward as far as the nineteenth century, where the boy who blacked the shoes, whoever he might be, was customarily known as 'Boots.'

Although Vertuous Life and his associates God's Promise and Good Fame have names composed of two words, approximating to the structure of a Christian name and a surname, they never register in Fulwell's interlude as such. It is true that Puritan and Anabaptist christenings were to produce names quite as outlandish as Jonson's parodic 'Zeal-of-the-Land Busy,' or 'Tribulation Wholesome': 'Faint-not Fenner,' for instance, 'No-Merit Vynall,' 'Weakly Ekins,' 'Helpless Henley,' 'Sorry-For-Sin Coupard,' and 'Flie-Fornication Andrewes,' the unfortunate last an illegitimate child, are all recorded combinations.[33] Fulwell, however, was writing before the Puritans began to reject orthodox Christian nomenclature. It looks very much as though he set out to distance these virtuous characters by giving them abstract names corresponding to nothing in the experience of the audience, treating them in their nomenclature as in their speech as essentially inhuman abstractions.

Only the unregenerate in *Like Will to Like* have recognizable first names: 'Tom Tosspot,' 'Rafe Roister,' 'Cuthbert Cutpurse,' 'Philip Fleming' or 'Haunce,' the Lowlands sot. Alliteration keeps them to some extent within the confines of type, yet these Christian names create intimacy all the same. Because of them, the spectators – including, after all, people who themselves answer to 'Tom' and 'Philip,' 'Nicholas' or 'Rafe,' but certainly not to 'Virtuous' or 'God' – cannot dissociate themselves completely from characters of whom the play officially disapproves. That may operate, on one level, as a salutary warning. Concurrently, however, through naming, a rivalry is set up between exemplary but chilly abstractions and a messy, reprehensible but somehow cozy fraternity of the dissolute. Comedy, as is its wont, is threatening to overturn the moral applecart, with the help of names.

Never, in morality drama proper, does this threat actually reverse the didactic current of the play, as embodied in its plot. Audiences may experience a sneaking sense of sympathy with 'Tom Tosspot' or 'Rafe Roister'; there will be no hope for these characters at the end unless they can somehow negotiate a change of name which, unlike the pseudonyms adopted by vice figures, sets the seal on a genuine change of heart. Such reformations are difficult, however, to achieve, partly because the determinism of names tends to be so absolute in this drama. Morality writers, manipulators of a system ruthlessly dividing sheep from goats, sometimes seem to occupy not so much the position of Adam as of Calvin's God. Names, especially those bestowed in infancy, come to look like a form of predestination, confirming virtuous characters in their expectations of salvation, while launching others irreversibly towards hell. The system runs the risk of being both undramatic (because the ending is predictable) and didactically unsound. Not only is there little point in striving to live a virtuous and godly life if one's name

54

is 'Worldly Man,' time lavished by the virtuous on the reform of such a character is likely to seem foolishly misspent. Either he is not open to persuasion, or his reform will be temporary at best, returning him sooner or later to being what his cratylic designation ordains. This, at least, is what the nomenclature of a Tudor interlude like William Wager's *Enough Is as Good as a Feast* (1560) contrives to suggest, and it often seems at odds with didactic purpose. Why, after all, should the 'Potfulofales' and the 'Aydrunkens' in the audience try to mend their ways if their names effectively condemn them to be forever what they are?

Rebaptism is one possible solution to the problem. It was employed as early as the anonymous *Occupacioun and Ydelnes* (c 1450), where Ydelnes (who has earlier tried to pass himself off as 'Besynesse') turns into 'Clennes' at the end, after a strenuous working over from Doctrine.[34] Later moralities, however, gravitating as they did in the direction of realism and the representation of contemporary social life, tended to be less comfortable with name-changes of this kind. Most sixteenth-century moral interludes, while rich in low-life rascals, nevertheless centre upon, and assume with respect to the audience, a prosperous, middle- or upper-class milieu: one in which surnames are established things, remaining constant throughout and indeed beyond an individual's life. Tudor moralities, moreover, tend to bestow upon their protagonists names still abstract, but more particularized than the old 'Everyman,' 'Humanum Genus,' or 'Mankind.' Dramatists who tried to ignore or defy the implications of this more restricted and inflexible nomenclature were likely to find themselves in trouble. In the anonymous *Interlude of John the Evangelist* (1520), the name Eugenio ('Good Spirit') makes no sense through much of the play, except as a prophecy of its bearer's eventual conversion. Even in *Misogonus* (1570), a prodigal play whose names were designed (like many of those in Lyly, Jonson, and Chapman later) to 'speak' only to those members of the audience with a classical education, there is something puzzling and clumsy about an ending that leaves its eponymous hero repentant and reformed, yet still encumbered with a name ('misbegotten') that contrasts him with his virtuous brother Eugonus in a manner no longer appropriate. The play itself offers no hint that Misogonus will sooner or later return to his wicked ways. Only his name does that, raising the spectre of a future relapse beyond the dramatist's control.

This problem was still dogging Jonson when he suddenly transformed 'Sordido' in *Every Man out of His Humour* (1599) into a figure of magnanimity and good will, not to mention positing the reform of an entire corrupt and aptly named court at the end of *Cynthia's Revels* (1601). Interlude-writers of the first half of the sixteenth century continued, in some cases, to resolve it by invoking the baptismal powers of the church, as when the godly sponsors of 'Imagynacyon' transform him into 'Good Remembraunce' at the end of *Hick Scorner*. 'Free Will,' in the same play, gets out of the trap more ingeniously by announcing from the start an unresolved potentiality: 'I tell you my name is Free Will; / I may choose whether I do good or ill.'[35] Rather more drastic was the solution adopted by the anonymous author of *Mundus et Infans* (1500), who simply allowed 'The World' to retitle 'Dalliaunce,' the protagonist, as he moved through the successive stages of his life, as 'Wanton,' 'Lust and Lykyng,' and 'Manhode,' before abandoning him as 'Shame,' a condition from which he is narrowly rescued at the last moment, ending his strange eventful history as 'Repentaunce.'

Plays of this kind have already recognized a difficulty common to much Elizabethan and Jacobean secular comedy: how to take advantage of the suggestiveness and economy of cratylic naming while also allowing characters the freedom to alter and change. An issue that was to become immensely important in the work of the great Elizabethan and Jacobean playwrights – Jonson, Middleton, and Shakespeare himself – indeed something which can be seen to shape their individual and distinctive modes according to how they respond to its challenge, it becomes openly a matter for debate in the mid-sixteenth century. So, in William Wager's interlude of 1559, *The Longer Thou Livest the More Fool Thou Art*, three stern characters called 'Discipline,' 'Piety,' and 'Exercitation,' determined to drag the wayward protagonist into salvation, are initially dismayed to discover that his name is 'Moros.' Piety, trying to defy augury, declares firmly for the hermogenean position: people ought to be judged by what they do and are, not by accidental names, whether those names are unflattering or propitious:

> Moros is a fool by interpretation,
> But wisdom goeth not all by the name;
> He that is a fool in conversation,
> As a fool in deed we may him blame.
> I know some that be named happy,
> And some good, blessed, and fortunable;
> Yet truly there be none more unlucky,
> Worse, more wicked and unprofitable.
> And though 'Moros' a fool doth signify,
> Yet you may be wise, as I trust you will
> If you will serve God as you ought diligently;
> He shall give you wisdom, if you pray still.[36]

Piety, like Wager himself, is a good Protestant. That, however, cannot be the only reason why he avoids here any direct confrontation with the historical Sir Thomas More of *Utopia* and Erasmus's punning *Encomium Moriae*: that wise and diligent servant of God, who had been martyred some twenty-four years earlier. Many members of Wager's audience must, however, have remembered More, and the seemingly inexhaustible verbal games that contemporaries liked to play with the glaring incongruity between that man's moronic surname and the brilliance of his mind and accomplishments.[37] To have made the juxtaposition explicit would have shattered Wager's modest play. As it is, *nomen omen*. Although Piety manages to gesture at the possibility of choice and change, Moros proves in the end ineducable. An irredeemable fool, he is finally borne off to Hell on Confusion's back, without ever doing anything that might challenge the determinism of his name. Some three decades later, Shakespeare would find it possible, in 2 *Henry IV*, to create a character called 'Francis Feeble' and make him conspicuously brave. For Wager, on the other hand, the cratylism inherent in morality drama as a form was still too powerful to be overturned, despite his underlying awareness that not only in life

57

as it is off-stage, but also in other contemporary plays, 'wisdom goeth not all by the name.'

By the time of *The Longer Thou Livest*, moralities were engaged in an increasingly unequal competition with other kinds of Elizabethan play. Dramatists exploring these newer forms often veered markedly in the direction of Hermogenes, while allowing themselves to remember, at times, some of the onomastic habits and strategies associated with the moralities. This was not merely a matter of introducing the occasional self-indicting name. In the anonymous *Mucedorus* (1590), where names (as was usual in romance drama) are glamorous but only distantly expressive, an engaging clown named Mouse exploits the same fluidity of surnames among the lower orders that Fulwell had tapped in *Like Will to Like*, when he announces himself as 'the Goodman Rat's son of the next parish over the hill.'[38] Mouse's genealogy, however, is unjudgmental. His interlocutor, moreover, puzzles as no one in Fulwell had over its ambiguous status as Christian or surname: 'What, plain Mouse ... who gave thee that name?' (Mouse's deliberately riddling replies leave open the possibility that with time he may blossom into a 'Rat' like his father.) An individual called 'Thrift' in *Common Conditions* (1576), another essentially hermogenean romance play, is so obviously misnamed that other characters take to addressing him as 'Fellow Un-Thrift.' They do so here, however, without reproach, let alone any sense of exposing hidden evil.

Many of those adoptious christendoms that characters invent for each other in Elizabethan comedy – Benedick's 'my Lady Tongue,' for instance, in *Much Ado about Nothing*, or Orlando's dig at Jaques as 'Monsieur Melancholy,' in *As You Like It* – seem to suggest for an instant some shadowy morality drama. Shakespeare often turns common nouns into derogatory nicknames in this way. He was not, however, above mocking the habit, and the kind of play from which, in most cases, it derived. When, in *Much Ado about Nothing*, the members of Dogberry's ancient and most quiet watch overhear Borachio's exclamation, 'what a deformed thief this fashion is' (III.3.130–1), and proceed to give the adjective an independent life as one 'Deformed,' a vile thief this seven years, who walks up and down like a gentleman, with a lovelock over one ear, they are not, like Dogberry, simply mistaking the meaning of a word. Deaf to the genuine villainy Borachio unfolds, George Seacole and the rest, as they sit listening on their church bench, ferret out (as they think) a hidden personification, as though they were spectators at some old, outmoded morality play.

Chapter Three

Medwall's *Fulgens and Lucres* (1497) is England's earliest surviving secular comedy. Its author, chaplain to Archbishop Morton, had previously written at least one interlude: the two-part *Nature* (1495), a traditional moral play touched by humanist thought, in which the Seven Deadly Sins display their usual ingenuity in providing themselves with misleading pseudonyms. In *Fulgens and Lucres*, by contrast, Medwall approached the matter of naming with caution. Most unusually for a comic dramatist, he took over without alteration all four of the names in his source, Bonaccorso of Pistoia's tale *De Vera Nobilitate* as printed by Caxton in 1481: 'Lucres,' her father 'Fulgens,' her rival suitors 'Gayus Flaminius' and 'Publius Cornelius.' These Roman titles he handles neutrally throughout, displaying not the slightest interest in anything they might mean. In a sub-plot of his own invention, Lucres' maid, designated merely as 'Ancilla' in speech prefixes, is addressed by the two *trompe l'oeil* servants who emerge from Archbishop Morton's hall to compete for her favours as 'Jone,' a generic English name for a peasant girl. 'Some men,' as Berowne was later to put it, in *Love's Labour's Lost*, 'must love my lady, and some Joan' (III.1.205). The servants themselves, however, despite their importance in the play as a whole, have no names at all. Distinguished from each other in speech prefixes only as A and B, they make no attempt to improve on an anonymity about which both they and the dramatist seem oddly self-conscious. Not only does A twice address B as 'what calt,'[1] when in Part II Lucres asks him, 'What ys your owne name, I wolde understonde?' he is obliged to inform her that, 'By this lyght, I have forgoten.' Amnesia of this kind, including the suggestion that he will need to consult 'som of my company' in order to repair it, is familiar. A, however, unlike vice characters, has no title to conceal. In Medwall's hands, an old ruse, purposeful in its morality context, seems to have become a joke about his own failure to give names.

Taken together, the anonymity of A and B and Medwall's acceptance of the names given in his source suggest a lack of onomastic confidence understandable perhaps in a man departing from native medieval forms in order to explore the relatively unfamiliar territory of comedy. A generation later, the farce-writer John Heywood was still shy about inventing individual designations. In his *Play of the Wether*, Jupiter and (significantly) the vice Mery Reporte stand out amid a cast of generically named characters: the Miller, Merchant, Launderer, Ranger, and Boy. In four of the five other interludes attributed to him, characters are almost invariably designated only by occupation, social condition, or (*The Play of Love* [1533]) amorous role. One 'Neybour Pratt' makes the briefest of appearances at the end of *The Pardoner and the Friar* (1519). The real exception, however, if indeed it is by Heywood, is *Johan Johan*. Behind that play lies a contemporary original, the French farce *Pernet*, whose names the English adaptor daringly replaced with others of his own choice. Place-names, both English and foreign, are as common in Heywood as they are in morality drama. Personal names, on the other hand, of the kind which by Heywood's time had long been glanced at in the dialogue of the moral plays – the disreputable 'Jack Poller,' 'Ann Thriftless,' and 'Wanton Sibley,' for instance, of *Hick Scorner*, or 'litle Margery' and 'fleyng Kat' of Medwall's *Nature* – seem in England to have required the sanction of classical comedy before they could attach themselves as a matter of course to the majority of speaking parts.

Nicholas Udall's *Ralph Royster Doyster* (1552), written for performance by the boys at Eton, has a fair claim to be the first London comedy. Indebted both to Plautus' *Miles Gloriosus* and to the *Eunuchus* (Terence's most Plautine play), it skilfully mingles Plautine with morality and actual English contemporary names. The original of 'Harpax,' a musician in Udall, can be found in Plautus' *Pseudolus*. 'Matthew Merygreeke,' for the shiftless

61

but witty parasite, a name out of the same stable as 'megge mery wedyr' in the N-Town play, deliberately seeks indulgence for its owner of the kind extended to Peniculus in the 'Greek' world of the *Menaechmi*. Lewis Loytrer, on the other hand, together with Watkin Waster, Davy Diceplayer and Nicholas Neverthrives, some of the parasite's invisible but meticulously named patrons, belong in the morally dubious company of Tom Tosspot and Cuthbert Cutpurse in Fulwell's *Like Will to Like*.

Among the speaking parts of *Royster Doyster*, alliterative Christian names and surnames remain the order of the day, but 'Tristram Trusty,' 'Gawyn Goodlucke,' 'Dobinet Doughtie,' 'Sym Suresby,' and 'Tom Truepenie' are discreet in their adumbration of positive personal qualities, while 'Christian Custance,' the name of the heroine, manages to suggest 'Christian Constancy' without reducing her to a bloodless abstraction like 'God's Promise.' Tibet Talk-apace and Annot Alyface ('ale-face'), Christian's maids, have less complimentary titles, diminutives yoked to nicknames that glance at their respective loquacity ('Ye were not for nought named Tyb Talk-apace') and affection for strong drink.[2] As for 'Mage Mumble-crust,' her nurse, the name both recalls Plautus' 'Artotrogus' ('bread-muncher') and, like the more dignified 'Custance,' 'Suresby,' 'Doughtie,' and 'Goodlucke,' seems to have been a familiar contemporary name.

One name stands conspicuously apart from all the others. By coining the absurd extra word 'doyster' (OED *dois*, a crashing noise), Udall fantasticated his protagonist, lifting him out of the comparatively realistic sphere of characters like Fulwell's 'Rafe Roister' into the one occupied by those grotesque braggart soldiers in Plautus upon whom he is really modelled: men with impossible compound names like 'Pyrgopolinices' and 'Polymachaeroplagides.' It is part of Royster Doyster's massive but naïve egotism that he should take pride in his title ('Royster Doyster is my name, / Royster Doyster is my name, / A lustie brute I am the same'),[3] while omitting to commit to memory either the praenomen or the surname of the rich widow he supped with the previous night and has now decided, without consulting her in the matter, to marry. Christian Custance happens to be betrothed already to Goodlucke, a merchant whose name is a virtual reassurance that he will indeed return safely from sea to rescue his lady from a Royster Doyster. Yet, before that occurs, the braggart stumbles upon an important psychological truth about diminutives and pet-names. Merygreeke's caressing repetition of the widow's name after she has lost her temper in Act IV – he addresses her by it eight times in the space of four lines[4] – is a characteristically intelligent stratagem. To over-use a person's name, in conversation, is a way of forcing intimacy and gaining the ascendant. In comedy, it manifests itself as early as the *Knights* of Aristophanes, in the scene where Paphlagon and the Sausage-seller, competing for the favour of Demos, continually reach out to him by name. More surprising is the way Merygreeke's playful manœuvre suddenly impells Royster Doyster to transform 'Christian' into 'Kit.' No one else ever calls her this. A blatant and high-handed attempt to impose on her a private, lover's name that she has only in her relationship with him, it foreshadows the technique later employed by Shakespeare's Petruchio, in *The Taming of the Shrew*. Royster Doyster's use of 'Kit' is less successful than Petruchio's of 'Kate,' but his instinct here is, for once, entirely sound.

If, as seems likely, Udall was also the author of *Jacke Jugeler* (1555) and of *Respublica* (1553), an interest in the psychology of names was one of his recurring characteristics. *Respublica* is a political morality, not a classical imitation, but it is unusually elaborate in its handling of the customary morality subterfuge whereby vices conceal themselves under virtuous names. In a scene to be surpassed for sheer comic brilliance only by that later one, in Redford's *Marriage of Wyt and Science* (1568), in which Idleness battles heroically to teach Ignorance his name, Udall's Flatterie, also known as 'Adulacion,' the most dimwitted of the crew, has to put so much feverish effort into remembering his new name of 'Honestie' as to be exasperatingly incapable of mastering the spurious titles of the others. More interesting still is *Jack Jugeler*, an adaptation of Plautus' *Amphitryon* in which the Jupiter/Amphitryon/Alcmena plot has been stripped away, leaving only the dilemma of the servant refused admission to his master's house by a double claiming his identity and name. Reduplication of name, something that in Plautus had been only part of the confusion, becomes in Udall its origin and centre. Robbed of a name which, in any case, no longer fits him, the once insouciant Jenkin Careawaye disintegrates. The play anticipates, remarkably, the interest later to be shown by Shakespeare and others in the shattering psychological effects of namelessness as a condition not freely chosen, but enforced.

By no means all pre-Shakespearean comedy was cratylic, either in Plautine or morality play terms. A few significant names put together from Greek and Latin ('Tellus,' 'Corsites,' 'Geron,' 'Protea,' 'Psyllus,' 'Maestius') call attention to themselves among the predominantly mythological cast of characters in the courtly comedy of John Lyly. Romance plays, however, a genre that became popular in the 1570s, seem, on the evidence of surviving texts and the titles of lost works, to have favoured hermogenean names intended to convey little beyond a sense of the glamorous, exotic, and strange: *Sir Clyomon and Sir Clamydes* (1570), *Philemon and Philecia* (1574), *Herpetulus the Blue Knight and Perobia* (1574), or *Cloridon and Radiamanta* (1572). Only among servants and clowns, or surviving Vice figures such as Subtle Shift in *Sir Clyomon and Sir Clamydes* and the eponymous Common Conditions (1576), is it usual in this type of play for names to describe the nature or behaviour of their bearers.

In general, the more urban and familiarly allied to the times Elizabethan and Stuart comedy is, the greater its interest in the life of ale-houses, small hamlets, and city streets, the more likely it will be to gravitate away from the hermogenean in the direction of descriptive names. These did not need to act as moral pointers, even in the tolerant, good-humoured fashion of *Royster Doyster*. The author of *Gammer Gurton's Needle* (1553), a university play often paired with *Royster Doyster*, but far less indebted to classical comedy for either characters or plot, is already using linked and expressive names quite unjudgmentally, in order to bring a closely knit village community into focus. Gammer Gurton takes her name from the village itself, almost certainly present-day Girton, near Cambridge. Around her, type names accumulate: 'Hodge' the slow-witted rustic, 'Tyb' and 'Doll' the maids, her pert serving boy 'Cocke.' Such designations function here, as in Greek New Comedy, as dramatic short-hand. The dramatist was also, however, concerned to locate his central characters within a continuum of particularized village life. Invisible but suggestively named figures help to realize this background: 'Mother Bee,' 'Kristian Clack,' 'Hob Fylcher,' 'Sim Glover,' 'Tom Simson,' 'Tom Taylor,' 'Thomas Tankard,' their shadowy off-stage existences interwoven with those of Gammer Gurton and her household, her gossip Dame Chat, Master Bayley and his servant Scapethryft, and the curate Doctor Rat.

The life of these villagers is everywhere entwined with that of the domestic animals upon whom their economy and well-being depend: geese and ducks, tithe-pigs, hens, Gammer Gurton's gravid brown cow and 'sandy sow,' her fair red cock with yellow legs, Tom Tankard's cow on the gad, and his big, bald curtal horse. Only one of these animals enjoys a name: 'Gyb,' Gammer Gurton's 'great cat,' with whose invasion of the milk pan all the troubles of the day originate. Like 'Tyb' or 'Hodge,' or 'Joan,' 'Gyb' is generic: equivalent to today's 'Tom' for a male cat. By the time its four-legged owner is actually produced on stage, at the end of Act III, he has become the centre of an unspecific but pervasive beast fable, a story (as Diccon the Bedlam beggar puts it) 'of cat, and Chat and Doctor Rat,' in which Dame Chat, Gyb's slyly suggested human counterpart, 'must be chiefe captaine to lay the Rat in the dust,'[5] and her alleged theft of Gammer Gurton's 'cocke' manages to confound bird with boy in an almost Aristophanic way.

※   ※   ※

Almost a century later, in the reign of Charles I, Ben Jonson was using a nomenclature similar to that of *Gammer Gurton's Needle* in order to recreate life under the young Queen Elizabeth in a little circle of villages on the outskirts of London, earthy hamlets populated by people called 'Tobie Turfe' and 'John Clay,' 'Squire Tub,' 'Clench,' 'Puppy,' 'Wispe,' and 'Canon Hugh.' By the time he wrote *A Tale of a Tub* (1633), however, Jonson had virtually reached the end of a lifetime of experiment with different comic nomenclatures and forms.[6] *A Tale of a Tub*, with its country setting and linked but morally neutral names, is the late and in many ways untypical work of a man whose bias through most of his life had been as instinctively towards the urban and cratylic as that of Shakespeare was towards the rural and hermogenean. With Jonson and Shakespeare, the old onomastic debate between Aristophanes and Menander, Plautus and Terence, seems to renew itself. Shakespeare's fundamentally romantic comedy, with its predilection either for country settings or distant and oddly ruralized cities (the Athens of *A Midsummer Night's Dream* or the Messina of *Much Ado about Nothing*) was generically unlikely to favour cratylic names. It also, however, seems that by temperament Shakespeare was not only inclined to be careless when it came to naming parts, but wary of onomastic determinism. Jonson, by contrast, stands apart from all his contemporaries in the centrality and significance he accords, in his work as a whole, to acts of truthful naming.

Even in *The Comedy of Errors* and *The Case Is Altered* (1597), two early comedies in certain respects uncharacteristic of their respective authors, Shakespeare and Jonson can already be seen to be operating very differently in relation to each other and to their Plautine originals when it comes to the naming of parts. In reworking the *Menaechmi* and part of the *Amphitryon*, Shakespeare jettisoned every one of Plautus' names. Udall had done this too in *Jacke Jugeler*, but he replaced the Greek and Latin personal names of his original with expressive English equivalents – 'Jugeler,' 'Careawaye,' 'Boungrace,' 'Ales Trype and Go,' 'Dame Coye' – and Thebes with his audience's own London. Shakespeare, already avoiding London as a setting for comedy, as he was to do all his life, moved the story of the brothers Menaechmus from Epidamnum to Ephesus. In doing so, he undoubtedly meant to invoke the latter city's Pauline associations: with witchcraft, sorcery, and the proper relationship between husband and wife. Equally important, however, the change forestalled any of those cratylic jokes, registered in the *Menaechmi* itself and widespread in classical literature, about the near-impossibility of not being damaged, perhaps damned,

in Epidamnum: 'propterea huic urbi nomen Epidamno indi-
tumst, / quia nemo ferme huc sine damno devortitur' – or, as
William Warner translated it in 1595, 'The verie name shows the
nature, no man comes hither *sine damno*.'[7] (The Romans, when
they took over Epidamnum, nervously changed the name.) If
Shakespeare, as Dr Johnson complained, was all too readily inclined to sacrifice everything for a quibble, he became uncharacteristically restrained and cautious as soon as it was a question
of word-play implying the determinism of proper names.

The *Menaechmi*, unusually for Plautus, leaves no fewer than
five characters, three of them major, unnamed. Otherwise,
its nomenclature is typical of its author. Not only the parasite Peniculus, but the courtesan Erotium ('little love') and her
fat cook Cylindrus have defining names. The twin brothers
Menaechmus are named, wittily, after a Syracusan mathemati-
cian of the fourth century BC who discovered a method of du-
plicating regular solids by conic sections,[8] while Messenio, as
slaves so often do in New Comedy, goes by a title designating
his place of origin: Messenia, in the Peloponnese. Significantly,
Plautus goes out of his way to explain how the brothers' identical names, necessary for the plot, but scarcely a confusion that
the parents of twin boys might be expected to perpetrate, came
about. The twin stolen from his father at the festival in Tar-
entum (*puer surreptus*) was always called 'Menaechmus.' Only
after his loss was the name of Sosicles, the remaining twin,
changed, in memory of his lost brother, and also to honour the
grandfather, himself called 'Menaechmus,' who brought him
up. It is precisely because of this rebaptism that even when the
twins have at last confronted each other on stage, and acknowl-
edged their startling physical resemblance, full recognition and
acceptance of their relationship is held up while each brother
disputes the other's possession of his own name. Only when
the foreign twin remembers that he was once 'Sosicles' (and also
supplies their mother's name, Teuximarcha), is the situation finally untangled.

To turn from the *Menaechmi* to *The Comedy of Errors* is to exchange onomastic neatness and lucidity for opacity, and also
a measure of contradiction. By adding twin servants, from

the *Amphitryon*, a living father and mother for the other pair of twins from Gower's story of Apollonius of Tyre, a goldsmith and a merchant to complicate the plot, and a Duke and a marriageable heroine out of his own liking for figures of this type, Shakespeare considerably increased Plautus' modest cast of characters. The names he chose throughout, a mixture of Greek, Latin, English, Semitic, and Italian, all of them functioning as praenomen, are, on the whole, uncommunicative. Only 'Pinch,' the equivalent of the nameless 'medicus' in Plautus, could be said to be defined by his name. A few others are gently suggestive: 'Angelo' for a goldsmith, 'Egeon' for a man once shipwrecked in that sea, the hint of contrasted dark and bright in the names of the two sisters, Adriana and Luciana. Otherwise, etymologies appear to be wholly irrelevant to character or function, as with 'Antipholus,' meaning 'one who returns another's love,' 'Aemilia,' the 'the flattering or winning one,' or 'Balthazar,' 'protect the king.'[9] Attempts to establish the literary or other origins of the names Shakespeare uses in the play tend to be similarly unhelpful, not because antecedents cannot be found, but because there are too many of them, and – given the arbitrary way names are attached to particular individuals – little possibility of determining the original context. There is, for instance, a heroine named 'Antiphila' in Terence's *Heautontimorumenos*, 'Antiphilus,' an ungrateful knight, appears in Sidney's *Arcadia*, and the name was recommended for a lover in the *Thesaurus Graecae Linguae* (1572) compiled by Estienne.[10] Any of these might have prompted Shakespeare when he was casting about for a name to replace 'Menaechmus.' None seems to shed any light whatever upon the play.

McKerrow's original contention that *The Comedy of Errors* must have been set up not from a prompt-copy but from Shakespeare's own manuscript has been widely accepted. If so, the Folio text would seem to reflect a striking degree of carelessness and inconsistency in Shakespeare's approach to the naming of parts. A printer's error might just be responsible for the way, on two occasions in the second scene of Act III, Luciana inexplicably becomes Juliana. The Nell/Luce confusion, on the other hand, looks very much as though the dramatist had originally called his fat kitchen-maid 'Nell' – thus allowing the terrified foreign Dromio to pun on her being roughly 'an ell' about the waist – and then, having no further use for the joke, mislaid the original name. Nell (or Luce) scarcely figures as a character in *The Comedy of Errors*, indeed is likely to have been only a description offered by Dromio and (in III.1) an off-stage voice. More interesting is the inconsistency and apparent carelessness in Shakespeare's handling of something that, in Plautus, had been both central and scrupulously explained: the naming of the twins.

In *The Comedy of Errors*, as in other plays, Shakespeare sometimes seems to forget that he has already named a character. In stage directions and speech headings, even quite late in the action, 'Egeon' can lapse into 'merchant' or 'father,' the Antipholuses into 'brothers.' He also uses two different methods of distinguishing the latter, as 'Antipholus Sereptus' (Plautus' *puer surreptus*) and the mysteriously titled 'Antipholus Erotes' (*?erraticus*), and then, more straightforwardly, as 'Antipholus of Ephesus' and 'Antipholus of Syracuse.' Most perplexing of all, although Egeon, recounting his family history to Solinus in the opening scene, claims at one point that his twin sons 'could not be distinguish'd but by names' (I.1.52), he goes on to liken the attendant of the Syracusan twin to his master in being 'reft of his brother, but retain'd his name' (I.1.128). Nowhere in this long speech does the old man indicate what his sons' names, or those of their twin servants, actually are, or clarify just how and when they became the same, if they were not so from the start. Nor does he name his lost wife. He himself remains anonymous, merely a condemned 'merchant of Syracusa,' until he has finished his tale. Only then does Duke Solinus allow him a particular, as opposed to a generic, identity: 'Hapless Egeon' (I.1.140).

In the *Menaechmi*, a play of some 1150 lines, the name 'Menaechmus' is spoken, in one or another of its grammatical forms, thirty-seven times. 'Antipholus,' by contrast, is pronounced only fourteen times in a considerably longer play of 1775 lines. Although the Syracusan twin panics as he recognizes that, in this strange city, 'every one doth call me by my name' (IV.3.3),

69

Shakespeare places far less emphasis than Plautus had done upon this particular aspect of the misunderstanding. The frequency of 'Dromio' is much higher than 'Antipholus,' but almost equally inconsequential. Where Udall, in *Jacke Jugeler*, had, if anything, magnified the bewilderment of Sosia in the *Amphitryon* at finding his own name usurped, Shakespeare, in the equivalent scene of *The Comedy of Errors* (III.1) reduces it almost to nothing. The Syracusan Dromio, unlike Plautus' Mercury, speaks to his double only from within the house, never actually showing himself. Such staging might seem naturally to throw more weight upon the duplication of names, but Shakespeare was content to assign a single line of protest to the Ephesian Dromio: 'O villain, thou hast stol'n both mine office and my name' (III.1.44). When he came, moreover, to rewrite the Plautine recognition scene at the end, Shakespeare rejected the Roman writer's powerful stress on names as initially a bar to recognition, and then a means of confirming it. Because her name has never previously been mentioned (although it easily might have been, in Egeon's initial narration), the self-revelation of the Abbess as 'Aemilia' carries far less significance than Plautus' 'Teuximarcha,' the remembered name of a woman both invisible and irrevocably dead. Nor does either of the Antipholus twins feel impelled to make an issue out of the 'theft' by a double of his own personal name, as the Menaechmi had. The two Dromios appear to be similarly unconcerned. In the *Menaechmi*, names had not only been expressive, but an integral part of the selfhood of their bearers. In *The Comedy of Errors*, they are neither. Shakespeare's interest in what might be called the psychology of names – how people use and feel about their own and those of other people – was to become something that not even Jonson in the period could rival. In this particular early comedy, however, for whatever reason, it is a concern striking only by its absence.

Ben Jonson seems to have intended that *The Case Is Altered* should be one of his 'lost' Elizabethan plays. The quarto edition that appeared in 1609, when Jonson had become a celebrated man, was certainly unauthorized, and abominably printed. Yet for all its mislineations, vagaries of punctuation, and obviously garbled passages, this Jonsonian adaptation of two plays by Plautus – the *Captivi* and the *Aulularia* – is, by comparison with *The Comedy of Errors*, a model of clarity in its handling of proper names. Like Shakespeare, Jonson rejected all the names in his Latin originals, and also changed the locale. Unlike Shakespeare, however, he abandoned the ancient world entirely, replacing the regulation public street and house fronts of what Gratwick has called 'Plautinopolis'[11] (purportedly ancient Athens in the *Aulularia* and a city of Aetolia in the *Captivi*) with a recognizably contemporary Milan of shops, modest back-gardens, and aristocratic interiors. The Shakespeare who, in *Measure for Measure* later, could cheerfully populate Vienna with native citizens called Claudio, Lucio, Froth, Elbow, Angelo, Escalus, and Mistress Overdone, might well have found Milan no bar to his own selection of Greek and Latinate names. For Jonson, this was impossible. To the French prisoners Gasper and Chamont, and their pages, and the resident aliens Jaques and Rachel de Prie, he gave appropriate French names. Otherwise, his nomenclature is almost entirely Italian, and realistic of its kind. Jonson even goes out of his way to supply, in many instances, both Christian and family name. The only anomalies are the cobbler 'Juniper,' and 'Peter Onion,' Count Ferneze's groom of the hall, both of whom sound English without apparently being so. They are also the only characters with blatantly expressive or 'speaking' names of the kind that make comic word-play, a deliberate confusion of the human with the non-human familiar both from Aristophanes and Plautus, and from much earlier English comedy, virtually inevitable.

Everything about *The Case Is Altered* suggests that, whatever he later came to think of the play, Jonson originally named its characters with great care. Each is identified for the audience as soon as possible in the dialogue, and he reveals not the slightest tendency to change or generically dissolve individual designations fixed on, almost certainly, before he actually began to write. Only two names are withheld until the closing moments: 'Melun,' the true name of Jaques de Prie, and 'Isabell,' the name that restores the supposed Rachel to her brother Chamont. At the same time Gasper is discovered to be 'Camillo,' the child lost twenty years ago at the sack of Vicenza, to whom Count Ferneze has continually alluded. 'Isabell' and 'Camillo,' despite very little prompting from either of Jonson's two source plays, are important recognition tokens. They reflect, indeed, not so much his understanding of Roman comedy, as his own, highly individual sense of the importance of names. The *Aulularia* did not provide the miser's daughter, the equivalent of Jonson's Rachel, with a new family and name – only with a penitent rapist turned husband who acknowledges paternity of her new-born child. In the *Captivi*, the slave Stalagmus revealed, under duress, that Gasper was the child he kidnapped so many years ago, whereas in Jonson a name ('Camillo') and a token – the tablet inscribed *In mimimo, mundus* under the figure of a silver globe, originally found with Ferneze's son – are the agents of recognition.

※   ※   ※

The scrupulous handling of names in *The Case Is Altered* is very Jonsonian. Less characteristic is the play's hermogenean bias. This, indeed, may have been one reason why Jonson excluded it from the Folio of 1616. *Every Man in His Humour*, in its original version of 1598, had also employed neutral, largely Italian names – 'Lorenzo,' 'Giulliano,' 'Musco,' 'Stephano,' 'Biancha,' 'Thorello,' 'Prospero,' 'Matheo' – in keeping with its Florentine setting. Only the water-carrier Cob, a man as much given to word-play on his own name as Peter Onion, and his wife 'Tib' seemed to have strayed in from a more northern clime. This comedy, however, prophetic of its successors in Jonson's first Folio, had always contained an exposition of humours. It was comparatively easy, when he came to revise it, to replace 'Lorenzo' by 'Kno'well,' 'Giulliano' by 'Downright,' 'Musco' by 'Brayneworme,' 'Thorello' by 'Kitely,' 'Prospero' by 'Wellbred': English names expressive of character as their Italian prototypes were not. It required, similarly, only a modest amount of effort to make the shadowy London of lodging houses and ordinaries, conduits, counting-houses, and fashionable residences that had always lurked below the surface of an ostensible Florence

72

emerge strongly into the light. Jonson could not have revised *The Case Is Altered* in this fashion without, in effect, writing a wholly new play.

With *Every Man out of His Humour* in 1599, Jonson committed himself whole-heartedly to London (thinly disguised under 'the fortunate Iland') as a setting and to cratylic naming. Thereafter, with the exception of *Poetaster* (1601), *Volpone* (1606), and the unfinished pastoral *The Sad Shepherd* (1637), all his comedies would take place either in or very near the metropolis where Jonson himself lived. He derived his expressive names in two instances (*Every Man out of His Humour* and *Volpone*) from Florio's Italian dictionary. *Cynthia's Revels* (1601) anatomizes the inhabitants of 'Gargaphie' (alias London and the court of Queen Elizabeth) by way of a largely invented Greek nomenclature not dissimilar to that employed on occasions by Lyly. In all the rest, except for *Poetaster* and *The Sad Shepherd*, which constitute special cases, English 'speaking' names prevail. Jonson's preference for contemporary London as a setting, a preference naturally impelling his comedy in the direction of satire, implies in itself the use of charactonyms. Other dramatists of the period, Fletcher and Marston, Massinger or Middleton, can also be observed veering sharply in the direction of cratylic naming whenever they choose London, as opposed to some more remote, exotic place – Sicily or Milan, Paris, Flanders, Hungary, or Tunis – as a comedy locale. Massinger's *The Guardian* (1633), for instance, set in Naples, although scarcely romantic in its handling of women, presents characters called Alphonso, Severino, Montecларo, Durazzo, Caldoro, Camillo, Iolante, Caliste, and Mirtilla, and discourages any attempt to discover significance in their names. Yet in his London play *The City Madam*, performed in the preceding year, he had employed such obviously defining titles as 'Frugal,' 'Plenty,' 'Goldwire,' 'Tradewell,' 'Stargaze' (an astrologer), 'Fortune,' and 'Shavem.'

Jonson's cratylism, however, unlike that of Massinger and many other contemporary dramatists, is not simply the result of his election of contemporary London as a setting. An ingrained habit of mind, it colours virtually all of his work, not only the comedies, but the nondramatic poems and the court masques

73

as well. In these latter forms, moreover, it reaches out to absorb the rival hermogenean position, turning it cunningly to its own ends. There are, in consequence, two characteristic kinds of name in Jonson, opposed but complementary. It is a cardinal rule of *Epigrams*, *The Forest*, and *Underwoods*, Jonson's three great collections of nondramatic verse, that the names of the noble and the good should come to epitomize their bearers, not so much through etymologies, or even mimological suggestion, as through association with the lives and virtuous qualities of their owners. The family name 'Sidney' may derive from 'St Denys' in France, or from a Saxon word meaning 'dweller by the wide well-watered land.'[12] That, for Jonson, is a matter of indifference. The name's meaning for him – like the meanings that accrue to stock New Comedy names in Menander – is entirely a product of the actions and characteristics of those who have borne it, and it requires (as in Menander) exploration and revalidation by each successive owner. ' 'Twill be exacted of your name, whose son, / Whose nephew, whose grand-child you are,' he informed the young William Sidney sternly, on the occasion of his twenty-first birthday.[13] Occasionally he will glance at the meaning of this type of name, as he does with the play upon 'lucent' in his epigram on Lucy, Countess of Bedford. The real stress, however, falls elsewhere. After imagining a woman 'faire, and free, and wise, / Of greatest blood, and yet more good then great,' a 'learned and a manly soul' housed in a soft yet radiant form, 'Such when I meant to feign, and wished to see, / My muse bade, Bedford write, and that was she.'[14] The surname, when finally released, is a representation in miniature of its owner's individual life and qualities.

> Praises should then, like definitions, be
> Round, neat, convertible, such as agree
> To persons so, that were their names conceal'd,
> Must make them known as well as if reveal'd.[15]

Jonson would have endorsed the words of Lord Herbert of Cherbury, in his elegy for John Donne, while also insisting that the converse was true: the names of those truly deserving of

74

praise become in themselves celebrations of worth. Particular surnames may even revert to the status of common nouns, something he imagines happening in the case of Sir Lucius Cary and Sir Henry Morison, who

> lived to be the great surnames,
> And titles by which all made claimes
> Unto the virtue. Nothing perfect done,
> But as a Cary, or a Morison.[16]

It is the expressed intention of Jonson's *Epigrams*, in particular, to lead forth 'many good, and great names as my verses mention on the better part to their remembrance with posterity.'[17] The individuals Jonson means to censure, on the other hand, are condemned even before their particular faults have been anatomized, simply by the fact that their real names have been replaced by exactly the kind of pejorative cratylic name he employs in his comedies: 'Sir Annual Tilter,' 'Sir Voluptuous Beast,' 'Lieutenant Shift,' or 'Fine Lady Would-Be.' The most contemptible of all (as in 'To One That Desired Me Not To Name Him' and 'On Something That Walks Somewhere'), denied even such caricature titles, become totally anonymous, a state Jonson regards as tantamount to non-existence.

In his court masques, those fictions of power linked with goodness that Jonson and Inigo Jones created for the Stuarts, at Whitehall, between 1605 and 1631, the two complementary naming strategies of the poems were translated into a peculiarly visible dramatic form:

> And who this king and queen would well historify
> Need only speak their names; those them will glorify:
> Mary and Charles, Charles with his Mary named are,
> And all the rest of loves or princes famed are.[18]

The world of the masques is one of onomastic order and transparency. It delights in anagrams – 'Charles James Stuart' revealed as 'Claimes Arthurs Seate,' 'Charles Stuart' as 'Calls True Hearts' – and in the kind of etymologizing which, in *The*

Haddington Masque (1608), could turn the bride's family name ('Radcliffe') into a stage setting: 'a high, steep, red cliff advancing itself into the clouds.'[19] *Hymenaei* (1606) depends in its entirety upon the correspondence Jonson teases out between 'Juno,' the patroness of marriage, and 'Unio,' the king's scheme for the unification of Britain.[20] Names indicate essence, whether by way of an overt cratylism that is both playful and serious, or through Jonson's tendency to nudge hermogenean surnames towards the expressive by allowing them to take colour from the lives and natures of their bearers. Never, in any case, do they lie. Although, as in morality drama, niggardly Plutus may attempt for a time to pass himself off as Cupid, Opinion as Truth, or Anteros as Eros, discovery is inevitable. Either such characters, in speaking, will reveal attitudes incompatible with their names, or their appearance will render the deception obvious to the iconographically adept.

In theory at least, the correct naming of masque personages or images, according to their appearance, attributes, and (sometimes) words, was one of the chief intellectual pleasures offered by these entertainments. Mindful of this, Jonson sometimes significantly delays the release of a character's name, as he does, for instance, with 'Heroic Virtue' in *The Masque of Queens* (1609) or 'Robin Goodfellow' in *Love Restored* (1612), in order to allow the audience to guess, from a combination of appearance and words, what he or she ought to be called. In the masque as printed, this strategy (as so often) tends to be obscured, the name declaring itself prematurely either in a speech prefix or stage direction. Masque texts, however, were special in their retrospective need to describe and so perpetuate the visual: costumes and scenic splendours, transformations, or a dance like the one in *The Masque of Queens* in which the participants apparently arranged themselves so as to spell out the letters of Prince Charles's name. Initially, at least, Jonson was scrupulous about recording in his text something else the reader could not otherwise divine: the names of the noble masquers.

In the enclosed world of Whitehall, the real identities of Anne of Denmark, the Countess of Bedford, or Prince Charles, despite their token vizards and silent, allegorical roles, must have been as transparent to most of the audience as Benedick's is to Beatrice, or Antonio's to Ursula in the revels scene of *Much Ado about Nothing*. The quarto texts of *The Masque of Blackness* (1605) and its sequel *The Masque of Beauty* (1608), *Hymenaei*, *The Haddington Masque*, and *The Masque of Queens*, lead forth the names of the masquers (together with those of Jonson's collaborators, Master Herne and Master Giles, Master Ferrabosco and Master Jones) to their remembrance with posterity as carefully, and for the same basic reasons, as those of the people honoured in Jonson's nondramatic verse. Then, in 1615, the Overbury scandal broke. In his Folio of 1616, Jonson not only removed the names of Frances Howard and the Earl of Essex, the unsavoury bridal pair, from the title-page of *Hymenaei*, but expunged the names of all the high-born performers in the masque as well. He continued to create masques for King James, and also to publish the texts. A diminution, however, in the value he placed on the masque performance, 'the short bravery of the night,' and the 'jewels, stuffs, the pains, the wit / There wasted,' is implied by his suppression henceforth of the performers' names.[21] Only in the first masques of the new reign, *Love's Triumph through Callipolis* (1631), in which King Charles himself deigned to perform, and *Chloridia* (1631), which featured the Queen, did he allow them to return.

In his nondramatic poetry, and in his masques, Jonson's attitude towards names and naming is remarkably constant and fixed. His decision no longer to record the names of the masquers represents a changed attitude towards the masque, but not towards naming itself. *The Gypsies Metamorphos'd* (1621), King James's favourite masque, is unique in entrusting speaking parts to its noble participants. In publishing this most spectacularly successful of his entertainments, Jonson nonetheless firmly omitted the names of Buckingham and his fellow-actors. (Their identities are recoverable now, and then imperfectly, only on the evidence of a contemporary.)[22] The names of those members of the audience, beginning with 'James the Just,'[23] who had had their individual natures and fortunes expounded by the pretended gypsies were another matter. Some are spoken in the dialogue; all were scrupulously signalled in the text as printed. There, they become expressive in the manner of 'Bedford' or

'Sidney' in the nondramatic verse. Against them, in what passes here for an anti-masque, Jonson sets fictional speaking names – Townshead and Cockerel, Paul Puppy and Tom Clod – just as he did in his *Epigrams*, and encourages play on their literal meanings.

Simple without being vicious, the rustics of *The Gypsies Metamorphos'd* escape, however, the opprobrium meted out to their equivalents in the *Epigrams*. The nomenclature Jonson devised for them looks forward, in fact, to *A Tale of a Tub*. In comedy, the fact that he became significantly less judgmental with time did gradually modify some of Jonson's onomastic habits. That increasing tolerance of human peculiarities which begins to manifest itself in *The Alchemist* (1610) impelled him both to qualify defining surnames with Christian names of an ordinary, neutral kind, and to make surnames themselves less morally constricting than they had been in the 'comicall satyres' of his late Elizabethan period. Jonson never returned to names as opaque and uncommunicative as those he had used in *The Case Is Altered*. But he did, increasingly, minimize titles like 'Sir Amorous La-Foole,' 'Epicure Mammon,' or 'Sir Glorious Tipto,' mingling or replacing them with designations – 'Abel Drugger,' 'Frank Penniboy,' 'Ned Winwife,' 'Ursula,' 'Pleasance,' or 'Laetitia' – allowing characters a space in which to manœuvre, and even change, that had been denied to most of the dramatis personae in *Cynthia's Revels* or *Volpone*. In *The New Inn* (1629), Jonson was even led to experiment with surnames ('Lovell' and 'Frampull') capable of meaning contrary things, and allowing the actions of their owners over the course of the play to justify the positive, as opposed to the negative, possibility.

Thomas Middleton, Jonson's only real rival as a dramatist of contemporary London life, also moved between 1603 and 1621 away from morally defining names in the direction of a more neutral and quietly suggestive nomenclature. There is a world of difference between an early Middleton play like *The Phoenix* (1604), set in a Ferrara that is patently London in thin disguise, with its damning 'Proditor,' 'Infesto,' 'Lussurioso,' 'Falso,' 'Latronello,' 'Furtivo,' and 'Tangle' set against the virtuous 'Phoenix,' 'Fidelio,' 'Castiza,' and 'Quieto,' and what Middleton was doing by 1613 in *No Wit, No Help Like a Woman's*. In the later work, characters called 'Jane Sunset,' 'Kate Lowwater,' 'Sandfield,' 'Weatherwise,' 'Overdone,' 'Gilbert Lambstone,' and the whole 'Twilight' family, 'Sir Oliver' and his nameless wife, 'Philip' and 'Grace,' create a pervasive atmosphere of stagnation and ageing, barrenness and shade strangely (and purposefully) at odds with the brisk plot of this formally most Plautine of Middleton's plays. In his last comedy, *Anything for a Quiet Life* (1621), the refusal to prejudge characters by way of their names has progressed even further than it was to do in Jonson's late plays. Only the lawyer 'Knavesby,' and a scattering of occupational names among lower-class characters ('Water-Camlet' the mercer, the barber 'Sweet-Ball,' 'Flesh-hook' the officer) remain as contrasts to 'Lord Beaufort,' 'Sir Francis Cressingham,' his sons 'George' and 'Edward' and daughter 'Maria,' the elder 'Franklin' and his son, 'Saunder,' and Water-Camlet's apprentices 'Ralph' and George.'

Jonson's belief in the significance of names, his respect for the position of Cratylus, never permitted him to go this far. Indeed, the comparison with Middleton serves in the end to demonstrate just how distinctive in their period, as well as consistent, Jonson's onomastics were. Like Plautus,[24] and also like the majority of his own contemporaries, Middleton seems to have been content, throughout his life, to leave major characters – the courtesan in *A Trick to Catch the Old One* (1605), the country wench and her father in *Michaelmas Term* (1606), the jeweller's wife in *The Phoenix*, Frank Gullman's mother in *A Mad World, My Masters* (1606), or the Welsh gentlewoman in *A Chaste Maid in Cheapside* (1611) – unnamed. Jonson, dedicated as he was to the idea of the revelatory name (whether cratylic or a matter of association), could never do this. There are no anonymous merchants, goldsmiths, fathers, mothers, courtesans, daughters, courtiers, or soldiers with major roles to be found in Jonsonian comedy. Peregrine, the young English traveller in *Volpone*, whose name is not spoken in the dialogue, constitutes a rare oversight on Jonson's part. Stage directions and speech prefixes, in any case, make it abundantly clear that he had, in fact, been scrupulously and appropriately named.

With the exception of a few, very common Christian designations ('Tom,' 'Edward,' 'Frances,' or 'John'), all of them overshadowed by a surname unique to the individual, or to members of his immediate family, Jonson never repeated names from one comedy to another. Middleton, by contrast, was as casual as Menander, Terence – or Shakespeare – in this respect, although usually more cratylic. He used twenty-six names twice or more, some as many as five, seven, or (in the case of 'Frank' and its associated forms) ten times.[25] In *Anything for a Quiet Life* (1621), he even managed to call two major characters 'George,' and put them on stage together. This duplication has sometimes raised suspicions of another hand in the comedy. More probably, it reflects an insouciance about onomastic repetition reminiscent not only of Shakespeare, but of John Heywood's awareness in *Johan Johan* that in real life acquaintances commonly share the same Christian names, and may as well do so on the stage.

Like Jonson, the younger Middleton occasionally derived his morally defining names from Florio's dictionary: 'Castiza,' which he used three times, or 'Sordido' and 'Lussurioso.' He was quicker, however, than Jonson to become concerned about the extent to which such names, whether Italianate or English, tended to immobilize characters, rendering them predictable, and precluding change. Even in his early play, *The Family of Love* (1602), the two young lovers, although sometimes mocked, had been set off from the knaves and fools around them, characters trapped by names like 'Glister,' 'Purge,' 'Lipsalve,' and 'Gudgeon,' by virtue of being simply 'Maria' and 'Gerardine.' The same distinction obtains in *Your Five Gallants* (1605), where the altogether admirable Fitzgrave and Katharine are again isolated by their names among a cast of characters called 'Tailby,' 'Frippery,' 'Pursenet,' and 'Bungler.' When Jonson, in *Volpone* the following year, wished to set two characters apart as rational human beings in a world of crows and foxes, parrots, vultures, and flies, he still burdened them with significant names: 'Celia' (the heavenly) and 'Bonario' (the good). Only, however, in *The Phoenix*, possibly Middleton's first comedy, and heavily indebted in a number of respects to Jonson's early humour

80

plays, are all the named characters, without exception, summed up by a single, morally revelatory designation.

At the end of *The Phoenix*, in a scene reminiscent of the purging of Crispinus in the last moments of *Poetaster*, the insanely litigious Tangle is cured, in public, of his obsession with the lawcourts through the ministrations of Quieto. His name, however, remains (like that of Sordido in Jonson's *Every Man out of His Humour*) to accuse him irrelevantly of habits and a disposition which he has now put aside. Middleton side-steps this problem, even as he had earlier evaded the question of just what Quieto himself had been called in the days when he too, by his own confession, was addicted to the law and 'mad, stark mad, nine years together.'[26] Because Tangle's reformation signals the end of the action, and also because *The Phoenix* as a whole is so episodic, and so uncomplicated in its characterization, such failures to explain hardly matter. Yet, in subsequent and more richly textured plays, Middleton grew more and more uneasy in his cratylism.

Like Jonson, he came increasingly to give major characters two names, and to allow the first of them – 'Richard' or 'Mary,' 'Oliver' or 'Jane' – to militate against the distancing, caricature effect of the second. In *A Mad World, My Masters*, he went further, experimenting here in a way Jonson never did with oxymoron. 'Richard Follywit,' 'Frank Gullman,' 'Bounteous Progress,' and 'Penitent Brothel' do not really have contrasting potentialities, in the manner of Jonson's 'Frances Frampull' and 'Herbert Lovell.' They are irresolvably contradictory names, exacting a divided response from the audience. So, in a slightly different way, does 'Allwit,' the name of that heartless but indomitable survivor in *A Chaste Maid in Cheapside* (1611). Referred to initially in the dialogue as 'Jack,' or simply 'the wittol,' he becomes 'Allwit' for the theatre audience only at the end of Act II. A redemptive transformation of 'wittol,' this surname when revealed manages to give with one hand while continuing, in a new sense, to take away with the other. Its belated release into the dialogue, a technique characteristic of Middleton,[27] has been carefully calculated: a discovery meant to correct what the audience now realizes was an oversimple and facilely dismissive first impression.

There is some evidence in the quarto editions of *A Mad World, My Masters*, in both of which 'Penitent Brothel' metamorphoses into 'Penitent Once-Ill' in stage directions after his reformation, that Middleton may have intended to change this character's name as soon as he amended his life. If so, unlike the formal rebaptisms of some morality plays, the new name would not have registered on stage, only in the printed text. On the other hand, the uncertainty over the name of the citizen cuckolded by Penitent – in stage directions, it changes from 'Harebrain' to 'Hargrave' and back, before concluding its career as 'Shortrod' – suggests that the printer was working from a manuscript that recorded several different stages in Middleton's naming of parts. Even as he found it natural to leave some characters entirely unnamed, so (as it seems) he was content to write dialogue for others whose names, up to a very late stage of composition, still hung in the balance. An approach inconceivable from Jonson, it is one of several onomastic habits which, despite the London settings and, for much of the time, the underlying cratylic bias, serve to link Middleton's comedy with that of a man with whom it is probable on occasion that he collaborated, as he could never have done with Jonson: William Shakespeare.

Chapter Four

In Sonnet 81, Shakespeare assures his friend, the 'lovely boy' who is lord of his heart, that long after both of them are dead,

> Your name from hence immortal life shall have ...
> And tongues to be your being shall rehearse,
> When all the breathers of this world are dead;
> > You still shall live (such virtue hath my pen)
> > Where breath most breathes, even in the mouths of men.

The young man's name, kept alive in Shakespeare's verse, is a word that will be perpetually on the lips of men. What, however, was his name? Shakespeare never says. Nor does he ever explain how, as a particular individual, the object of his praise will be able to 'pace forth' against 'death and all-oblivious enmity' without it (Sonnet 55). The rival poet, and the 'woman coloured ill' who appears at the end of the sequence, are equally anonymous. Only Anne Hathaway, in a sonnet that seems to have strayed in from some earlier and unrelated work, has her surname glanced at, in 145: ' "I hate" from hate-away she threw.' In some of the late sonnets, Shakespeare puns wryly on his own Christian name of 'Will.' With respect, however, to 'the onlie begetter' of the majority of the poems, the man for whose immortality such extraordinary claims are made, there are only the initials 'W.H.,' and they were supplied by Thomas Thorpe, the publisher of the 1609 quarto, not by Shakespeare.

It is easy to imagine how Ben Jonson might have handled the situation in the *Sonnets*. The young man would have been named directly as 'Henry Wriothesley, Earl of Southampton' –

or, perhaps, 'William Herbert, Earl of Pembroke.' The rival poet might have appeared as 'Impertinax Scribbler,' the dark lady as 'Mistress Bed-lust': insulting substitutes for their real names. Jonson's way with personal names, however, is not Shakespeare's. Jonsonian comedy sometimes seems almost as thickly sown with the names of specific contemporaries as that of Aristophanes. It introduces the names of Elizabethan poets: Sidney, Spenser, Daniel, indeed Jonson himself, alchemists like Dr Dee and the less reputable Simon Read, the actors Nathan Field, Richard Burbage, and Dick Robinson, the Archbishop of Spalato, Archie the King's fool, even particular racehorses of the time called 'Puppy,' 'Peppercorn,' 'Whitemane,' and 'Franklin.' There is nothing even approaching this flood of contemporary reference to be found anywhere in Shakespeare.

It is not that Shakespeare is oblivious to the power that can reside in the names of living men. Henry v before Agincourt encourages his soldiers by predicting how, in time to come, his own name, and the names of those great nobles of England who are to fight beside them – 'Harry the King, Bedford and Exeter, / Warwick and Talbot, Salisbury and Gloucester' – will be familiar in their mouths 'as household words' (IV.3.52–4), to be remembered and pledged on each succeeding St Crispin's Day. When the battle is over, Henry reads the roll-call of the illustrious French dead: 'Charles Delabreth, High Constable of France, / Jacques of Chatillion, Admiral of France, / The master of the cross-bows, Lord Rambures, / Great Master of France, the brave Sir Guichard Dolphin' (IV.8.92–5) and so on, down through a list that almost vies with the Salic Law speech earlier in its length and particularity. It is immediately after this list that Shakespeare, in the Chorus speech describing Henry's victorious return to London, makes one of his exceedingly rare allusions to a contemporary. The crowds that assemble to greet the king are compared to those which might turn out now, were 'the general of our gracious Empress' to enter the city from Ireland, 'bringing rebellion broached on his sword' (V.30–32). Shakespeare clearly means the Earl of Essex but, characteristically, he refuses to name him, any more than he would name Elizabeth herself, at least during her lifetime, either here or in *A*

Midsummer Night's Dream, except through such circumlocutions as 'gracious Empress,' or the 'fair vestal throned by the west' (II.1.158). He does not name Christopher Marlowe either, except as 'dead shepherd' in *As You Like It*, with the result that scholars are still arguing about whether Touchstone's earlier reference to 'a great reckoning in a little room' (III.3.15) really does refer to Marlowe's death in a tavern brawl at Deptford, or not. Who, if anybody, was the mysterious 'Mistress Mall' in *Twelfth Night*, whose portrait needed to be curtained off and hid (I.3.126–7)? Again, no one knows.

Shakespeare did, on one notable occasion, get into trouble over a name. The historical Sir John Oldcastle, Baron Cobham had been a Lollard martyr in the time of Henry V. His descendants, in particular Sir William Brooke, seventh Baron Cobham, were proud of him and they did not relish his theatrical reincarnation in *1 Henry IV* as 'that trunk of humors, that bolting-hutch of beastliness, that swoll'n parcel of dropsies, that huge bombard of sack' (II.4.449–51): the character Shakespeare subsequently, as a result of their protest, rechristened 'Falstaff.' In the epilogue to *2 Henry IV*, he was even driven to offer a public apology: 'For Oldcastle died a martyr, and this is not the man.' Ben Jonson, unlike Shakespeare, was perpetually being accused of pillorying real individuals on the stage. It is difficult, however, to imagine him ever giving this particular kind of offence. The historical Oldcastle, in common with other Lollards, suffered from a predictably bad Catholic press during the fifteenth and even sixteenth century.[1] The Protestant tradition, on the other hand, well represented by John Bale, by Foxe's encomium in *The Book of Martyrs*, and subsequently dramatized in 1599 by the four collaborators responsible for the first part of *Sir John Oldcastle*, is unequivocal. Oldcastle may have penitently accused himself (like St Augustine, or Prince Hal) of having been wild in his youth. The gallant soldier and loyal servant of the crown, finally martyred by a reluctant king when he refused to abjure his faith, could never, even during Jonson's own Catholic period, have been put by him to comic use, any more than he could have bestowed the name 'Sidney' on a fool.

85

Shakespeare was less punctilious. As far as he was concerned, Oldcastle was some two hundred and fifty years dead. The name itself had fallen into disuse, and it had already been irreverently (although briefly, and far less strikingly) employed in the anonymous *Famous Victories of Henry V* (1586). He brushed aside, if he had not actually forgotten, the historical facts of Oldcastle's life when he took over this name, with its in-built potential for amusing word-play (Hal's 'old lad of the castle'), from the older history and reused it in his own. Surprised, presumably, by the resulting fuss, he seems also to have been somewhat annoyed. In the quarto text of *The Merry Wives of Windsor*, the absurdly jealous husband of Mistress Ford chooses 'Brooke' as an alias when he sneaks off in disguise to The Garter Inn to encourage Falstaff's courtship of his wife. This looks like a dig at the Brookes, Oldcastle's irate descendants, and a daring one, considering that the comedy was almost certainly written for performance at court. As such, it is uncharacteristic, which may explain why, after the storm had blown over, Shakespeare altered the alias to 'Broome' in the Folio text, expunging the contemporary allusion.

Apart from 'Brooke,' the infant Elizabeth in *Henry VIII*, and perhaps (in the most distant and shadowy way) Henri IV, Biron, de Mayenne, and Longueville in *Love's Labour's Lost*, there is only one clearly identifiable, named contemporary in all of Shakespeare's plays: the bear 'Sackerson,' invoked by Slender in *The Merry Wives of Windsor*. Setting *Henry VIII* aside, even near-contemporaries are rare. Machiavelli, who had died in 1527, is generalized, on the rare occasions when he is mentioned, into a quasi-fictional personage, verging indeed upon a common noun. Only Julio Romano, who died in 1546, before Shakespeare was born, comes across as a recognizable, historical individual removed by less than a generation from Shakespeare himself. In *The Winter's Tale*, everyone gathers at the end to admire the statue of Hermione that Paulina has in her keeping: 'a piece many years in doing and now newly perform'd by that rare Italian master, Julio Romano, who, had he himself eternity and could put breath into his work, would beguile Nature of her custom, so perfectly he is her ape' (v.2.95–100). Most of the members of Shakespeare's audience, at least at Black-friars, would have recognized Romano's name, and probably have known something about his work. Not, however, until the play was over could they possibly have puzzled out why Shakespeare had, so startlingly, introduced him. The recovery of Hermione from a death of sixteen years is something so delicate and emotionally fraught, a thing that 'Were it but told you, should be hooted at / Like an old tale' (v.3.116–17), that it required a palisade of safeguards, of which Julio Romano, a tangible Renaissance figure, is one. It is under the aegis of this Italian artist's demonstrable reality that what is arguably the most implausible event in the entire Shakespeare canon comes safely home.

❊   ❊   ❊

Jonson's In-and-In Medlay, in *A Tale of a Tub*, thought that the godfatherly task of giving names required much skill as well as luck: it is 'a maine mysterie,' he opines.[2] Shakespeare's own attitude seems to have been closer to that of his character Berowne, in *Love's Labour's Lost*:

> These earthly godfathers of heaven's lights,
> That give a name to every fixed star,
> Have no more profit of their shining nights
> Than those that walk and wot not what they are.
> Too much to know is to know nought but fame;
> And every godfather can give a name.   (i.1.88–93)

Jonson could never have imagined Volpone without his name. The Fox, in all his complexity, and much of his play, emerges from his title. Even in his later comedies, where characters' names have become more hermogenean, the signs are that for Jonson characters and their names took shape simultaneously. Shakespeare, on the other hand, appears to be describing his own method of composition when he has Theseus affirm, in *A Midsummer Night's Dream*, that the poet's eye, glancing from heaven to earth, from earth to heaven, bodies forth the forms of things unknown through the power of the imagination, then 'turns them to shapes, and gives to aery nothing / A local habitation and a name' (v.1.16–17). The name is the last stage of the creative process, added only after the fictional idea has acquired both a particular shape and a context in which to dwell.

Unlike Jonson, Shakespeare rarely invented his comedy plots. Occasionally, he took over one or more of the names he found in his source material, accepting designations already present in Boccaccio or Cinthio, Lodge, Whetstone, or Robert Greene. Far more often, in fact about ninety-three per cent of the time, he availed himself of the comic dramatist's age-old prerogative and replaced them.[3] The way in which he did so, even by comparison with the onomastic habits of Middleton, let alone the carefully premeditated approach of Jonson, seems to have been remarkably *ad hoc* and unsystematic. Both quarto and Folio texts, as Greg and McKerrow have demonstrated, provide ample evidence of Shakespeare's willingness to postpone the giving of a name, or to change one already bestowed, well after he had launched himself into the writing process. *The Comedy of Errors*, with its 'Nell'/'Luce,' 'Luciana'/'Juliana' confusions, and its shifting designation of the Antipholus brothers, is by no means the only play to bear out this contention. In *The Merchant of Venice*, for instance, it seems to have taken him some time to make up his mind whether the clown should be called 'Gobbo' or 'Jobbe.' There is a terrible editorial tangle in *Love's Labour's Lost* created by Shakespeare's initial indecision as to how the three ladies who attend upon the Princess of France should be named, and which was to be paired off with which of Navarre's lords.[4] Dr Johnson long ago surmised that the reason why there seem to be two friars in *Measure for Measure* playing remarkably similar small parts is that the dramatist failed to remember when he handed out the name 'Peter' in Act IV that he had already called the same character 'Thomas' in Act I.[5] It is equally possible, of course, that he simply changed his mind at this stage, and omitted to cancel the earlier designation. Near the end of *Henry V*, Pistol announces that his wife 'Doll' is dead, 'i' th' spittle / Of a malady of France' (v.1.81–2). When Pistol said goodbye to 'the quondam Quickly' in Act II, bidding her

88

look to his chattels and his moveables, she was called 'Nell.' It seems unlikely that Pistol can already be looking forward, sub-consciously, to a liaison with his old enemy Doll Tearsheet, 'the lazar kite of Cressid's kind' (II.1.76). For all his faults, it is not her second husband who has forgotten that Mistress Quickly's first name was 'Nell,' but Shakespeare, her creator.

These are only a few examples among many that seem to point not only to a certain casualness about naming on Shake-speare's part, but to a characteristic reluctance either to start from names, or to regard them, once given, as necessarily fixed. If Hand D in *The Book of Sir Thomas More* (1595) is indeed Shake-speare's own, it looks as though he found it natural to write out a page of dialogue initially without speech prefixes. These he added later in the margins, and then in a somewhat rushed and inconsistent fashion.[6] The printed texts of his plays, in par-ticular those derived from the author's foul papers, bear wit-ness to a remarkable fluidity of character-designation during the act of composition. Sometimes, halfway through a com-edy, Shakespeare will replace the name of a character with that of the actor he had in mind to play the part. So, in *Much Ado about Nothing*, 'Dogberry' and 'Verges' suddenly appear in Act IV as 'Kemp' and 'Cowley.' Such unthinking substitu-tions were perhaps inevitable from a man as closely and pro-fessionally involved as Shakespeare was with the personnel of the Lord Chamberlain's/King's Men: someone who thought of his plays, at least in the first instance, primarily as texts to be performed by particular actors in a particular place. More in-dicative (and complex) is the way, in speech prefixes and scene headings, 'Dogberry' and 'Verges' dodge back and forth not only between 'Kemp' and 'Cowley,' but between being 'the Constable and the Headborough,' 'Dogberry and his compart-ner,' 'Keeper,' 'Andrew,' and finally mere first and second con-stable, as though Shakespeare had forgotten, or become ten-tative about, the highly distinctive appellations he had earlier awarded.

However hesitant and untidy, such a method of composition by no means implies a lack of interest in names and their func-tions. Henry James, a writer whose onomastic habits were in some respects very similar to Shakespeare's, derived great pleasure from mimological games. According to Edith Wharton, he was fascinated by

the magic of ancient names, quaint or impressive, crabbed or melodious. These he would murmur over and over to himself in a low chant, finally creating characters to fit them, and sometimes whole families, with their domestic complications and matrimonial alliances, such as the Dymmes of Dymchurch, one of whom married a Sparkle, and was the mother of little Scintilla Dymm-Sparkle, subject of much mirth and many anecdotes.[7]

When it comes, however, to serious creation, the *Notebooks* reveal an artist inclined to defer the naming of parts. On 28 November 1892, James roughed out the sketch for a new work based on

a simultaneous marriage, in Paris ... of a father and a daughter – an only daughter. The daughter – American, of course – is engaged to a young Englishman, and the father, a widower and still youngish, has sought in marriage at exactly the same time an American girl of very much the same age as his daughter. Say he has done it to console himself in his abandonment – to make up for the loss of the daughter, to whom he has been devoted. I see a little tale, *n'est-ce pas*? – in the idea that they all shall have married, as arranged, with this characteristic consequence – that the daughter fails to hold the affections of the young English husband, whose approximate mother-in-law the pretty young second wife of the father will now have become[8]

And so it goes on, James thinking his way through the material, until *The Golden Bowl* is essentially there, in outline, on the page. The plot, at least, is present, the places where it might happen, and the proposed age, nationality, relationships, even something of the nature of the characters, their feelings and pasts. What is significantly not there is any indication of what these people might be called.

The next entry but one in James's *Notebooks* reads as follows:

NAMES. Bernal – Veitch (or Veetch) – Arrow – Painter – Melina – (xtian name) – Peverel – Chaillé (de Chaillé) for French person – Brasier – Chattock – Clime – Lys – Pellet – Paraday – Hurter – Collop – Hyme – Popkiss – Lupton – Millington – Mallington – Malville – Mulville – Wiffin – Christopher (surname) – Dark – Milsom – Medway – Peckover – Alum – Braby (or of place) – Longhay – Netterville – Lace – Round – Ferrard – Remnant (noted before) – Polycarp (xtian name) – Masterman – Morrow (house-place) – Marrast ...[9]

The list continues to a natural stopping point: the moment at which James found he had exhausted the 27 December issue of *The Times*. He did not, on this occasion, strike upon 'Maggie' or 'Adam Verver,' 'Charlotte Stant,' 'Fanny Assingham,' or the house-name 'Fawns.' (Although 'Veitch' or 'Veetch,' the second name on his list, was to find a local habitation some four years later in *The Spoils of Poynton*.) James was not, however, specifically looking on 27 December for help with the new novel gathering shape in his mind. He was merely continuing – the *Notebooks* are filled with lists of this kind – to build up a bank of possible names, some for houses or places, but the majority for people: names to which he could return, sifting them through, when he arrived, in the composition of a story or a novel, at the stage of naming parts.

Shakespeare is unlikely to have collected proper names for future use as James did, or Dickens, who was accustomed to ransack the Education Lists for the purpose. He must also, on some occasions, have thought of a character and a name simultaneously. It is clear from the *Notebooks* that James often does have names for some of the people in a fiction he is pondering, even before beginning to write. There is no reason why this should not have been true of Shakespeare as well. Yet there remains a fundamental difference between artists like Aristophanes or Ben Jonson, for whom naming usually forms part of a primary stage of creation, and those for whom it is secondary, like Shakespeare and Henry James. To name a character is, in a sense, to pin that character down. This is especially true if the name is a cratylic one, yet even more neutral designations tend to create certain parameters, however shadowy, within which the bearer will be confined. 'Every bearer of a name I yield to the temptation of writing,' James recorded in his *Autobiography*, 'insists on profiting promptly by the fact of its inscription – very much as if first tricking me into it and then proving it upon me.'[10] For some writers, such a delimitation provides a useful focus in the early stages of creation. Others prefer to discover names gradually, experimenting with a variety of alternatives, as Dickens did, for instance, before settling on 'Murdstone,'[11] or else leaving characters wholly undesignated for some time, allowing them to reveal at the right moment what they are called. Bernard Shaw once asserted that he habitually began by writing dialogue for characters he could not name and scarcely knew: 'Then they become more and more familiar, and I learn their names.'[12]

✻   ✻   ✻

While to name, however creatively, is always in a sense to limit, not to name is also, paradoxically, reductive. Like Middleton and many other contemporary playwrights, Shakespeare often seems to have decided to leave one or more important characters in a play anonymous throughout, designated in the dialogue, and in speech prefixes and scene headings only by rank or occupation. The Princess of France in *Love's Labour's Lost*, the King and the old Countess of Rousillion in *All's Well That Ends Well*, the Host of the Garter in *The Merry Wives of Windsor*, the Bawd in *Pericles*, and Cymbeline's wicked queen are among those deprived of personal names, while in *Timon of Athens* the stage fills with characters designated only as 'Poet,' 'Painter,' 'Jeweller,' 'Merchant,' or 'Banditti.' The situation with regard to *Timon* is complicated by the fact that the play may be unfinished, a preliminary draft, and also was probably written in collaboration with Middleton.[13] It raises in an acute form the question of whether Shakespeare intended at a later stage to supply at least some of the missing names, or whether a kind of studied impersonality, reminiscent of morality drama, is part of the very nature and quality of the work. Some such generalizing impulse does seem to govern the namelessness of the Bawd in *Pericles*, and possibly of the Host in *The Merry Wives of Windsor*. Anonymity of a somewhat different kind, associated less with morality or 'estates' drama than with the wicked characters of fairy-tale, serves to warn readers and audience alike that the psychology of Cymbeline's wicked queen is not to be enquired into over curiously. Namelessness need not but in practice often does emphasize the generic over the individual. So, in *The Comedy of Errors*, Shakespeare's insistence upon bestowing a personal name (Adriana) upon the anonymous wife in Plautus' *Menaechmi*, while at the same time reducing Plautus' spirited 'Erotium' flatly to 'Courtesan,' accompanies a radical reversal in the respective importance and complexity of these two characters. On the other hand, both the self-willed and stubborn King and the remarkably individual Countess in *All's Well That Ends Well* are nameless without being in the least 'types.'

It was, of course, relatively easy for any Elizabethan or Jacobean dramatist to name a character, signal that name clearly in the authorial manuscript that went to the playhouse, by way of speech prefixes, scene headings and stage directions, but not to notice that because the name happens never to be spoken in the dialogue, it cannot communicate itself to a theatre audience. Cast lists were not distributed at The Globe, any more than they were in the medieval theatre, or in that of Dionysus. Some omissions of this kind, however, look deliberate: a theatrical strategy obscured by the practical necessities of the prompt-book, whose version was subsequently carried over into the printed text. In the case of *Hamlet* and of *Measure for Measure*, editors have almost invariably chosen to retain 'King' and 'Duke' in the speech prefixes throughout, even though the former character is silently introduced as 'Claudius' on his first appearance, both in the second quarto and in the Folio, by way of the scene heading, and the latter (with less authority) called 'Vincentio' in the list of dramatis personae printed in the Folio. In doing so, they honour the play as performed, the experience of the audience as opposed to the one potentially, at least, available to the reader.

L.A. Beaurline, the most recent editor of Fletcher's *The Noble Gentleman* (1626), has spoken out strongly in his Textual Introduction to this play against the 'gradual shift' in editions since 1647 away from generic to proper names. Three major characters in *The Noble Gentleman* remain anonymous throughout, both in dialogue and in the prefixes and directions of the text as printed. Others, he claims, including the 'noble gentleman' of the title, are named so late and glancingly in the dialogue that a theatre audience would scarcely be able to register their designations. For modern editors gratuitously to supply 'Monsieur Marine' throughout in prefixes and stage directions, where the original reads only 'Gentleman' or (later) 'Duke,' is to obscure with 'novelistic identifications' the elemental force of a work intended to come across on stage as 'a morality play transformed into a farce.'[14]

The argument is persuasive, a reminder of how persistently readers – from those ancient scholiasts who bestowed the name 'Mnesilochus' upon the nameless relative in Aristophanes' *Thesmophoriazusae* onwards – have wanted to resist an anonymity which, in the theatre, rarely seems troubling. Fletcher's intentions, however, at least seem clear. Far more problematic (and characteristically Shakespearean) is the situation in *Timon of Athens*, where Timon's honest steward makes his first appearance, in a scene heading, under his generic title, is then addressed (at I.2.157) for the one and only time in the play as 'Flavius,' a name he retains in the speech prefixes until the end of the scene, after which he relapses again into 'Steward.' On the only occasion after this when the name 'Flavius' recurs in the text it appears (confusingly) to be attached to another, and minor, character. The Riverside editor, faced with this inconsistency, has chosen to designate Timon's steward as 'Flavius' throughout, and to amalgamate the second 'Flavius' with Timon's steward 'Flaminius.' The second decision may well be right. The first is dubious, a 'novelistic' tampering, as Beaurline would call it, with the nature and quality of the play.

In printing 'Steward' all the way through, even in the group of five Folio speech prefixes that employ 'Flavius,' the Arden and Oxford editors certainly seem closer to the generalizing spirit of *Timon*, and to the play in performance. There is, however, a limit to what play-readers as opposed to play-goers can be asked to tolerate – or imagine. Otherwise, it might be tempting to argue, for instance, that editors ought really to replace the Folio prefix 'Viola' in *Twelfth Night* with 'Lady' and 'Cesario,' or 'Volumnia' in *Coriolanus* with 'Mother,' on the grounds that both these personal names are held back in the dialogue until late in Act v. In neither case does the long delay in their release look accidental. There are very definite reasons why both 'Viola' and 'Volumnia' should have to wait as long as they do to be spoken, reasons recoverable from the text when read as well as performed.[15] On the other hand, to have tried to duplicate on the printed page the theatrical effect of such belated revelations would have been to run the risk of misinterpretation: of imposing a false suggestion of type upon characters for whom, unlike those of *The Noble Gentleman*, it would be inappropriate.

Both *Twelfth Night* and *Coriolanus* are, in different ways, highly self-conscious about naming and names. In the latter, however, Shakespeare adhered to normal tragic practice in taking over the names he found in Plutarch, while in *Twelfth Night*, he sought out his own. The nomenclature of the comedy is characteristically hermogenean, with a larger-than-usual admixture (in the below-stairs world of Olivia's household) of the cratylic which may owe something to Shakespeare's awareness, at this stage in his career, of Jonson's rival kind of comedy. Certainly the incidence of pejorative speaking names for major characters – 'Malvolio,' 'Aguecheek,' 'Belch' – is for Shakespeare relatively high. Even more reminiscent of the early Jonson is the fact that none of the three could be said to contradict his name, as Feeble does, for instance, in *2 Henry IV*, or the unexpectedly sprightly Constable Dull in *Love's Labour's Lost*. Significantly, all three of them are involved in that most Jonsonian of activities, a gulling plot. This plot, moreover, unlike the benevolent one which unites Beatrice and Benedick in *Much Ado about Nothing*, but very like that which unmasks Parolles (another character transfixed by a name he never defies) in *All's Well That Ends Well*, has as its aim only the comic humiliation and exposure of its victim.

The onomastic mainstream of *Twelfth Night* is, however, the one usually associated with Shakespeare. 'Olivia,' 'Viola,' 'Maria,' 'Fabian,' 'Orsino,' 'Sebastian,' 'Antonio' – even 'Feste,' attached to a surprisingly thoughtful fool – are at most suggestive, in no sense judging characters or holding them captive. Nor, at least in the case of 'Maria,' 'Sebastian,' and 'Antonio,' are they unique to this play. Like Menander, Terence, and Middleton – and unlike Jonson – Shakespeare continually repeated characters' names. Although his comedies are dotted with inspired coinages ('Shylock,' 'Dogberry,' or 'Aguecheek'), names which could not possibly designate more than one character, for the most part he seeks out neutral praenomens regularly employed by other dramatists of the time, and reuses them across a range of plays. There are, for instance, four comic characters in Shakespeare named 'Sebastian,' four 'Balthazar,' two 'Ferdinand,' four 'Helen,' two 'Claudio,' two 'Angelo,' three 'Katherine,' and no fewer than seven 'Antonio.' The majority of these are figures of some importance, who also have (in most cases) no discernible surnames to distinguish them from each other. 'Angelo' – what? 'Antonio' – who? Only intermittently, as with the Ford and Page families of *The Merry Wives*, or the 'Minolas' in *The Taming of the Shrew*, does Shakespeare say.

Middleton had named two characters 'George' in *Anything for a Quiet Life*. Shakespeare perpetrates duplications of this kind in three plays: with the two brothers 'Dumain' in *All's Well That Ends Well*, Jaques the malcontent and Jaques the second son of Sir Rowland de Boys in *As You Like It*, and (most alarming of all) the two Bardolphs in 2 *Henry IV*. When, in the first scene of that play, someone knocks on the gate of Northumberland's castle of Warkworth, is asked for his name, and replies, 'Tell thou the Earl / That the Lord Bardolph doth attend him here' (I.1.2–3), it seems for a moment as though something has gone terribly wrong with the New Year's Honours List. How can the Bardolph of 1 *Henry IV*, Falstaff's thievish, sodden, and disreputable follower, conceivably have elevated himself in this fashion? The Bardolph of Warkworth is, of course, a new and quite different character. The audience's old acquaintance will shamble on in the next act. *He*, however, on the evidence of certain uncancelled speech headings and prefixes surviving in the quarto edition, seems to have begun life in Part I as 'Russell.' It is conceivable that Shakespeare's decision to abandon the aristocratic 'Russell' was enforced, for reasons similar to those affecting 'Oldcastle.' It would, on the other hand, be entirely like him to have decided, at a relatively late stage in the composition of Part I, that 'Russell' was wrong for this particular character as he had developed, and 'Bardolph' (a surname known to have existed at Stratford-upon-Avon), better. Dickens might easily have done this too. What Dickens would not have done was to repeat 'Bardolph,' once it had occurred to him, as the name of another and very different minor character in the same work.

Attempts have sometimes been made, as they have with Menander and Terence, to demonstrate that certain favourite names carry specific associations for Shakespeare, that family resemblances can be discerned among the characters to whom he gives them. It would be difficult to argue for any connection between the two Bardolphs. On the other hand, the various Antonios do tend to be fatherly, the three major 'Helen' characters (in *A Midsummer Night's Dream, Troilus and Cressida* and *All's Well That Ends Well*) are all self-willed and rash; both the Ferdinands are royal, 'Balthazar' is always given to a servant or subordinate, and the two Claudios (in *Much Ado about Nothing* and *Measure for Measure*) both experience serious difficulties in getting married. 'Claudio,' as it happens, is a name frequently used for young lovers in *commedia dell'arte*. To think of it in that context is to see at once that, by comparison with a nomenclature such as the one developed in the Italian improvised theatre of the mid-sixteenth century, Shakespeare's naming is fairly random. The particular 'Antonio' who plots and schemes in *The Tempest* is not very 'fatherly' – although the single, mysterious reference to his 'brave son' (I.2.439) may reflect a customary pattern of association that Shakespeare decided, in this instance, not to develop, and then forgot to erase. His accomplice 'Sebastian' is not in the least like his namesake in *Twelfth Night*; the Katherine of *Love's Labour's Lost* has little in common with Petruchio's shrew, nor has the goldsmith 'Angelo' in *The*

Comedy of Errors with the corrupt deputy of *Measure for Measure*. A half-conscious network of private preferences, rather than a code designed to supply the audience with advance information about a character's temperament, age, and social status, shared names in Shakespeare cannot be relied upon to display the kind of consistency we expect from 'Pantalone' and 'Arlecchino,' or even from 'Myrrhine,' 'Parmenon,' and 'Charisius' in Menander.

❊   ❊   ❊

In 2 *Henry VI*, the young Shakespeare toyed briefly with the idea that names, under very special circumstances, might possess a kind of magic power. Peter, a young apprentice, has accused his master, the armourer Horner, of speaking treason against the crown. He is terrified when he learns that a trial by combat is to decide the issue. Unskilled at 'fence,' he expects to be killed by Horner, a man well trained in the art. Just before the contest begins, the Earl of Salisbury enquires Peter's surname and, learning that it is 'Thump,' enjoins him to 'thump thy master well' (II.3.84). This, against all the odds, is exactly what Peter proceeds to do. Horner, who confesses to treason before he dies, had made the mistake of entering the lists drunk, but it is also true that Thump's name – which Shakespeare invented – seems in some obscure but telling way to have dictated the outcome.

The same play also contains the strange prophecies – again, invented by Shakespeare – that the Duke of Suffolk will die 'by water,' and that Somerset ought to shun castles: 'Safer shall he be upon the sandy plains / Than where castles mounted stand' (I.4.68–9). Both predictions are vindicated, but in a fashion so pernickety and verbal as to make the witches' equivocations with Macbeth seem almost straightforward by comparison. Suffolk, banished in Act III, might well be expected to remember the ominous prognostication of the wizard when Queen Margaret tells him to flee to France. In fact, he gives no indication of thinking that a sea voyage might be fatal. Even after he has been captured by pirates in the English Channel, he remains

98

self-possessed. It is only when he is told his captor's name ('Walter Whitmore') that Suffolk collapses: 'Thy name affrights me, in whose sound is death' (IV.1.33). The contemporary pronunciation of 'Walter' was 'Water' and, although Suffolk tries desperately to translate it into its French equivalent – 'Thy name is Gaultier, being rightly sounded' (37) – he cannot escape his fate. Learning that his prisoner is 'the Duke of Suffolk, William de la Pole,' Whitmore turns cratylist, brutally seizing upon the origin and true meaning of Suffolk's name: 'Poole! Sir Poole! lord! / Ay, kennel, puddle, sink, whose filth and dirt / Troubles the silver spring where England drinks' (71–2). Contemptuously declining a ransom, he chops off the Duke's head as a public service. As for Somerset, he dies in Act V at the hands of the future Richard III but not, as might be expected, in or beside an actual castle. The victim of a name, a name again claiming equivalence with the thing it signifies, Somerset lies in death 'underneath an alehouse' paltry sign, / The Castle in Saint Albons' (V.2.67–8). The coincidence, Richard observes, 'hath made the wizard famous,' but it is an odd kind of fame. One does not know quite how to take it.

There is something risible about all three of these egregiously nominal catastrophes in 2 *Henry VI*, as there will not be when Birnam Wood comes to Dunsinane, or Macduff informs Macbeth that he is not of woman born. Shakespeare chose to introduce Peter Thump, Walter Whitmore, and the alehouse sign, and to make them all real enough agents of death. Yet, in elaborating his sources in this way, he seems to be smiling covertly at the very idea that names might possess a magical and determining power. Certainly it is far more typical of him, even in his other early plays, to treat identifications of name with thing straightforwardly as a joke, as he does with Dromio's spherical kitchen-maid, 'Nell,' with Petruchio's puns on the name 'Kate' in *The Taming of the Shrew* – 'Kate of Kate-Hall, my super-dainty Kate, / For dainties are all Kates' (II.1.188–9) – Feste's wish in *Twelfth Night* that his sister 'had no name,' because 'her name's a word' and, in an age of quibbles, 'to dally with that word might make my sister wanton' (III.1.16–20), or the constable's solemn announcement in *Measure for Measure* that 'my name is Elbow. I do lean upon justice, sir' (II.1.48–9). The most fanciful and elaborate of these equations of name with thing occurs in *The Two Gentlemen of Verona*. Determined to prove to her maid Lucetta that she is not at all the sort of young lady who would countenance a clandestine correspondence, Julia impetuously rips up Proteus' love letter. Then, forced to piece it together again, bit by bit, she entertains the notion that she might actually have injured Proteus himself by mutilating his written name, and that she ought to heal his imagined wounds, and also punish herself, by cherishing that particular scrap of paper in her bosom, while she tramples on those that contain the word 'Julia,' or invokes a whirlwind to lose them in the sea. The basic conceit is familiar from Elizabethan sonnet sequences. Sidney's Astrophil, for instance, had professed a worried inability to destroy certain verses, although he knew they were inferior, 'because their forefront bore sweet STELLA'S name.'[16] Julia, to her credit, is as aware as her creator that fancies of this kind, however witty and amusing, are only fancies.

Shakespeare may be sceptical about the magical power of names, and about their cratylic correspondence with people or things. He is even more sensitive than Jonson to the importance that individuals other than poets attach to them, and to the psychological complexities of their everyday use. Again and again, in Shakespeare as in Jonson, characters who either possess or (more often) are anxious to acquire a measure of control over another person feel impelled, in conversation, to over-use that person's name, reiterating it for reasons (often quite unconscious) which have their roots in primitive convictions that to allow another person to know and use one's true name is to surrender independence and possibly identity into that person's hands. As early as *The Taming of the Shrew*, Lucentio, eager to cajole his servant Tranio into helping him woo Bianca, addresses him by name five times in eleven lines (II.1.148–58). Falstaff, in *The Merry Wives of Windsor*, his confidence badly shaken by the buck-basket incident, harps on the name of the man he knows as 'Master Brook' thirteen times in the course of telling him all about the dreadful experience, and explaining why he has not yet managed to earn Brook's money by lying with Mistress Ford

(III.5.61–138). Shylock, abandoned by Jessica, reaches out compulsively to Tubal by name, trying to bind his friend to him (*The Merchant of Venice* III.1.125–130), Benedick, once he has decided to be 'horribly in love,' does the same with 'Beatrice' (*Much Ado about Nothing* IV.1.255–325), and Malvolio in his dark house with 'Sir Thopas.'

In Act II of *Measure for Measure*, Escalus is enchanted to discover that the rascal before him has a surname – 'Bum' – which makes his grandiloquent praenomen of 'Pompey' even more absurd. He is unable, especially with Angelo out of the way, to resist punning on it: 'Troth, and your bum is the greatest thing about you, so that in the beastliest sense you are Pompey the Great' (II.1.217–19). Thanks to the ineptitude of Constable Elbow, Escalus is obliged to let Pompey off on this first occasion with nothing more than a warning. The number of times, however, that he repeats his first name in the course of delivering this warning reflects not only his own private delight in its incongruity, but also a degree of command and authority over its bearer. Lucio will do the same thing, but in a less attractive spirit, later on in Act III: 'Farewell, good Pompey. Commend me to the prison, Pompey. You will turn good husband now, Pompey, you will keep the house.'

POMPEY
I hope sir, your good worship will be my bail?
LUCIO
No indeed will I not Pompey, it is not the wear. I will pray, Pompey, to increase your bondage. If you take it not patiently, why your mettle is the more. Adieu, trusty Pompey.   (III.2.68–77)

Not only does Lucio refuse to stand bail for his old acquaintance, he compounds the insult by the condescending over-use of his name.

Petruchio's reiterated naming in *The Taming of the Shrew* has a more positive purpose. His first words to the girl whose social behaviour he means to transform are, 'Good morrow, Kate, for that's your name, I hear' (II.1.182). In fact, it is not her name, as she proceeds to make quite clear: 'Well have you heard, but something hard of hearing: / They call me Katherine that do talk of me' (183–4). Petruchio will have none of this:

> You lie, in faith, for you are call'd plain Kate,
> And bonny Kate, and sometimes Kate the curst;
> But Kate, the prettiest Kate in Christendom,
> Kate of Kate-Hall, my super-dainty Kate,
> For dainties are all Kates, and therefore, Kate,
> Take this of me, Kate of my consolation . . .
> Myself am mov'd to woo thee for my wife.   (185–90, 194)

It is the first, carefully calculated step in the taming process. Although Katherine has been glancingly addressed or referred to as 'Kate' twice before, once by her sister Bianca (II.1.21) and a second time by her father (II.1.167), as soon as Petruchio meets her the name becomes his special prerogative, employed by no one else. Apart from two purposeful deviations into 'Katherine' during the public wager scene at the end (V.2.121, 130), Petruchio clings stubbornly to the abbreviated form: a new name for a new and gentler person, the name of the girl he wants 'Katherine' to become. His continual hammering on this name when speaking to her is part of the power struggle, an instrument of control. Yet it also has, from the beginning, a less minatory potential. By the end of the comedy, Katherine has accepted 'Kate,' not only because she was frustrated and unhappy as 'Katherine' and (after a rough start) being 'Kate' has turned out to be much more fun, but because it is the intimate, private name that belongs to her in her relationship with her husband, a man she has grown to love.

Early though it is, *The Taming of the Shrew* is already very subtle in its understanding of how people feel about personal names. Whatever the status of that anonymous comedy *The Taming of a Shrew* (printed 1594), whether it is a bad version of Shakespeare's play or, as used to be thought, its source, the two texts are strikingly different in that everybody in *A Shrew* addresses Katherine as 'Kate.' In other ways too, Shakespeare's play is more imaginative than the rival version in its attitude to names. In the Induction, for instance, of *The Taming of the Shrew* the lord who persuades the drunken tinker Christopher Sly that he is really a nobleman, just recovering from an unnatural sleep of fifteen years, has no name. He does not even assume one for the purposes of the game, unlike his equivalent in *A Shrew*, who calls himself 'Simon.' Apart from the page Barthol'mew, named once when the lord gives instructions that he should dress up as Sly's lady wife, Shakespeare's aristocratic household is anonymous. Names, in the Induction, are reserved for the lower orders of being: for the lord's dogs, 'Brach Merriman,' 'Clowder,' 'Silver,' 'Belman,' and 'Echo,' or for Christopher Sly himself, who prides himself on the unlikely fact that the Slys 'came in with Richard Conqueror' (Induction 1.4–5). Not only does Sly have a name of his own, with which he is very loath to part, even if the change seems to be to his advantage – 'I am Christophero Sly, call not me honor nor lordship' (Induction 2.5–6) – his head is crammed with incidental proper names, most of them belonging to people who never appear in the play: 'Marian Hacket,' the fat alewife of Wincot, 'Cicely Hacket,' her maid, 'Stephen Sly, and old John Naps of Greece, / And Peter Turph, and Henry Pimpernell, / And twenty more such names and men as these' (Induction 2.93–5).

Absent presences, they are telling all the same against the elegant, witty, but also somewhat chilly and inhuman world of that anonymous, upper-class milieu to which Sly finds himself so inexplicably translated. When he greets the travelling players, the lord remembers the face of one of them from a previous visit, and even the part he played, that of a farmer's eldest son, but 'I have forgot your name' (Induction 1.86). The omission is scarcely as consequential as Coriolanus' inability to remember the name of the poor citizen, now a prisoner of war, who was once his host in Corioles and used him kindly. Yet in both cases, a certain aristocratic disdain for the individuality of social inferiors, an individuality bound up with their proper names, makes itself (not very attractively) felt. Significantly, Shakespeare's Sly, unlike his equivalent in *A Shrew*, is not only dissatisfied with a situation that the anonymous lord regards as quite normal, that of being addressed all the time as 'your honour' or 'your lordship,' rather than by a personal name, he is distressed to discover that his supposed wife, who also speaks to him as 'my lord,' is herself nameless. 'What must I call her?,' he asks. Told that the correct form of address is 'Madam,' he remains unhappy: 'Al'ce madam, or Joan madam?' 'Madam, and nothing else,' the lord instructs him, 'so lords call ladies' (Induction 2.108–11). But Sly cannot bring himself to do this. No one will disclose his wife's Christian name, so he makes do with 'Madam wife' or 'Madam lady,' something less individual and satisfying, certainly, than 'Cicely Hacket,' but at least miming the structure of a surname and Christian name, and so preferable to unadorned 'Madam,' a title that is entirely generic and unparticularized.

Katherine Minola in the inset play ends by embracing a new name. Sly also has his usual name taken away from him, but he cannot make himself comfortable with the neutral title that replaces it, whatever its material advantages. That the Slys came in with the Conqueror is almost certainly a fib. The surname, recorded in Stratford-upon-Avon in Shakespeare's time, as well as being that of one of his fellow shareholders among the Lord Chamberlain's Men, is not Norman in origin. Yet Christopher Sly's name is intimately connected with his individuality, not quite in the honorific way he thinks, and certainly not in any sense that Plato's Cratylus would have understood – there is nothing either 'Christ-bearing' or particularly clever, cunning, or artful about this roistering demolisher of Marian Hacket's glasses – but simply because it is his: a name that registers in a raffish, untidy world of alehouses and unpaid bills, pedlars, bear-wards, and patched shoes, the world that he shares with other people called 'John Naps,' 'Peter Turph,' and 'Henry Pimpernell.' Although it plays off the named against the nameless, Shakespeare's strategy here is not Jonsonian. Indeed, it turns the system governing Jonson's *Epigrams* upside-down. The named, although vital, are unexemplary and disreputable, the nameless, however respectable, unmemorable and dull. Although possibly the first, it was by no means the last time that Shakespeare was to do something like this: use proper names, many of them attached to people who never appear in the play, to suggest a rich, essentially unjudgeable substratum of human life, one against which certain of the characters and ideals presented more directly in a particular fictive society will be measured, and found wanting.

Chapter Five

When Bertram, Count of Rousillion, in *All's Well That Ends Well*, declines to marry one Helena of Narbon, a mere physician's daughter, the King of France quickly reminds him that the quality and worth of individuals is not to be deduced from their names:

> Good alone
> Is good, without a name; vileness is so:
> The property by what it is should go,
> Not by the title. (II.3.128–31)

Helena herself remembers the King's distinction. At the end of the play, she is redeploying it as a way of describing her own predicament: officially Countess of Rossillion, but because unacknowledged as such by her husband, the mere 'shadow of a wife ... the name, and not the thing' (V.3.307–8). These two passages have their analogue, perhaps their origin, in Montaigne, in the 1603 translation of the *Essais* by Florio that Shakespeare knew: 'There is both name, and the thing: the name, is a voice which noteth and signifieth the thing: the name, is neither part of thing nor of substance: it is a stranger-piece joyned to the thing, and from it.'[1]

Montaigne's nominalism was extreme and special in its period. His allusions to the *Cratylus* tend to be dismissive, as when (in the essay 'Of Names') he remarks that some attempted etymologies for French names are *even* as crude as those in Plato.[2] Yet the man who carefully suppressed his family surname ('Eyquem') in favour of 'Montaigne,' the more aristocratic

106

place name deriving from his estate (he may have been responsible himself for the obliteration of 'Eyquem' in his father's record book) was certainly not impervious to the quality and significance of names. Indeed, not only do his essays sometimes play with etymologies, he is profoundly interested in the way people feel about names, their own or those of others. The contradiction here is more apparent than real. Like Cratylus, the disciple of Heraclitus, although on alien philosophical grounds, Montaigne believed that reality was unknowable. Unlike Cratylus, he declined to place any trust in names as fixed and constant indications of truth in the midst of flux. There is nothing whatever that *verba* can say about *res* itself. They can, on the other hand, communicate eloquently about man's concept of *res*, a thing fallible, arbitrary, and often intimately bound up with precisely the thing that engages Montaigne: the psychology of the individual. It is better, for instance, to have a 'well-sounding and smooth name' than one that is harsh and difficult to remember, because such a designation is more likely to stick in the memory of kings. A licentious young man might very credibly be recalled to virtue by his appalled discovery that the name of the prostitute he was about to lie with was 'Mary.' People cannot help imagining that some names are fortunate, others ill-omened, or from musing on the way the heroic names of the past – 'Grumedan,' 'Quedragan', or 'Agesilan' – naturally seem to describe men very different from 'Peter,' 'Guillot,' or 'Michell.' Names are on one level mere 'dashes, and trickes of the pen, common unto a thousand men.' There is nothing in the old fable of *nomen omen*, nothing to prevent 'my horse boy' from calling himself '*Pompey* the great.'[3] But then there is nothing either – as the Shakespeare who christened Mistress Overdone's servant 'Pompey Bum' would readily have agreed – to stop the bearer of such an incongruous title, or his associates, from constantly holding the name up against the person, in ways crucial to an understanding both of how that person views himself and how he is perceived by others.

As G. Wilson Knight once observed, even when Shakespeare does allow himself to give an obviously expressive or 'speaking' name, 'Bottom' or 'Parolles,' 'Aguecheek,' 'Proteus,' 'Overdone,' 'Pistol,' or 'Belch,' it tends to 'point affinities' rather than operate as an overruling definition.[4] Many of his charactonyms glance at occupation, like those of Bottom the weaver and his friends in *A Midsummer Night's Dream*, but even those that comment on the quality of an individual are likely to do so in an oblique and partial way. By preference, he leads characters with what initially threaten to be defining names to overturn them. So, Justice Silence in *2 Henry IV* is the noisiest man at the party, Sampson Stockfish sells fresh fruit, and Speed, in *The Two Gentlemen of Verona*, never manages to turn up on time.

In the recruiting scene in Justice Shallow's Gloucestershire orchard, in Act III of *2 Henry IV*, Shakespeare allowed what looks very like his own distaste for the literal interpretation of names to come to the surface. Falstaff is at his callous and predatory worst in this scene, the man who could say of his miserable soldiers in Part I, 'food for powder, food for powder; they'll fill a pit as well as better' (IV.2.65–7), displayed now at greater length. All the men Shallow has assembled for Falstaff's consideration have strongly defining surnames: 'Rafe Mouldy,' 'Simon Shadow,' 'Thomas Wart,' 'Francis Feeble,' and 'Peter Bullcalf.' Falstaff proceeds to interpret them in the most straightforwardly cratylic way. It is time, he announces brutally, that Mouldy were 'us'd' or even 'spent.' Shadow will prove but 'a cold soldier,' but convenient enough to sit under in a summer campaign. Wart is 'a very ragged wart,' whose whole frame 'stands upon pins,' Francis Feeble will predictably be about 'as valiant as the wrathful dove, or most magnanimous mouse,' and Bullcalf is enjoined to 'roar again.'

Superficially, the word-play here resembles that engaged in by Bottom in Titania's bower when introduced to the (supposedly) tiny servants of the Fairy Queen. Bottom's response to the discovery that the fairies were called 'Cobweb,' 'Peaseblossom,' and 'Mustardseed' had been playfully to pretend that they really were the entities signified by their names: that Cobweb might bind up a cut finger, Peaseblossom be the child of Master Peascod and Mistress Squash, and that Mustardseed comes from a family that makes the eyes water, and has been much victimized in the past by roast beef. No offence was intended, or taken, in this light-hearted verbal game played out in the heart of the forest. Bottom's confounding of categories, the animate and inanimate, human and vegetable, was quintessentially comic, a type of confusion stretching back at least to Aristophanes' *Acharnians*. Falstaff, however, makes us uneasy. Justice Shallow may find his name-play wonderfully funny: 'Ha, ha, ha! most excellent, i' faith! Things that are mouldy lack use. Very singular good, in faith, well said, Sir John, very well said' (III.2.107–9). The recruits themselves are not amused. Mouldy angrily questions the idea that he ought to be 'spent'; Bullcalf is not attracted by the suggestion that the wars will kill off his roaring cough by also killing him, while Francis Feeble, the woman's tailor, unfeebly announces, in tones anticipating Hamlet, that 'a man can die but once, we owe God a death. I'll ne'er bear a base mind. And't be my dest'ny, so; and't be not, so. No man's too good to serve's prince, and let it go which way it will, he that dies this year is quit for the next' (234–8).

The difficulty here is not just that the individuality of the recruits, however briefly displayed, wars against Falstaff's dehumanizing attempt to reduce them to their surnames, but that a strategy associated with comedy becomes, in the different genre of the history play, threatening. Wart and Feeble, Shadow, Bullcalf, and the rest really do constitute potential cannon-fodder: Falstaff's onomastic play is consequential and sinister, not (like Bottom's) merely a verbal fantasy. Removal from its accustomed context complicates comic naming, yet also sheds light on the way it works. Though history and indeed tragedy usually have little to tell us about Shakespeare's naming of parts, at the margin of these genres, as limiting cases, a great deal can be learned. This is especially true of 1 *and* 2 *Henry* IV, plays in which comedy continually tests itself against historical truth, as it is (in a different sense) of *Romeo and Juliet* and *Othello*: Shakespearean tragedies whose special relationship to comedy depends to a large extent upon their unusual use of invented names.

Falstaff's callous and unimaginative cratylism in the recruiting scene is the more striking because of the acute understanding of naming psychology that he displays elsewhere. The diminutive 'Harry' had already been employed, without any particular historical justification, by the author of the anonymous *Famous Victories of Henry v* (1586). 'Hal,' on the other hand, the name critics significantly favour when referring to the prince, would appear to be Falstaff's invention and (like Petruchio's 'Kate') virtually his prerogative.[5] 'Hal' occurs thirty-seven times in Part I and, with the exception of two glancing and probably parodic uses by Poins (I.2.112, II.4.3), only on Falstaff's lips. The sudden eclipse of the name in Part II (only five instances) is directly related to the fact that, until the moment when Falstaff, disastrously, addresses Henry v returning from his coronation as 'king Hal, my royal Hal!' the prince and his companion are together for only one short scene.

'Hal,' as it happens, is a name Shakespeare uses only in the Henry IV plays, and then as one character's private designation for another. Transparently a pet name, its attempt to signal intimacy is not only a little too insistent, but glaringly one-sided. The Prince does not reciprocate in kind. Sir John Falstaff is 'Jack' to *all* his 'familiars,' not exclusively to 'the son of the King nearest his father' (2 *Henry IV* II.2.119–20, 132–3). Insofar as the Prince does coin his own, personal appellations for Falstaff ('grey Iniquity,' 'father Ruffian,' 'Vanity in years,' 'Satan'), they are distancing terms, radically different from those 'pretty, fond, adoptious christendoms' invented by lovers and close friends: the category to which 'Hal' aspires. Falstaff's renaming of Henry of Monmouth, like Royster Doyster's 'Kit' and Petruchio's 'Kate,' is on one level a strategy of appropriation. He claims, as comic dramatists have always done, the right to rechristen in order to possess. Unfortunately, the character he hopes to control, although given (especially in Part I) to making forays into the world of comedy, belongs fundamentally to that of history. And history, as Falstaff will discover to his cost, refuses to countenance the existence of 'King Hal.'

Although 'Hal' is a unique name in Shakespeare, 'Harry' is not. It appears in *Richard III*, *Henry VIII*, *1* and *3 Henry VI* and, in the *Henry IV* plays, it identifies no fewer than three major characters: Harry Percy and King Harry IV, as well as Harry Monmouth, Prince of Wales. Three 'Harries' in a play might well be thought a little confusing, especially since none of the three men seems historically to have attracted or answered to this soubriquet. Shakespeare, however, having invented the situation, keeps it under tight control, using it to create troubled connections, contrasts, and lines of force. So, in Part I, the fact that his enemy Harry Percy and his son the Prince of Wales both answer to the same Christian name encourages Henry IV to make constant comparisons between them, all to the disadvantage of his own Harry. In everything but their age and names, the two seem to be opposites: the one, 'sweet Fortune's minion and her pride,' a continual rebuke to the disreputable, tavern-haunting other. It even occurs to the King to wish someone would discover that Northumberland's son and his own had been mysteriously exchanged in their cradles: 'Then would I have his Harry and he mine' (*1 Henry IV* I.1.90) The theatre audience constructs its own comparisons between the two Harries, by no means as unequal as the King's, but it is left in no doubt that these are curiously dissimilar twins. Hotspur himself anticipates their encounter at Shrewsbury as a clash of shared names: 'Harry to Harry shall, hot horse to horse, / Meet and ne'er part till one drop down a corse' (*1 Henry IV* IV.1.122–3). The meeting itself, bringing together two strangers for long intensely aware of each other, begins with an almost ritualistic exchange of their common name:

HOTSPUR
If I mistake not, thou art Harry Monmouth.
PRINCE
Thou speak'st as if I would deny my name.
HOTSPUR
My name is Harry Percy.   (*1 Henry IV* V.4.59–61)

One of the Prince's most powerful lines of defence when summoned before an exasperated father in Act III had been to argue that Harry Percy 'is but my factor, good my lord, / To engross up glorious deeds on my behalf' (III.2.147–8). At Shrewsbury, he repeats the promise, this time to Hotspur himself. And, as Percy dies, it seems to him that this is exactly what the Prince

111

of Wales has done: 'I better brook the loss of brittle life / Than those proud titles thou hast won of me' (78–9). There are now only two Harries in the play: the King, and a son who seems not only to have eliminated his father's most dangerous enemy, but in some mysterious way to have taken over with his 'titles' the chivalric qualities of his fallen foe. That, at least, is how it looks for a few moments at the end of Part I, as what Harry Monmouth has described as the 'double reign / Of Harry Percy and the Prince of Wales' (v.4.66–7) comes to its unexpected close.

How little the King's victory at Shrewsbury has actually accomplished becomes depressingly plain in Part II. A few people – Hotspur, Blunt, Vernon, and Worcester, not to mention Falstaff's anonymous ragamuffins – are now dead. Lady Percy and Mistress Quickly have been widowed. For the others, however, nothing has essentially changed. The Archbishop is still in arms against the crown; Northumberland is confronting the same decision he faced before Shrewsbury, and King Henry is still trying, unsuccessfully, to get to the Holy Land. Falstaff is no closer to living 'cleanly as a nobleman should do' (v.4.164–5), and Prince Hal continues to play the fool with the time as though the noble horseman of Shrewsbury had never existed. The heroics of Part I are replaced in its sequel by a world of quotidian detail, one in which proper names, already a conspicuous feature of the first play, increase from a stream to a torrent: the recruits, Falstaff's annually disappointed Ursula, Jane Nightwork and her son Robin, Shallow's godchild Ellen, Scoggin – whose head the young Falstaff broke at the court gate – Master Dommelton the mercer, Master Surecard, Sneak, Goodwife Keech, William Visor, and Clement Perkes of the Hill, old Double, Sampson Stockfish, Will Squele (a Cotswold man), Francis Pickbone, or Black George Barnes. Apart from a flicker in the Jack Cade scenes of 2 Henry VI, there is nothing like this in Shakespeare's eight other histories, even in scenes purportedly lower-class. In Richard II, the gardeners talk generally about lopping, weeding, or binding up errant apricots before they get down to political matters but it never occurs either to Shakespeare or to us that they need proper names. In 1 Henry IV, by contrast, in a scene roughly one third the length, it seems

112

natural, not only that the two carriers at Rochester, whose only appearance in the play this is, should be identified as 'Tom' and 'neighbour Mugs,' but that they should allude to a man now dead: Robin Ostler, who never joyed since the price of oats rose. Even their pack-horse, currently afflicted with sore withers, answers to 'Cut.'

This is Falstaff's world, one upon which he touches at almost every point. Through his agency and mediation, the Prince of Wales for a little while can enter it, participating in what for most people is the trivially ordinary but which, without Falstaff, would have remained as unknown to the heir apparent as what there might be on the moon. The Prince's engagement, even in Part I, is limited and somewhat wary. In Part II, however, it becomes joyless, and the weariness is compounded by a new royal impatience both with the particularities of life as lived by lesser folk and the associated acts of naming and noting. 'What a disgrace is it to me,' he tells Poins brutally in Act II, 'to remember thy name, or to know thy face tomorrow, or to take note how many pair of silk stockings thou hast ... or to bear the inventory of thy shirts' (II.2.13–17). Such indifference to the quotidian augurs ill for Falstaff, and it is, significantly, in Part II that the fat knight for the first time refers to the Prince as 'Harry.' He does so only three times, (II.2.120, IV.3.117, V.1.79), and always in the Prince's absence, but his use of this more public designation, in place of his customary 'Hal,' seems to reflect not only the physical distance separating the two men after Shrewsbury, but the fact that, for Falstaff as for everyone else, the Prince is insistently twinned now, not with Harry Percy, but with the man he will succeed: Harry the Fourth, England's ailing king.

It is Falstaff's tragedy to believe that 'Harry' will retain the tastes and interests of 'Hal.' Even after Gaultree, when he has been forced into strategic retreat in Gloucestershire, Falstaff is still planning how he may verbally transport this country backwater to London, how to make the prince see and laugh at life in Justice Shallow's miniature realm: 'I will devise matter enough out of this Shallow to keep Prince Harry in continual laughter the wearing out of six fashions, which is four terms, or two actions, and 'a shall laugh without intervallums' (v.1.78–81). Gloucestershire is the place of details and particularities par excellence, where names and private memories of the past mingle with today's need to supply a new link for the bucket, sow the hade-land with red wheat, and price a yoke of bullocks at Stamford Fair. Falstaff is right to seek refuge from the Lord Chief Justice and the cold eye of Prince John in this particular haven, one in which individuals exaggerate (and occasionally lie and scheme) but at least drink together in good faith, where Shallow's man Davy can ask his master to countenance William Visor of Woncot because, although 'an arrant knave,' 'the knave is mine honest friend,' and Shallow naively exclaim of Bardolph's promise to stick loyally by Davy when they are in London together, 'Why, there spoke a king' (v.1.50, 3.69). He is wrong, however, to believe that the weary prince of Part II, a man already impatient with himself for knowing the details of Poins's wardrobe and private life, would find interest and amusement in Falstaff's Gloucestershire tales.

Observing that even his own brothers look nervous during the first moments of his reign, Henry v assures them that 'not Amurath an Amurath succeeds, / but Harry Harry' (v.2.48–9). That is the name which everyone will use henceforth, on the field of Agincourt, and beyond. When Falstaff tries to insist that 'Hal' has succeeded 'Harry' – 'God save thy Grace, King Hal! my royal Hal!' – the response is deadly:

> I know thee not, old man, fall to thy prayers.
> How ill white hairs becomes a fool and jester!
> I have long dreamt of such a kind of man,
> So surfeit-swell'd, so old, and so profane;
> But being awak'd, I do despise my dream.   (v.5.107–8)

The deposed Richard II, meeting his queen in a London street, had counselled her to 'think our former state a happy dream, / From which awak'd, the truth of what we are / Shows us but this' (v.1.18–20). For King Harry, by contrast, his past as Prince of Wales has been a dream and he is only now, as England's king, awake. Nor does he need to fear, as his father did, that

114

his reign will be haunted by spectres from that past, men who shared his life before he became king. Falstaff, the man without kindred or sons, is no Northumberland. Indeed, the king has already managed, as it seems, to forget his name.

When, just before Agincourt, Fluellen tells his sovereign that 'one Bardolph, if your Majesty know the man' (III.6.101–2) is about to be executed for robbing a church, it becomes apparent that King Harry has forgotten this name too. 'We would have all such offenders so cut off' is the only reply he vouchsafes to Fluellen's questions (107). *We* don't know Bardolph, although there was once an *I*, a Prince of Wales, who actually struck the Lord Chief Justice in defence of this very man (*2 Henry IV* I.2.55–6). And indeed, even in the ordinary world outside the courts of kings, the memory of the prince's former companions is fading fast. Fluellen recollects that Harry Monmouth 'turn'd away the fat knight with the great belly doublet. He was full of jests, and gipes, and knaveries, and mocks – I have forgot his name' (*Henry V* IV.7.47–50). It seems a harsh fate for the man who once claimed that 'I have a whole school of tongues in this belly of mine, and not a tongue of them all speaks any other word but my name' (*2 Henry IV* IV.3.18–20), not foreseeing that when the belly went the way of all flesh so would the name.

❧   ❧   ❧

Shakespearean comedy may be only infrequently cratylic. It tends to look darkly upon people, even the hero of Agincourt, who suppress or are neglectful of proper names. When Angelo, in *Measure for Measure*, is asked 'What shall be done, sir, with the groaning Juliet? / She's very near her hour,' he replies: 'See you the fornicatress be remov'd' (II.2.15–16, 23), coldly stripping Juliet of her individuality along with her name. The strategy turns against him. In the same moment, he loftily gives admittance to 'the sister of the man condemn'd,' an anonymous appellant who becomes unsettling at the same time that she becomes 'Isabel,' first in Angelo's private thoughts, and then (shockingly) when he speaks her name aloud for the first time: *Isabella*. 'My brother did love Juliet, / And you tell me that he shall die for't.' *Angelo.* 'He shall not, Isabel, if you give me love' (II.4.142–4). Although Angelo's fall from impersonal rectitude into sensuality scarcely renders him lovable, it is at least humanizing, the kind of failure with which comedy has always been much concerned. The watershed of the play, however, the moment at which it decisively rejects its tragic potential, is signalled by a very different act of naming: Pompey's invocation, near the end of Act IV, of all those invisible prisoners, Master Caper, Master Rash, Master Starve-lackey, and the others. Unseen, unheard, their shadowy presence nonetheless marks the turning point of the action. Pompey's roll-call effectively strips the prison of its menace.

Names used in this way, to establish the rule of comedy, need not be (although they usually are) defining. In the opening, spring stanzas of the song that concludes *Love's Labour's Lost*, people are dealt with entirely by way of generic and collective nouns, 'married men,' 'shepherds,' 'maidens,' and 'ploughmen.' Only in the final, winter stanzas does Shakespeare introduce individuals: 'Dick the shepherd,' 'Tom,' 'Marian,' and 'Joan,' names of unrelieved ordinariness and neutrality. These lives are harsher and more demanding than those of the anonymous shepherds piping on oaten straws in stanza one, or the carefree and equally anonymous maidens bleaching their summer smocks, but they are also more genuinely social and, despite the inclemency of the season, warm. The owl's note in winter sounds unexpectedly merry, as against the cuckoo's springtime 'word of fear,' largely because named individuals, their day's work done, listen to it indoors, clustered around a fire, talking, and sharing a meal. A comment on the entire comedy it crowns, the song is also a hopeful prognostication. Navarre and his bookmen are themselves about to enter a winter world, to be separated for a year and a day from the women who cannot trust their vows. The spring meadows of their youth need to be left behind, and so do certain careless, self-regarding ways of treating other people. What they go out to find, however, is adumbrated in the winter stanzas of the song that dismisses them: a genuine community, not an artificial, single-sex construct like the Academe at the beginning. The daily lives of red-nosed Marian and greasy Joan, on the one hand, and Rosaline and the Princess of France, on the other, will be in certain obvious ways very different. They draw together, nonetheless, in that all are rooted in marriage and social relationships, in the way Navarre's initial pursuit of fame prohibited, but which comedy, especially Shakespearean comedy, sanctions and approves.

The insistent naming of insignificant or invisible characters creates a dense social texture, something comedy finds particularly congenial. In Shakespeare, this kind of naming may appear suddenly, as it does with Pompey's list of prisoners, the winter stanzas of the dialogue between the owl and the cuckoo, or the introduction in *Much Ado about Nothing* of Hugh Oatcake and George Seacole, members of Dogberry's ancient and most quiet watch, in order to signal the dispersal of a tragic threat. In *Romeo and Juliet*, on the other hand, the abrupt withdrawal of this kind of naming, endemic up to the mid-point of Act III, announces the onset of tragedy. The play begins by embracing an entire civic order, a crowded and populous Verona, which seems to have more in common with the Ephesus of *The Comedy of Errors*, or *Measure for Measure*'s Vienna, than it does with Rome, Elsinore, Athens, or Dunsinane. Shakespeare accepted with only slight modifications the names provided for him in Brooke's *Tragicall Historye of Romeus and Juliet*: 'Tybalt,' 'Friar Lawrence,' 'Mercutio,' 'Escalus,' 'Paris,' 'Peter,' as well as those of the two lovers and their families. That was to be expected. What is surprising is his insistence upon also cramming the play with names of his own devising, those of men and women who, with two important exceptions, impinge upon the tragic action only slightly, or not at all.

Certainly that meticulous listing of the guests invited to the Capulet's house in Act I accords far more with comic than tragic practice: 'Signor Martino,' 'County Anselme,' 'the lady widow of Vitruvio,' 'Signior Placentio,' Mercutio's brother 'Valentine,' 'Rosaline,' 'Livia,' 'Signior Valentio,' 'Lucio,' and 'the lively Helena' (I.2.64–70). At the event itself, there is talk of one 'Lucentio,' who died before his son came of age. Mute characters, 'young Petruchio' and 'the son and heir of old Tiberio' are pointed out, and instructions given to admit 'Susan Grindstone' and 'Nell,' presumably extra servants hired to help in the kitchens. The Nurse, nameless in Brooke, but addressed once in Act IV as 'Angelica,' had a daughter, now deceased, called 'Susan.' Even tiny speaking parts tend to attract names: 'Sampson' and 'Gregory,' 'Potpan,' 'Anthony,' 'Abram,' or the three musicians, 'Hugh Rebeck,' 'Simon Catling,' and 'James Soundpost.' Only a few of these names, generally the English intrusions, are defining. All of them, however, as they accumulate, build up the sense of an ordinary, unremarkable continuum of life, a background to the story of the lovers, from which Romeo and Juliet gradually distance themselves as the story veers towards tragedy.

In Brooke, Romeus's closest friend, 'the trustiest of his feeres,'[6] had (like the Nurse) been anonymous. 'Benvolio' (one who means or wishes well), the name Shakespeare invented for this character, is the opposite of 'Malvolio,' the designation he was to bestow, in *Twelfth Night* a few years later, upon that archenemy of Sir Toby Belch, Feste, and the comic spirit generally. Although Shakespeare's imagination must have been stimulated by the suggestion of 'mercurial' embedded in Brooke's 'Mercutio,' Benvolio is the only major character in *Romeo and Juliet* who possesses a truly defining name: one that can be seen to govern his nature and behaviour. In every scene in which he appears, Benvolio functions as the voice of common sense. This young man deplores extremes, whether of hate or love, delights in arranging maskings, in parties and badinage, is affectionately concerned for his friend Romeo, but knows that if one love suit is unsuccessful, there are still plenty of fish in the sea. He, far more than Mercutio, or even the Nurse, is the relaxed and genial spokesman for comedy in the play.

Throughout Acts I and II, and in the first scene of Act III, Benvolio patiently urges comedy's attitudes of tolerance, compromise and equability upon characters whose own natures drive them towards violence or excess. On his first appearance, in the opening scene, he is occupied in the vain attempt to prevent hostilities from breaking out between the two warring households, even asking Tybalt to help him restore peace. His advice to Romeo, that if Rosaline really has taken a vow of chastity, he ought to direct his attentions elsewhere, falls initially upon deaf ears, only to be acted on that evening in a spirit Benvolio could scarcely have foreseen. Characteristically, he attempts to restrain Mercutio from conjuring up Romeo by way of a bawdy description of Rosaline, because 'if he hear thee, thou wilt anger him' (II.1.22). Act III, scene one, finds him trying to persuade Mercutio to come indoors:

> I pray thee, good Mercutio, let's retire.
> The day is hot, the Capels are abroad,
> And if we meet we shall not scape a brawl,
> For now, these hot days, is the mad blood stirring.   (III.1.1–4)

He is unsuccessful with Mercutio and, a few moments later, in reasoning with Tybalt. When Mercutio is hurt, as he and Romeo try to part the combatants, there is nothing Benvolio can do but help the stricken man into a house, return to announce his death, and (for the second time in the play) provide a measured account, this time to the prince, of violence which, if only people had listened to him, would never have erupted at all. That is the end of Benvolio's part in the play. A major character for almost half of it, he vanishes without explanation at the end of this scene, never to reappear.

In the 'bad' quarto of 1597, old Montague announces at the end of the play that 'My wife is dead tonight' / 'and yong Benvolio is deceased too: / What further mischiefe can be found?'[7] Clearly, those responsible for the memorial reconstruction of Shakespeare's text were sufficiently puzzled by Benvolio's disappearance to try to account for it, linking it clumsily to the lines in which Shakespeare's Montague had spoken merely of his wife's death (v.3.210–11). Like the unexplained disappearance of Lear's Fool, also in Act III, Benvolio's departure, so puzzling in literal, plot terms, signals to us simultaneously from another level. When this character mysteriously melts away from Romeo's side, comedy leaves the play with him. The centre of gravity shifts abruptly towards tragedy, in ways that Friar Lawrence alone will be powerless to redress.

It seems to be part of this shift that Old Capulet should undergo an abrupt change of character, the tolerant host who was happy to countenance Romeo's presence at the ball, who restrained Tybalt, and assured the County Paris in Act I that as far as his daughter's marriage was concerned, 'my will to her consent is but a part' (I.2.17), metamorphosed into the tyrant who proposes to draw Juliet to church on a hurdle, or throw her out to 'hang, beg, starve, die in the streets' (III.5.192). Even the part of the Nurse undergoes a sea change. The woman who liked to tease her mistress in Act II by telling her that 'Paris is the properer man,' watching her turn 'as pale as any clout' (II.4.204–6), is still doing this in Act III: 'I think it best you married with the County. / O he's a lovely gentleman! / Romeo's a dish-clout to him' (III.5.217–19). The verbal echo only underlines the fact that what formerly was humorous has turned ugly, that a character who was once unequivocally comic can now be referred to as 'ancient damnation, O most wicked fiend!' (III.5.235) and that Juliet must act alone.

In the light of Juliet's new perception of evil beneath the naïve garrulity of her old companion, Shakespeare's naming of the Nurse, for the first and only time, in the next act becomes ironic. Like the corrupt deputy Angelo in *Measure for Measure*, the Nurse is only superficially 'angelic.' The revelation jars, and not least because it stands out so glaringly amid preparations for a second banquet at the house of the Capulets at which, in sharp distinction from the first, none of the supposed guests are named. In vanishing, Benvolio appears to have taken with him that continuum of ordinary Veronese life in which the lovers were protectively enfolded during the first half of the play. Apart from those three lugubrious musicians, Simon Catling, Hugh Rebeck, and James Soundpost, who arrive to perform at a wedding and discover that ' 'tis no time to play now' (IV.5.109), incidental naming of the old, lavish kind disappears entirely. The curious little scene with Peter in which they gloomily pack up their unsounded instruments seems to embody the last stand – and defeat – of comedy in a play obsessed now with the mistakes of a few tragic characters. Only that meticulously observed apothecary, with his stuffed

120

alligator and tortoise, 'green earthen pots, bladders, and musty seeds, / Remnants of packthread, and old cakes of roses' (v.1.46–7), from whom Romeo buys poison in Mantua, momentarily suggests an existence, however wretched, defiantly independent of the tragic action. The apothecary turns out, however, to be tragedy's agent. Unlike Benvolio, he is only superficially comic, which is why he can manifest himself so late in the action, and also why Shakespeare declines – just as he does with the gravediggers in *Hamlet*, the Porter in *Macbeth*, or the countryman with the asps in *Antony and Cleopatra* – to endow him with a proper name.

※   ※   ※

It has become something of a critical commonplace to point out that the place where Shakespearean comedies normally end is the place where the tragedy of *Othello* properly begins. The end of Act I, with the heroine successfully married to the man she loves, the unwanted rival suitor defeated, the senex compelled by higher authority to acquiesce in the marriage he passionately didn't want his daughter to make, is reminiscent of the relationships finally worked out among Hermia, Lysander, Demetrius, old Egeus, and Duke Theseus at the end of *A Midsummer Night's Dream*, or between Jessica, Lorenzo, Shylock, and the court of justice in *The Merchant of Venice*. But there is another, and even more distinctive respect in which *Othello*, not merely in its first act, but throughout, allies itself with comedy. The names of its principal characters, with a single exception, do not derive from Shakespeare's source, the seventh story of the third decade of Giraldi Cinthio's *Hecatommithi*, in the way that those of *Macbeth* and *King Lear* had from Holinshed, those of the later Roman plays from Plutarch, or those of *Romeo and Juliet* from Brooke. In Cinthio's novella, no one, apart from Disdemona, had possessed a personal title. Characters were identified only by rank, social relationship, or, in the case of the hero, race and geographical origin. We read about an ensign, the ensign's wife and child, a capo di squadro, a courtesan, a woman skilled in embroidery, and a Moor. Dialogue, however, as opposed to

121

narrative, is difficult to write for characters never able to address or refer to one another except as 'him,' 'her,' 'ensign's wife,' or 'the lady who does wonderful embroidery.' In deciding to re-work Cinthio's story, Shakespeare was forced to do something which, however customary in his comedies, is unique to this tragedy: he invented almost all the characters' names. Having done so, moreover, he proceeded to hold them up for scrutiny, exacting for these names comedy's distinctive attention to what they mean: in themselves, and in their interaction with each other.

In *Twelfth Night*, a comedy close in date to *Othello*, Shake-speare used anagrams to create a trio of linked names. 'Vi-ola' and 'Olivia' are words that mirror each other, blurred only slightly at the edge by the extra 'i' in 'Olivia.' In 'Malvolio,' these two names are enfolded, under the mildly threatening control of a first syllable that seems to menace both woman with 'ill-will.' A pattern devised, as it seems, chiefly for the reader of *Twelfth Night* – given that Viola's name is not spoken in the di-alogue until late in Act V – it nonetheless calls attention to itself obliquely by way of the feigned letter from Olivia ('M O A I doth sway my life'), where Maria anticipates, correctly, that sooner or later Malvolio will recognize that 'every one of these letters are in my name' (II.5.141). There are some anagrams in *Othello* too. 'Othello' itself, a name apparently coined by Shakespeare, has long been recognized as an anagram of 'Thorello,' the name of the insanely jealous husband in that quarto version of Jonson's *Every Man in His Humour* in which we know Shakespeare acted. More sinister in its implications is the chiming echo of 'Iago' in the last two syllables of the name 'Roderigo.' This infiltration of the latter name by the former is suggested the very first time 'Roderigo' is spoken: 'It is as sure as you are Roderigo, / Were I the Moor, I would not be Iago' (I.1.56–7). By way of a partial anagram, akin to the ones in *Twelfth Night*, Iago's name with all its malevolent self-obsession – the 'I,' 'I,' 'I-ego' adumbrated by its diphthong – has invaded that of his dupe. Its enclosure there prefigures Roderigo's extraordinary structural and psychologi-cal isolation from everyone in the play but Iago: a stranglehold so complete that, after his assault in the opening scene upon

Brabantio's peace, Roderigo speaks only sixty-one words in the entire play to anyone except Othello's ancient, forty-eight of these in asides addressed to himself.

Even more disturbing, however, are 'Disdemona,' the single name Shakespeare inherited from Cinthio, and the three he invented to go with it: 'Cassio,' 'Emilia,' and 'Othello,' for Cinthio's 'capo di squadro,' 'ensign's wife,' and 'Moor.' The most distinctive group of names in the tragedy, these four do not interact anagrammatically. They are linked by the fact that all of them harbour at their centre a singularly literal form of what Genette has called 'noms cachés': a single, pejorative word operating here as a latent possibility. This word, controlled and rendered harmless by the name as a whole, is nonetheless potentially (and ominously) detachable from it, awaiting a moment of liberation. An onomastic scheme prompted, no doubt, by the composition of the one pre-existing name, Shakespeare used it to provide a subtle, underlying commentary on the action of the play.

The name 'Michael Cassio' is the second to be spoken in *Othello*, at line twenty of the first scene, just after that of Iago: 'Forsooth, a great arithmetician, / One Michael Cassio, a Florentine.' It is an anomaly in the play. Cassio, at least up to the mid-point of Act III, is the only speaking character possessed of a surname as well as a Christian name. Iago's insinuating reference, 'For Michael Cassio, / I dare be sworn I think that he is honest' (III.3.124–5), is the eleventh, and also the last, time Othello's lieutenant is identified as 'Michael Cassio,' or as 'Michael' alone. After that, he is always 'Cassio,' a word that mysteriously moves forward, as in Bianca's 'O my dear Cassio, my sweet Cassio!' (v.1.76), into the position of a given, as opposed to a family, name.

'Michael' is extremely rare in Shakespeare, found only here and in *1 Henry IV*, where Shakespeare had bestowed it on a tiny, quite unhistorical character: 'Hie, good Sir Michael,' the Archbishop of York commands, 'bear this sealed brief, / With winged haste to the Lord Marshal' (IV.4.1–2). 'Winged' makes the chain of association clear. 'Michael,' the name of the warlike angel who overcame Lucifer and his power, leader of the host of Heaven, is appropriate for the messenger chosen by the Archbishop in what for him is a holy war. It also helps to characterize the Cassio encountered in the early sections of *Othello*: the generous herald of Desdemona's arrival in Cyprus after the storm, an officer hated by the diabolic Iago, but loved and confided in by Othello and his lady. 'Michael,' however, accords less well with those sides of Cassio's character that become visible in Cyprus: not merely his relationship with a courtesan, but the callous way he treats Bianca, the insolence and irresponsibility of the drinking scene, the nagging suit to the General's wife for reinstatement. So Shakespeare strips away the protective and positive first name from Othello's former officer, leaving us to contemplate without qualification the beast latent at the heart of 'Cassio.' 'The ass in compound with the major part of your syllables,' as Menenius puts it in the very different context of *Coriolanus* (II.1.58–9), is inevitably less dominant in a five-syllable designation than it becomes when those syllables are reduced to three. Cassio is not summed up henceforward by the word 'ass.' The maimed and bleeding man who can say gently at the end, 'Dear general, I never gave you cause' (v.2.299) is worthy of respect. Yet, as surely as Othello himself, he has demonstrated that he may 'as tenderly be led by th' nose / As asses are' (I.3.401–2).

In Cinthio, the noble ladies and gentlemen who listen to the story of Disdemona, the ensign, the capo di squadro and the Moor profess themselves astonished 'that such malignity [as the ensign's] could have been discovered in a human heart.'[8] But they also blame Disdemona's father for giving his daughter such an unlucky name (it means 'unfortunate'). 'The party decided,' Cinthio writes, 'that since a name is the first gift of a father to his child, he ought to bestow one that is grand and fortunate, as if he wished to foretell success and greatness.' Shakespeare glances at this etymology only once, in Othello's exclamation near the end: 'O ill-starr'd wench' (v.2.272). Basically, he is less interested in the Greek root of the name than in its onomatopoeic potential as a cry of pain: something especially striking in the variant form 'Desdemon,' in which the final 'a' is cropped: 'O Desdemon! dead, Desdemon! dead' (v.2.281).

Instances of this abbreviated form are particularly frequent in the last two acts of the tragedy, where they seem to serve an emotional, rather than any metrical, need.

Even more important, however, than its plangently melodious sound, is that sinister word 'demon' hidden at the centre of the name: a dark potentiality which, thanks to Iago, not only comes in Othello's mind to assume the status of fact, but to govern the whole name of which it is rightly only a shadowy and unrealized part. 'Devil, devil,' he calls her in the first scene of Act IV (240, 244), and 'fair devil' in Act III (3.479) – a paradox, since devils were thought to be black. He discovers 'a young and sweating devil' in her hand (III.4.42) and, in the 'brothel' scene, pretends to encounter her sexually as though she were an inhabitant of hell. 'Her name,' he finds (in the quarto text), 'that was as fresh / As Dian's visage, is now begrim'd and black / As mine own face' (III.3.386–8). As it does with Cassio earlier, the metaphoric sense of 'name' as 'reputation' fuses here with its literal meaning.

The fact that Desdemona's worst faults are youth and inexperience (leading her to lie nervously about the handkerchief), plus a kind of childish inability to let a subject drop, is one of the most painful aspects of the tragedy. Honest Iago, and not she, as the audience knows all along, is really the 'fair devil' of the play. Yet the 'demon' lurking in the centre of her name is not there only for Othello to discover and misconstrue. It answers to an attitude towards women generally, a set of hostile assumptions, for which Iago is the most forceful spokesman but which, Shakespeare implies, is universal in this male society, to be found even under the surface of Cassio's courtliness and respect. Othello himself, although an outsider in Venice, a stranger to its ways, is not a stranger to its prejudices about the opposite sex. (Presumably, the cannibals and anthropophagi were familiar with them too.) It is true that these generalities have not hitherto seemed to have anything to do with his own marriage, which is a unique and miraculous thing. But when Iago, whose honesty is a byword with everyone, suggests that the only unusual thing about it is what it reveals about Desdemona's abnormal sexual tastes, all the old truisms come flooding back. That is one reason why Iago's task is no more difficult than it is.

In the first scene of Act II, while awaiting Othello's arrival in Cyprus, Desdemona dismisses Iago's slanderous descriptions of women as wildcats and devils, noise-makers and idlers, who 'rise to play, and go to bed to work' (115), as 'old fond paradoxes to make fools laugh i' th' alehouse' (138–9). So they are, but the laughter continues to ring out all the same, and the prejudices that generate it are not left behind with the empty tankards at closing time. In *Othello*, we actually hear this unlovely hilarity from Cassio, who 'cannot restrain / From the excess of laughter' (IV.1.98–9) at any mention of Bianca. Bianca is no divine Desdemona, to whom 'tempests themselves, high seas, and howling winds' (II.1.68), in Cassio's Petrarchan imagination, pay homage. In a play that works out its black and white symbolism so carefully, the name 'Bianca' – whiteness itself – has not been bestowed upon Cinthio's 'courtesan' without thought. Uncontrolled and embarrassing though it is, there is something genuinely innocent about Bianca's hopeless love for Cassio, who enjoys her body, and her little suppers, gratis. It was not pleasant to hear Othello call Desdemona an 'impudent strumpet' (IV.2.81). But Iago's 'O notable strumpet' (V.1.78), addressed to Bianca, who has rushed to the aid of the stricken Cassio without regard for her own safety, jars too, as does Emilia's echo: 'O fie upon thee, strumpet!' (121).

Bianca's retort to Emilia – 'I am no strumpet, but of life as honest / As you that thus abuse me' (122–3) – bears interestingly upon Emilia's own name. Emilia is certainly not a strumpet (neither is Bianca in her relationship with Cassio) in the sense of asking money for sexual favours. Iago may or may not be right in suspecting that she has been unfaithful to him: 'How many lovers had Iago's wife?' is not a question the play proposes to answer. The real force of Bianca's comparison, coming as it does immediately after the willow scene, is to remind the audience that the Emilia who, at the beginning of III. 4, replied 'I know not, madam,' to Desdemona's distraught enquiry, 'Where should I lose the handkerchief, Emilia?' (23–4), is most certainly not honest, in the sense of 'truthful,' and that the one who hints to Desdemona at the end of the willow scene that the right way to handle a jealous, brutal, or unfaithful husband is to make him a cuckold is recommending dishonesty in the sexual sense as well. There is a link, moreover, between these two different failures in honesty.

Emilia has been celebrated as a feminist heroine, but that neither accounts for her conduct in the play, nor for the word hidden in the centre of her name (lacking one letter, but clear in the pronunciation): the monosyllable 'ill.' A word prominently featured in the concluding couplet of her attack upon husbands – 'Then let them use us well; else let them know, / The ills we do, their ills instruct us so' (IV.3.102–3) – it is another of those latent possibilities, like the 'ass' in Cassio, the 'demon' in Desdemona, destructively liberated in the course of the tragedy. Emilia not only lies when questioned directly by Desdemona about the handkerchief; she hears her mistress being savagely interrogated about its loss, watches her marriage fall apart, yet never lets her know that she has picked the token up and given it to Iago. Her silence springs neither from cowardice nor from loyalty to the husband who consistently abuses her. It seems to relate to a cynicism about men – ' 'Tis not a year or two shows us a man: / They are all but stomachs, and we all but food' (III.4.103–4) – as sweeping and destructive as male generalizations about women. If it wasn't the handkerchief, it would be something else that made Othello jealous. 'Men,' she tells Desdemona, 'are not ever jealous for the cause, / But jealous for they're jealous' (III.4.160–1).

At the end, with Desdemona dead and Iago's villainy revealed, Emilia knows why she should have looked further. She dies remembering Desdemona's willow song, the ballad broken off when Desdemona realized the lines were in the wrong order, that her mind had jumped forward to 'let nobody blame him, his scorn I approve,' when what should have followed was 'I call'd my love false love; but what said he then? ... / If I court moe women, you'll couch with moe men' (IV.3.52, 55, 57): a classic statement of antagonism and misunderstanding between the sexes. There is something very dispiriting about this vicious circle of betrayals, in the song, and as subsequently rec-

127

ommended by Emilia. Desdemona listens to Emilia's worldly and disabused counsel, and then rejects it: 'God me such uses send, / Not to pick bad from bad, but by bad mend' (104–5). She says that partly because of the person she is, but also because of the nature of the marriage she and Othello almost and – as she, tragically, thinks at that moment – still might have.

As for the Moor, the man who fails her, although constantly discussed and referred to, he is not actually named in the play until an astonishing three hundred and thirty lines have gone by, one hundred and forty-six lines after his first appearance on stage. 'Valiant Othello,' the Duke announces, 'we must straight employ you / Against the general enemy Ottoman' (I.3.48–9). There is from the start something disquieting about this beautiful, sonorous name that Shakespeare has invented for his hero. It has an indefinable foreign quality, emphasized in the assonance which links it with 'Ottoman.' (Jacobeans would probably have pronounced it 'Ot-hello.') More important is the fact that in rearranging the letters of Jonson's 'Thorello' to form 'Othello,' Shakespeare fixed at the centre of the name, as a complement to 'Des-demon-a,' the monosyllable 'hell.'

'Black is the badge of hell, / The hue of dungeons, and the school of night,' Navarre says in *Love's Labour's Lost* when attacking Rosaline, a lady whose blackness is not even African but a matter of white skin set off by dark hair and eyes (IV.3.250–1). Othello, however, although he can be hideously misled, is not a stereotype of evil, like black Aaron in *Titus Andronicus*. He turns out to be admirable, in ways made possible by the new Renaissance interest in primitive societies and in the christianizing and redemption of black peoples, but also in ways that reflect Shakespeare's creative concern with moral oxymoron. Much of the language of the play is tautly ambiguous in its handling of the counters of black and white. Yet when Desdemona, Othello's 'fair warrior' in the reunion at Cyprus, becomes as he thinks his 'fair devil,' the hellish potentiality contained in his own name is released to destroy them both.

Othello does, fatally, what the heroes of Shakespearean comedy never do so close to the end of their plays: he returns to the exclusively male bonding of his military life before he met

Desdemona. It is Iago's assurance, 'I am your own forever,' that he accepts, not that of his wife. It is precisely because the play, even here, long after it has abandoned any pretence to comic plotting, continues to raise issues central to comedy, that the triumph of evil is so wrenching. The mimology of a name, in Genette's terms, has spawned implications so large as to be almost metaphysical. Othello, accepting them, consigns himself literally to hell:

> when we shall meet at compt,
> This look of thine will hurl my soul from heaven,
> And fiends will snatch at it . . .
> Whip me, ye devils,
> From the possession of this heavenly sight!
> Blow me about in winds! roast me in sulphur!
> Wash me in steep-down gulfs of liquid fire!   (v.2.273–5, 277–80)

Othello has been accused of lacking any true sense of what he has done to Desdemona and himself. His final response, however, to his own name suggests that the Moor's intelligence, as always, remains surer at the level of language than in its knowledge of motives and hearts. Not content with acknowledging the dark core of his name, he also rejects its enveloping brilliance: 'valiant Othello,' the commander heroically bound up with his occupation, the 'Pride, pomp, and circumstance of glorious war.' Shakespeare had been responsible for stripping Michael Cassio of part of his name. Othello becomes wholly nameless by his own choice. In the rushed, accidental phrasing of Lodovico's enquiry, 'Where is this rash and most unfortunate man?,' the Moor discerns and immediately articulates a personal truth: 'That's he that was Othello' (v.2.283–4). Lodovico tries to give him back his name – 'O thou Othello, that was once so good' (291) – and Cassio, his lost occupation: 'Dear general, I never gave you cause' (299). But Othello knows better. In executing justice on himself, he deliberately confounds his identity with that of an anonymous man, the malicious and turbaned Turk he once punished in Aleppo. It is largely because of his acceptance of namelessness, a condition associated formerly with his inferiors, that Othello can be allowed the partial recovery and reconciliation of his last words to Desdemona: 'I kiss'd thee ere I kill'd thee. No way but this, / Killing myself, to die upon a kiss' (v.2.358–9). The pronouns here are both intimate and blameless, shying away from those fateful proper names that in the course of the tragedy have come to mean too much.

Chapter Six

Once upon a time, there was a miller who had a daughter so beautiful and accomplished that he could not help boasting about her to the King, adding that she could even spin straw into gold. The King, liking the sound of this, summoned her to his castle, put her in a room with a great deal of straw, and told her to spin it into gold by morning or he would cut off her head. Transforming straw into gold happened not to be one of the poor girl's talents. She was in despair until an anonymous, little grey man appeared from nowhere in particular, and did the job for her in exchange for the necklace she was wearing. On the second night, when the King put her into a larger room, with even more straw, the little man again saved the situation, in exchange for her ring. The third night found the miller's daughter in an enormous room, facing a mountain of straw, but this time the King had said that if she succeeded by daybreak he would not only not cut off her head, but would marry her. When the little man appeared again, the girl had nothing left to give him, and she was forced to promise him her first child. After the birth of the prince, the little man turned up and claimed him. The Queen offered all the treasure of her kingdom to be released from her bargain, but the little man merely observed that a living creature was dearer to him than wealth. Still, he was sorry for her, because she wept so bitterly, and he told her that if she could guess his name within the next three days, she could keep the royal child. The Queen made lists of all the names she knew, and sent messengers over her kingdom to bring back uncommon and unusual names, but when she tried them out, the little man always said, 'That's not my name.' On the third day, one messenger returned and reported that he had not been able to find any new names, but that he had seen something very odd at that 'corner of the wood where the foxes and hares bid each other goodnight': a tiny house, a fire, and a grotesque little man hopping around it and singing,

> Tomorrow I brew, today I bake,
> And then the child away I'll take;
> For little deems my royal dame
> That Rumpelstiltzkin is my name.[1]

When the little man reappeared, the Queen, relaxed now and at her ease, permitted herself the luxury of playing with him: 'Is your name, "Conrad?"' 'No.' 'Is your name "Harry?"' 'No.' 'Is your name, perhaps, "Rumpelstiltzkin?"' 'Some demon has told you that,' screamed the little man and, as the brothers Grimm report, with characteristic ferocity, 'in his rage drove his right foot so far into the ground that it sank in up to his waist; then in a passion he seized the left foot with both hands and tore himself in two.'

The Rumpelstiltzkin story returns us to the name taboo of the Nambikwara, as described by Lévi-Strauss, or to those sorcerers who conjure names into leaves or straw, to be burned or scattered. Rumpelstiltzkin's power is bound up with his concealment of his name. Once that name has been discovered, as the result of his own carelessness, he has not only lost his contest with the Queen; he has to destroy himself. Clint Eastwood, in such films as 'High Plains Drifter' and 'The Dollar Trilogy,' has made his fortune by playing the part of a Rumpelstiltzkin who doesn't get found out. To be firmly settled in the possession of one's true name, but voluntarily to choose anonymity, is not only to be strong, but almost inhuman. That, at least in sophisticated societies, is what makes it a position so difficult to maintain. Even Rumpelstiltzkin was unable to resist pronouncing his name aloud as he danced around his fire, communicating it not only to the hares and foxes but, inadvertently, to the Queen's messenger, who happened to be riding by.

132

The Rumpelstiltzkin story offers evidence, from the depths of the folk tradition tapped by the brothers Grimm, of the possibilities surrounding the concealment or revelation of a name, possibilities that are ambiguous and rich. One of the reasons why the little man is so frightening through much of the story is that he seems perfectly at ease with total namelessness in his dealings with the Queen. He does not even have a generic social designation: of rank, like the King and Queen, or occupation, like the miller. This fact renders him both more and less than human. Certainly he is unlike most tricksters who wish to conceal their identity, the great majority of whom, in hiding a real name, carefully replace it with a pseudonym.

One special class of assumed name runs the condition of being nameless very close. 'Outis' ('Nobody'), the designation Odysseus craftily offers the Cyclops Polyphemus in Homer, both is and is not a name. The means by which he gets himself and what is left of his men back to their ship alive, it is a weapon not (as is sometimes suggested)[2] a weakness. Indeed, like 'Eperitos,' the 'stormy' alias Odysseus ('the troubler' and 'troubled') cunningly offers on his return to Ithaca, it manages simultaneously to conceal and indicate his real name. The distinctive epithet attached to Odysseus in Homer is *polymetis* – literally, 'many-witted.' *Metis*, however, is a Greek word which, besides meaning 'intelligence,' operates as an alternative negative to *outis*. As Norman Austin points out, in 'Name Magic in the *Odyssey*,' these two negatives are ironically juxtaposed just after the blinding of Polyphemus in ways that make it plain that 'Outis' is not simply a momentary expedient on Odysseus' part, but a ruse retaining contact with his customary form of identification: 'not pseudonym but cognomen.'[3] Weakness only manifests itself later, in Odysseus' moment of triumph, when he cannot resist blatantly naming himself to his enemy, violating that ancient taboo which those who care for him in the poem (Penelope, Telemachus, Eumaeus) can be seen so scrupulously to observe.

None of the Cyclops' kindred on the island have come to the rescue of the stricken giant – understandably, since he insists that 'nobody' is hurting him. He cannot even plot revenge for his blinding against a wholly anonymous and, in a sense, non-existent man. Then Odysseus, safely (as he thinks) under sail and leaving the land of the Cyclops, ignores the advice of his companions and reveals his true name: 'Say that Odysseus, the sacker of cities blinded [you], even the son of Laertes, whose home is in Ithaca.'[4] The consequences of this self-advertisement (as in the case of Rumpelstiltzkin) are dire. Instantly, the Cyclops calls upon his father Poseidon, asking that 'Odysseus, the sacker of cities, may never reach his home, even the son of Laertes, whose home is in Ithaca,' or that if he must, it should take a very long time and that he should arrive to find trouble in the house. The ritual repetition of Odysseus' name, that of his father, and that of his homeland, is striking. Without those words, the Cyclops' curses would have been ineffectual, and Penelope would have been reunited with her husband much earlier than she was. The lesson is painful, but Odysseus learns it thoroughly. Even when he reaches the friendly, known land of the Phaeacians, he remains for a long time evasive about his name.

The idea of the hero who gets out of a tight scrape by becoming 'Nobody' was not new in the *Odyssey*, although earlier European and Asian versions seem to have employed the formula 'Myself' rather than Homer's linguistically more interesting 'Outis.'[5] Essentially a comic device, part of the immemorial lore of the trickster, it declares its nature unequivocally in Euripides' satyr play, the *Cyclops*. Euripides' Odysseus announces his true name, but not those of his father and his country, immediately after he has escaped from the cave, while Polyphemus is still groping murderously after him: 'Out of reach / I assure ye, I ward Odysseus's body from your fury.'[6] The Cyclops queries this new name, but then remembers that an oracle had foretold his blinding by 'Odysseus,' adding that his enemy would be doomed to wander the seas for many years. The myth enforces this future, but Euripides minimizes Odysseus' troubles to come, even as he does his folly in revealing his name, and the connection between that mistake and Polyphemus' curse. At the end of the *Cyclops*, the Chorus of satyrs eagerly enlists in 'the crew of Odysseus,' not only because (like Caliban) they have discovered that the man 'bears celestial liquor,' but because he is so wonderfully resourceful and shrewd.

The 'Outis' gambit may be used for satiric purposes, as it is in Jonson's late masque, *The Fortunate Isles* of 1625 ('Know ye not *Outis*? Then you know nobody'),[7] or in that curious, early Jacobean play, *Nobody and Somebody* (1605), in which 'Nobody' is a character guilty of 'over-much releeving of the poore, / Helping distressed prisoners,'[8] and other benevolent actions the corrupt officers at court would like to curtail. Essentially, however, it is a comic ruse, even when – as in the *Wasps* of Aristophanes – it happens not to work. When Philocleon tries to escape from the house in which his son Bdelycleon has imprisoned him, he imitates Odysseus, clinging on to the underside of a donkey the is being driven to market. Bdelycleon, however, who has two eyes, both in working order, easily discovers the fraud. Not content with the traditional reply, 'Outis,' in response to his query 'Who may you be?' he presses an additional demand: 'Where do you come from?' 'Ithakos Apodrasippidou,' Philocleon suggests hopefully: 'Ithaca. I'm the son of Abscondippides.'[9] Wearily, Bdelycleon returns this very exasperating parent to captivity.

Although Aristophanic comedy is much concerned with trickery, it displays little interest in mistaken identity. In Homer, Odysseus had slyly introduced himself to his aged father Laertes at the end under the pseudonym 'Eperitos.' Philocleon's ruse, however, marks one of the very rare occasions on which a character in Aristophanes avails himself of an alias at all, even one as intangible as 'Outis.' Dionysus, in the *Frogs*, does try to gain entry to the underworld under the name 'Heracles' and, according to whether he thinks the people at the gate regard the real Heracles' previous treatment of their watch-dog Cerberus with admiration or resentment, he either maintains this identity or hastily exchanges it for that of Xanthias, his slave. Neither subterfuge profits him. More characteristic is the situation in the *Thesmophoriazusae*. Euripides' anonymous relative is wholly unable to produce a pseudonym when required to identify himself at the Festival of Women. Interrogated fiercely by the genuinely female participants, he gets no further than the idea that he might be wife to 'what-d'ye-call-him from Cothocidae.'[10] Even in the *Plutus*, when Aristophanes was experimenting with comedy of a different kind, it does not occur to the god of wealth, when pressed by Chremylus to reveal his name, that he might wriggle out of the situation by supplying a false one.

In what survives of the comedy of Menander and his Greek contemporaries, characters who assume an alias – although certainly not unheard of – remain comparatively minor and rare. It seems to have been Plautus, with his interest in the wily slave, and enormous magnification of this role, who was responsible for the striking increase in Roman comedy of disguisings and bogus names. Plautine practice ultimately left its mark on English comedy, either directly or by way of Italian classical adaptations. In the work of Peele and Lyly, Greene, Heywood, Dekker, and their contemporaries and successors, it joined hands with that native medieval dramatic tradition in which vice characters had found it natural to assume pseudonyms when they set out to deceive. Sixteenth- and seventeenth-century English comedy is filled with characters who voluntarily suppress a real name in favour of one that is fraudulent. Almost always, the move places them in a position of advantage. In Shakespeare alone, Julia in *The Two Gentlemen of Verona*, posing as 'Sebastian,' manages to execute Proteus' commission to Sylvia in a manner that does her far more good than it does her false lover; Master Ford gains ascendancy over Falstaff in *The Merry Wives of Windsor* by spying on his movements as 'Master Brook,' and Portia's impersonation of 'Balthazar' in *The Merchant of Venice* both saves Antonio and allows her to discover how dangerous a rival he is for Bassanio's affections.

To change one's name as an act of free choice is one thing; to be compelled to give it up, whether because that name is denied by everyone else, or because it becomes, for one reason or another, impossible to use, is an incipiently tragic predicament, linked (as the 'Outis' ruse is not) with the nothingness and non-being of death. In so far as namelessness can be seen to be forced upon characters in comedy, it is likely to indicate vulnerability rather than strength. This is true initially of

Rosalind's assumption of the name 'Ganymede' in *As You Like It*. Forced into exile by Duke Frederick, Rosalind reaches for a male pseudonym out of necessity, not (like Julia, Portia – or Odysseus) in order to further a design of her own. It is only afterwards, when she arrives in Arden to find Orlando there before her, and freely elects to remain 'Ganymede' rather than declaring herself to her father and lover, that her alias can be seen as unequivocally comic. She is fortunate, however, in that for Celia and Touchstone, her companions in exile, she never ceases to be 'Rosalind,' and also in persuading Orlando to address her in 'jest' by her real name.

Viola's disguise as 'Cesario' after she has been shipwrecked into Illyria, is more sombre than Rosalind's. There is from the start something negative about her decision to serve Orsino, concealing her true sex and name. Sebastian, her twin, who adopted the pseudonym 'Rodorigo' after the wreck, is able to abandon it on his very first appearance, entrusting Antonio with his real name and parentage (II.1.17). There is no one, however, to whom Viola can make a similar confession. An enforced and frustrating period of marking time, her disguise comes to seem more and more ominous in a play obsessed with the tragic brevity of youth, the idea that women's beauty, like that of the rose, unfolds and withers in an hour. Viola, however, is different from all the other Shakespearean heroines who adopt pseudonyms in that her true name is concealed not only from the other characters, but from the theatre audience as well, until the final scene.

The heroine of *Twelfth Night* arrives in Illyria merely as 'lady' or 'madam,' the titles by which the sea-captain addresses her. She subsequently becomes 'Cesario,' for us as for the other characters. The fact that her real name is never spoken until V.1.241 does not, for once, look like an example of Shakespearean carelessness: a simple failure to notice that 'Viola' has not been registered in the dialogue. Nor is it a silence dictated by the fact that she is a stranger in Illyria. She might easily have communicated her name to the audience at a number of points. Sebastian, speaking to Antonio about his sister in the same act, has to go out of his way to avoid mentioning it. In *Gl'Ingannati* (1531), a

Plautine imitation at several removes, and Shakespeare's probable source for the main plot of *Twelfth Night*, the audience (not to mention a number of the other characters) had known all the time that 'Fabio,' who like 'Cesario' has usurped her brother's name and masculine attire, is really 'Lelia.' Shakespeare was striking out boldly from his Italian model when he suppressed his heroine's true name, revealing her as 'Viola' only when she and her twin finally confront one another.

There are, as it happens, some scattered examples in Elizabethan drama of delayed naming that seem to function along Aristophanic lines. The most striking of them, probably, occurs in *The Revenger's Tragedy* (1605). There, in a play with marked comic components, where virtually all the characters possess morally defining names, the hero is not revealed as 'Vindice,' vengeance incarnate, until late in Act III. Only when he whispers the name into the ear of the Duke he has finally succeeded in poisoning, with the aid of 'the bony lady,' does the audience discover what the false 'Piato,' Hippolito's nameless brother, is really called.[11] The belated release of 'Viola,' however, is not (like 'Vindice' or 'Dicaeopolis') the celebration of a thing done, nor can the name itself be made to speak cratylically. After the play is over, its anagrammatic reduplication in 'Olivia' and 'Malvolio,' together with certain mimological associations (with 'viol,' for instance, and 'violet') may tease the imagination. Its prime function within the comedy as performed is restorative: returning the anonymous 'lady,' the pretended 'Cesario,' to her family, her social identity, and estate.

When the twins at last meet, alone together on a crowded stage, Sebastian is the one who needs to ask questions. His sister has already (III.4.366) been addressed as 'Sebastian' by Antonio. She has a shrewd suspicion that her brother lives, even before he presents her with her mirror-image. To his four pressing enquiries – about her possible kinship to him, her country, her parentage, and name – she gives three immediate replies: her country is Messaline, her father's name was Sebastian, and she had a brother called 'Sebastian' too, identical in appearance with the man who stands before her. About her own name, she pointedly says nothing at all. It is left to Sebastian, the only character, apart from Viola herself, who knows that name, to release it into the play, providing Viola as he speaks it with the single confirmation of his identity she seeks. As brother and sister go on to exchange knowledge of the birthmark on their father's brow and of the anniversary marked by his death, Viola repeats the name as her own. She refuses to embrace her twin until she has put off her 'masculine usurp'd attire,' and provided an account of her life since they were parted, but 'Viola,' the talismanic name offered and accepted, has established their relationship beyond any real need for further proof.

※　　　　　※　　　　　※

The recognition scene of *Twelfth Night* echoes and deliberately invokes classical comedy. Yet it also seems to reach back beyond Plautus and Terence. The most celebrated brother/sister recognition in ancient drama had been tragic: Electra's reunion with Orestes, which precedes the murder of Clytemnestra. In none, however, of the three versions of the story that survive, by Aeschylus, Sophocles, and Euripides, is disclosure of the stranger's name important. For Sophocles' Electra, his possession of her dead father Agamemnon's signet ring had been the determining factor. Euripides, mocking Aeschylus' symbolic establishment of blood relationship by way of matching footprints, embroidery, and hair, replaced the older emphasis on kinship within a royal house by the Old Man's visual recognition of a childhood scar, something that is more individually and accidentally the property of Orestes himself. It is only, however, in Euripides' *Iphigenia in Tauris*, one of those 'mixed' plays from which, according to Satyrus, New Comedy itself derived, that the agent of recognition is, quite specifically, a name.

In *Iphigenia in Tauris*, the shipwrecked Orestes' discovery of a different sister, long believed dead, averts catastrophe instead of bringing it on. When interrogated by the priestess Iphigenia, whose unwelcome task it is to sacrifice strangers to the goddess Artemis, Orestes flatly refuses to identify himself. Cast away on an unfriendly coast, far from home, dogged by his mother's Furies even there, and now destined to die like an animal, he

139

clings to anonymity as a means of preserving some pathetic remnant of dignity. He will resign his body to slaughter, but not his name: *anonumoi thanontes ou gelometh'an* ('If I die nameless, I shall not be mocked').[12] 'Dustucheis' ('unfortunate'), he suggests bitterly, is what he ought to have been called. Then, by 'chance,' Iphigenia herself speaks his name. She will permit Orestes' companion Pylades to return to Greece, on condition that he deliver a letter from 'Iphigenia' to her brother, called 'Orestes – so, twice heard, hold fast the name.'[13] Orestes and Iphigenia subsequently confirm their relationship by exchanging the names of their grandparents, together with a shared knowledge of their childhood and the history of their house, but the happy ending has really been brought about through discovery of the brother's (and to a lesser extent, the sister's) name.

'Orestes' and 'Iphigenia' can carry the weight imposed on them here partly because of the semi-comic nature of Euripides' play, one in which the chain of disasters in the house of Atreus comes, at least in part, to seem like a misleading tragic fiction, something it is possible, in the light of subsequent knowledge and developments, drastically to rewrite. But it also matters that, in themselves, these events and their protagonists are unique. Although a certain amount of duplication does occur among mythological names, there seems never to have been another 'Orestes,' or a second 'Iphigenia.' Nor did these names later become attractive to ordinary parents seeking designations for their children, probably because of their unpropitious associations, even in the happier versions of the Atreid myth, with matricide and an early, sacrificial death. Other, less ominous mythological names did acquire currency. In the *Helen*, another of Euripides' explorations of the comic variant of a tragic myth, Menelaus is momentarily baffled by the news that 'Helen,' calling herself Zeus' daughter, child of Tyndarus, hailing from Sparta, has been languishing in Egypt during the entire Trojan War:

> Can any *man* that bears this name of Zeus
> By Nile's banks dwell? One is there, he in heaven.
> And where hath earth a Sparta, save alone

140

There where Eurotas' streams are fair with reeds?
Do two men bear the name of Tyndarus?
Is there a land twin-named with Lacedemon
Or Troy? I know not what to say hereof:
For on the wide earth many, as men grant,
Bear like names, city bearing city's name,
And woman woman's: marvel none is here.[14]

His pragmatism is misplaced: the Helen beleaguered in Egypt
is indeed his loving wife, and her transportation there, while at
Troy men fought and died for a phantom 'Helen,' was marvel-
lous in the extreme. His is still the world of myth, one in which
the appropriateness of name to individual, although something
usually assumed rather than explored, means that a girl initially called 'Eido,' because she was her mother's pride, will,
when she is discovered to have the gift of prophecy, be renamed 'Theonoe' ('God's Purpose') for reasons that Cratylus
would have approved.[15] Yet for a moment, Menelaus' practical cognizance of the 'like names' randomly borne by different
cities, women, and men outstrips the context in which it is contained, reminding the spectators of their own populous, urban
environment, an historical Greece in which both 'Helen' and
'Menelaus' had indeed become ordinary given names.

Theirs was, or shortly would become, the world of New Comedy: blatantly fictional in its plotting, but otherwise familiar,
domestic, and in its account of social relationships, closely observed. In no surviving New Comedy text is the discovery of
the name of a lost brother, son, or daughter crucial in establishing identity. Infants exposed shortly after birth were, of course,
likely to be named by a foster-parent, rather than by the father or mother who abandoned them. The names of older children, lost through some accident, might reasonably be expected
to carry more significance. Menander and his contemporaries,
however, having elected to work with a repertory of standard
comedy names, could scarcely employ them as crucial tokens
of recognition between siblings or between parent and child. In
Shakespeare's *Pericles*, the King knows he has found his daughter when she tells him that her mother's name was 'Thaisa,'

and that she herself is 'Marina.' But for Glycera, in Menander's *Periceiromene*, to invoke her name when she finally confronts her father would be a little like pinning her hopes of recognition on 'Jones' after being abandoned in Swansea. Far more distinctive and persuasive are the tokens originally left with her in that shady place beside the spring: the necklaces, the woven girdle, the gold headband, and the box in which they were contained.

Plautus and Terence followed their Greek originals in making the name of the recovered child, where it figures at all, merely ancillary. Sometimes, as in the *Menaechmi*, a 'wrong' name briefly delays or impedes identification. In Terence's *Andria*, the father who has already, on other grounds, joyously accepted Glycerium as 'certe meast' ('undoubtedly my own') is suddenly assailed by a doubt: 'nomen non convenit.'[16] 'Pasibula,' the alternative her lover hastily produces as the name she has often told him she had as a child, merely sweeps away the last obstacle to a recognition already, in effect, accomplished. Similarly, at the end of Plautus' *Captivi*, the revelation by the slave Stalagmus that Tyndarus, the male child he kidnapped long ago, was originally called 'Paegnium' confirms Hegio in his acceptance of his son, without being central to the discovery.

In the *Rudens* of Plautus, a play often cited as the classical harbinger of Shakespeare's final romances, the slave-girl Palaestra is restored to her father Daemones, her mother Daedalis and her rightful freeborn status only because she can describe trinkets, a tiny gold sword and an axe inscribed with her parents' names, in a casket that has been stolen from her. Her own name, although Daemones already knows and has addressed her by it, apparently provides no clue to her identity. That might have been explained on the grounds that (like 'Glycerium' in the *Andria*) it was not her parents' original choice. More probably, like 'Crateia' in the fragmentary *Misoumenos* of Menander,[17] the equivalent of Palaestra in the Greek original by Diphilus upon which Plautus built simply had a name too common for it to be able to function as a token of identity. 'Daemones' and 'Daedalis,' on the other hand, are names arrestingly out of the ordinary.[18]

Roman audiences, unlike those for whom Menander and his contemporaries wrote, must have felt that the single, Greek character names in Plautus and Terence corresponded to little or nothing in their own, ordinary experience. Nor is their knowledge of Hellenistic comedy likely to have been sufficient to allow them to identify its stock names as such. Plautus' tendency, moreover, towards the invention of highly individual, defining names, some of them contaminated by Latin, many absurd, often means that his nomenclature seems at odds not only with Greek New Comedy naming practice, but with the logic of his inherited plots. In the *Poenulus*, a comedy that has been shown to contain a number of contradictions and inconsistencies arising from an imperfect assimilation of its Greek original,[19] one of the indignities confronting the two stolen sisters on the day that condemns them to a future as prostitutes is specifically said to be an enforced change of names.[20] 'Adelphasium' and 'Anterastilis,' the respectable family names they are about to lose, are unusual individually, and even more so as a pair. Yet Plautus neglects their usefulness as a means of recognition. It is, as so often, the circumstances and place of loss, together with a name at one remove, in this case that of their nurse 'Giddenis,' which restores the sisters to their father Hanno. Most striking of all, perhaps, is the situation in the *Curculio*. 'Therapontigonus Platigorus,' the name of the soldier who has unwittingly purchased his own sister Planesium from a pimp, is one of Plautus' most outrageous onomastic jokes: a comic fabrication Roman not only by virtue of its Latin construction, but because Planesium's brother has *two* names, not one, as was customary at the time in all other Indo-European languages, including Greek. Yet Planesium (although she cherishes a ring given her by this very brother when she was a child) never notices his unique and unforgettable designation. 'Periphanes,' 'Cleobula,' and 'Archestrata' – the remembered names of father, mother, and nurse – remain, as their equivalents must have been in the Greek original, the only onomastic sources of enlightenment.

※ ※ ※

The recognition scene of *Twelfth Night* conforms to the usual New Comedy pattern by invoking the name of the twins' dead father – another 'Sebastian,' as we have already been told (II.1.17–18). To him Shakespeare transfers that physical singularity (the mole upon his brow) that in New Comedy had usually served to establish the identity of the missing child. 'Viola,' however, is the most potent name in the scene, as central to the discovery of its owner's true identity and kin as 'Orestes' in the *Iphigenia in Tauris*. Not until he came to write *Pericles* did Shakespeare invest the name of another 'lost' girl with such transformative, almost magical power. In *Pericles* as in *Twelfth Night*, he may have been remembering Euripides. Closer to hand, however, there lay a distinctive group of sixteenth-century English plays, part of the popular romance tradition Shakespeare was reviving in *Pericles* and its successors, in which names had played a disproportionately large part in effecting the reunion of separated husbands and wives, brothers, parents and children, or lovers and friends.

In the anonymous *Sir Clyomon and Sir Clamydes* (1570), the earliest of the group, a primitive belief in names as an essential, and potentially vulnerable, part of the self lies close to the surface. No reason is ever advanced as to just why Clyomon, son to the King of Denmark, should promise his father, before setting out on his adventures, never to reveal his name to anyone 'unlesse by force he make it to be knowen.'[21] That it is, however, a protective device, a precaution out of the same folklore tradition that produced the Lohengrin and Rumpelstiltzkin stories, is obvious. Certainly Clamydes, Clyomon's knightly rival for most of the play, who fails to guard himself in this fashion, suffers in consequence. When Clamydes comes round from the enchanted sleep into which he has been cast by the cowardly Bryan sance foy, and finds himself robbed of his shield, his clothes, and (worst of all) the serpent's head which was the price of the princess Juliana's hand, he has no option but to hope 'that her grace / Will credit give unto my words, when as I shew my cace / How they were lost.'[22] What he has not bargained on is an even more impudent theft: that of the name 'Clamydes.' Not only is Bryan sance foy under this title given an ecstatic welcome by Juliana and her father the Danish king, when the real Clamydes turns up he finds himself rejected by his lady and by the whole court as an imposter: *Clamydes.* 'How darest thou attempt to usurpe the name of me?' *Juliana.* 'You lie Sir Knight, he doth not so, gainst him you have it done.'[23] Only the revelation that Bryan is a coward – a trait incompatible with the associations 'Clamydes' has gradually acquired – can resolve the situation, in a way the Jonson of the *Epigrams* would have understood.

Juliana, at least, might have been expected to notice, particularly when the two men stood before her, that Bryan sance foy's features and voice were not those of her beloved Clamydes. She is by no means unique, however, in finding this kind of simple physical identification difficult. At the very end, Clyomon (whose parentage, and consequently identity, has finally been harmlessly deciphered, in preparation for his re-entry into a social world) examines and rejects a beautiful, anonymous lady presented to him by his mother as a suitable bride. He does so out of loyalty to Neronis, his lost love. The lady happens to be Neronis herself, but she is obliged to tell him so – 'And now let this suffice my deare, I am *Neronis* whom you see' – before he can recognize her.[24] That Clyomon earlier should have failed to know Neronis, when she was serving him in male dress as his page, was understandable, given Elizabethan theatrical conventions. (She was unable herself, at that point, to recognize her lover 'strangely disguised.') Clyomon's inability, however, to identify his beloved's undisguised voice and appearance in the final scene, his dependence upon her name to identify her for him in an unfamiliar context, seems strange. Yet it is consistent with the importance given to names throughout: an importance unrelated to their meanings, which are characteristically opaque. Something very like it, moreover, persists in a number of later romance plays, written during the last decade of the sixteenth century.

In the anonymous *Thracian Wonder* (?1599), for instance, based on a story in Warner's *Albion's England*, a young husband and wife called Radagon and Ariadne, banished by a cruel father, are shipwrecked, and washed up separately on the same coast.

They then proceed to wear out some twenty years of existence in the same pastoral community – long enough for their small son Eusebius to be lost, grow up in Africa, and become a great warrior – themselves strangely attracted to each other but, 'thinking each other dead,'[25] incapable of surmounting the psychological barrier of their respective pseudonyms.

RADAGON
Can it be possible that we should live
So long together, and not know each other?
ARIADNE
I knew Menalcas, but not Radagon.
RADAGON
I Mariana, not my beauteous wife.[26]

Heywood's *The Foure Prentises of London* (1600) traces the fortunes of the four sons of the banished Earl of Bulloigne, separated when their ship was wrecked on Goodwin Sands, and each believing himself to be the sole survivor. This conviction renders the brothers incapable of recognizing one another whenever (as frequently happens) their paths and swords cross en route to Jerusalem. Not until they finally assemble before the walls of the Holy City itself does suspicion ripen into certainty as, for the first time, they invoke each others' names:

GODFREY
I had a brother, sir, resembled you.
EUSTACE
I had a brother too resembled you.
CHARLES
The *Bullen* Duke, if ever you have heard
of such a man, had once a sonne like you.
GUY
I, and another sonne as much like you.
GODFREY
My brothers name was *Eustace*.
EUSTACE
Godfrey mine.

GUY

That Duke cal'd his sonne *Charles.*

CHARLES

    Mine cal'd his *Guy.*

GODFREY

My brother *Eustace!*

EUSTACE

    Godfrey!

CHARLES

Guy!

GUY

    And *Charles!*

ALL

Brothers![27]

'This accident,' a noble bystander confesses, 'breeds wonders in my thoughts.'

As far as Francis Beaumont was concerned, *The Four Prentises of London* as a whole bred hilarity rather than wonder. Although Beaumont does not parody the recognition scene itself in *The Knight of the Burning Pestle* (1607) – those intrusive citizens George and Nell had, after all, only one apprentice to supply – Heywood's popular extravaganza clearly fathered the ludicrous Ralph plot in that play. The Shakespeare who put together the 'very tragical mirth' of the 'Pyramus and Thisbe' interlude in *A Midsummer Night's Dream* had found earlier Elizabethan romance dramas of the type of *Sir Clyomon and Sir Clamydes* equally risible. Yet, by 1608, at roughly the same time that Beaumont, some twenty years his junior, was briskly mocking Heywood's *The Four Prentises of London*, Shakespeare seems to have felt impelled to look again at plays of this type, including, it seems likely, both *Clyomon and Clamydes* and *The Thracian Wonder* themselves.[28] The result of this scrutiny was not parody, but a rehabilitation of 'wonders' in a new, highly sophisticated comic mode of his own. In its attitude to names, quite as significantly as in other respects, this late style is distinctive.

Only in the romances are we ever told why certain characters have the given names they do. Most refer explicitly to the un-

147

happy circumstances surrounding their owner's birth. Pericles calls his child 'Marina' because 'she was born at sea' (III.3.13), in a storm in which her mother, apparently, died. 'Posthumus' was bestowed upon the last of the Leonati by King Cymbeline himself, the foster-parent of an orphan whose own father, Sicilius Leonatus, died before his son's birth, and his mother as a result of it. Perdita is so named by Hermione 'for the babe is counted lost forever' (III.3.32–3). Miranda in *The Tempest* is, like her fortunes, 'wonderful,' a source of admiration. Apart from 'Posthumus,' which he picked up from Holinshed, where it belonged to the grandfather of Brute, legendary founder of Britain, these names seem to have been coined by Shakespeare. There is no record of their previous existence. All are 'speaking,' but what they say bears upon plot rather than character, in a fashion characteristic of the late plays, directing attention away from the nature and individuality of their bearers to the story in which they are enmeshed. The name 'Viola,' when finally spoken at the end of *Twelfth Night*, had seemed to rise, anagrammatically and in terms of association, out of the total context of the comedy, but it did not depend upon its action as these later designations do.

When she is spirited away from Tharsus by pirates, Marina loses the name her father gave her. In the brothel at Mytilene, the Bawd instructs the pander to 'take the marks of her, the color of her hair, complexion, height, her age' (IV.2.57–8), and proclaim them through the city. There is no mention of the virgin's name. In subsequent scenes, Marina is addressed or referred to as 'young one,' 'peevish baggage,' 'pretty one,' 'mistress,' 'fair one,' or 'lady.' Her own name, like her parentage and past, remains unspoken, concealed (like Clyomon's) from all the other characters she meets either in the brothel or after her escape. Not even Lysimachus, or the 'lord' who suggests that they have 'a maid in Meteline' (v.1.43) who might persuade King Pericles to speak, has any name to call this maiden by. Only King Pericles' question, on board the Tyrian galley, can release 'Marina' once again into the play: 'Thy name, my most kind virgin? / Recount, I do beseech thee.' (v.1.140–1) Reiterated four times in the course of the next thirteen lines, 'Marina' continues to sound through the remainder of the scene. Supplementary names of the kind favoured by New Comedy – 'Thaisa,' the name of Marina's lost mother, or 'my good nurse Lychorida' – provide additional proof. 'Marina,' however, is the talismanic word in which identity and reunion reside: a name that says nothing about the character and nature of the girl who bears it, but in which the crucial circle of her fortunes, 'born at sea, buried at Tharsus, / And found at sea again' (v.1.196–7), is closed.

Marina is unlike Viola and Imogen in that she loses her name for a time without assuming an alias, even one as circumlocutory as Clyomon's substitute designation: 'The Knight of the Golden Shield.' Her total anonymity, like that of Helena as a nameless pilgrim to St Jaques le Grand in *All's Well That Ends Well*, is a kind of death: a nothingness from which the recovery of her name restores her. Imogen, in *Cymbeline*, does adopt a pseudonym: 'Fidele,' a witness to her own constancy contrasted with Posthumus' 'great fail.' Yet her boy's disguise, adopted at the urging of Pisanio after she learns that the husband she has raced to meet at Milford Haven has arranged her murder, is the product of despair. In the final scene, Posthumus' agonized repetition of his wife's real name – four times in less than three lines (v.5.225–7) – restores Imogen from a melancholy kind of half-life to a wholeness of existence intimately bound up with the recovery of her name.

Posthumus, too, loses his name when he returns to Britain after the 'murder' of Imogen, but he invents no substitute. It is as an anonymous peasant that he defeats Iachimo, stands beside Belarius and the two princes in the narrow lane, and as an equally nameless Roman that he impatiently awaits death in his prison cell. Like Orestes in *Iphigenia in Tauris*, it is his anonymity he is concerned to preserve, not his life. Imogen's husband, however, as the dream vision reminds us, has two names to conceal. Both of them relate to his birth, but 'Leonatus' (the 'lion-born') is a family 'sur-addition' originally bestowed upon Sicilius by Cymbeline's father King Tenantius (much as Cominius bestowed 'Coriolanus' upon Caius Martius) for valour in his wars, and extended to his sons. Its Latin construction reflects the close contact between Britain and Rome made possible by a long period of peace. (Cymbeline himself admits [III.1.69–70] to having been one of those British youths who, according to Holinshed, were 'trained and brought up among the Romans,' in order to learn the skills of war and arts of civilization.)[29] Significantly, it is by this noble family designation, rather than by 'Posthumus,' the individual name of the unhappy, orphaned child, that Iachimo inadvertently summons Imogen's husband back into existence in the final scene (v.v.201). 'Leonatus' too is the name featured in the riddle: 'When as a lion's whelp shall, to himself unknown, without seeking find, and be embrac'd by a piece of tender air ...' (v.4.138–40). The identification of the 'lion's whelp' with Leonatus – 'the fit and apt construction of thy name' (v.v.444) – is transparent. The more difficult and elliptical phrase 'to himself unknown' the soothsayer applies to Imogen herself, 'unknown to you, unsought' (451). But it is also a telling description of the young man, lavishly admired by his contemporaries as a courtier, a glass of fashion and a mould of form, who nonetheless at the beginning of the play had yet to justify his warlike sur-addition, 'Leonatus.' This Posthumus does only in Act v. As the ghosts of his two brothers point out in the dream-vision, they themselves, loyal subjects of Tenantius, 'striking in our country's cause / Fell bravely and were slain' and now, with a happier issue, 'Like hardiment Posthumus hath / To Cymbeline perform'd' (v.4.71–6). The valour displayed by the anonymous soldier, a man hitherto 'to himself unknown' in terms of his martial capabilities, establishes (paradoxically) his true possession of the family name.

Although Perdita, in *The Winter's Tale*, loses her name when she and Florizel are forced to abandon Bohemia for Sicily, her predicament is very different from that of either Marina or Posthumus-Leonatus. The name Hermione instructed Antigonus to give her child when he abandoned it on the sea-coast of Bohemia is a name of loss. Although Florizel and everyone else addresses her by it during the sixteen years of her life as a shepherd's daughter, 'Perdita' ceases to be appropriate once Leontes' daughter sets foot in her own kingdom of Sicily. At this point, it vanishes from the play. She is addressed and referred to as 'Princess,' the 'daughter of a king,' from that time forward. Initially a make-believe title, a despairing ruse, it becomes publicly true as soon as the fardel is opened. No one adduces 'Perdita' among the various recognition tokens – Hermione's mantle, her jewel, the letters of Antigonus – found within it. Spoken only once again in the play, by Paulina, the name reappears briefly only in order to be cancelled out: 'Turn, good lady, / Our Perdita is found' (v.3.120–1).

In exchanging 'Perdita' for 'Princess,' the recovered royal child loses nothing. She merely crosses over to join the ranks of those characters, many of them important, for whom Shakespeare in these late plays preferred generic over individual designations: 'Queen,' 'Old Shepherd,' 'Clown,' 'Bawd,' 'Pander,' 'Boatswain,' or 'Jailor,' not to mention a host of highly articulate but quite anonymous attendant Lords, Ladies and Knights. The 'First and Second Gentlemen' of *Cymbeline* or *The Winter's Tale* might have been carelessly distinguished in earlier comedies. (One remembers the 'Salanio'/'Salerino'/'Salerio' tangle in *The Merchant of Venice*.) They would almost certainly have enjoyed at least some individualizing title. The tragicomic form of the romances may be responsible in part for the anonymity of many of its lower-class figures, imposing upon them the namelessness associated with such humble intruders into tragic events as the Porter in *Macbeth*, the gardeners in *Richard II*, or the Apothecary in *Romeo and Juliet*. On the other hand, generic designations of this kind are typical of folk and fairy-tales, where they are by no means confined to the lower social orders. Usually anonymous themselves, the creators of such stories have always found it natural to speak of a King, a Queen, a Prince or Princess, as well as of a Woodcutter, a Soldier, or a Fisherman. They are not unaware of the existence of personal names. The Queen's servants in the Rumpelstiltzkin story, despatched across her kingdom to discover individual examples, bring them back to her by the cart-load. Yet, apart from Rumpelstiltzkin himself, every one of the characters in this story – the miller, his daughter, the king, the successful messenger, the infant prince – is anonymous. In tapping material of this kind, as he did in his late plays, Shakespeare seems to have been as sensitive to its onomastic silences as to any of its other features.

In the Rumpelstiltzkin story, naming is of no importance at all, and also the only thing that matters. Folk and fairy-tales generally, where they do bestow individual designations, select them carefully. Names tend to be cratylic, but in ways that bear upon circumstance or appearance rather than moral nature or personality. This is particularly so with the names of heroines: 'Cinderella,' 'Beauty,' 'Snow-White,' 'Goldilocks,' 'Wooden-gown,' or 'Thumbelina.' 'Marina' and 'Perdita' are really names of this kind and so, in *The Tempest*, is 'Miranda.' That is why, under the special and perilous conditions of the island, it cannot be revealed lightly. Prospero specifically enjoins his daughter not to tell Ferdinand her name (III.1.36–7). When she disobeys this command, she breaks a taboo as old as anything likely to be found in Prospero's necromantic books. Her father, who had probably foreseen her disobedience, treats it with indulgence. Yet the surrender of Miranda's name, altogether happier in its consequences than that of 'Rumpelstiltzkin' or 'Odysseus,' is like them in shifting the balance of power within a relationship. In divulging it, Miranda transfers her principal loyalty from the father who for so many years has dominated her existence to the young man only just entering it. It augurs well, however, that Ferdinand did not really need to be told this name: 'O you wonder!' he exclaims intuitively at the first sight of Miranda (I.2.427). When actually revealed in Act III, 'Miranda' merely confirms something he had already divined: 'Admir'd Miranda, / Indeed the top of admiration!' (III.1.38–9). When, at the end of Act II of *Love's Labour's Lost*, Berowne, Dumain, and Longaville stole guiltily back to Boyet to discover the name of the lady to whom each was attracted, the information left them little wiser than before about this particular Katherine, Maria, and Rosaline, and how she ought to be valued and approached. 'Miranda' is different. A name talismanic and unique, it delivers into Ferdinand's hands virtually all that needs to be known about its bearer.

Chapter Seven

In the fourth book of his *History*, Herodotus describes a land in Africa where individuals have no names:

Ten days' journey from the Garamantes is yet another hill and spring – this time the home of the Atarantes, the only people in the world, so far as our knowledge goes, to do without names. Atarantes is the collective name – but individually they have none. They curse the sun as it rises and call it by all sorts of opprobrious names, because it wastes and burns both themselves and their land. Once more at a distance of ten days' journey there is a salt-hill, a spring, and a tract of inhabited country, and adjoining it rises Mount Atlas ... The natives (who are known as the Atlantes, after the mountain) call it the Pillar of the Sky. They are said to eat no living creature, and never to dream.[1]

Herodotus makes it plain that the Atarantes, who have no personal names, and the Atlantes, who do not dream, are distinct and separate peoples. His readers, however, seem to have felt compelled from an early date to confuse them. By way of Pliny and the early Roman geographer Pomponius Mela, the notion ultimately found its way into the work of Camden. 'The savages of Mount Atlas in Barbary,' Camden noted in *Remains concerning Britain* (1605), 'were both nameless and dreamless.'[2] The conflation is understandable. To be able to dream has traditionally suggested, at least in Western civilizations, individuality: a self that cannot be obliterated even in sleep, when the light of sense goes out. A unique and sleepless 'me' goes on spawning images, ransacking a personal past, summoning up its particular terrors and desires. To be nameless, however, in the manner of the Atarantes, implies a selfhood so nebulous and frail that its nights will presumably be vacant, passed in an oblivion resembling death.

Even dogs and cats dream. They also attract names. In the modern Japanese novel *I Am a Cat*, it is one of the principal grievances of Sōseki's hero that after two years spent in the schoolmaster's household, no one has thought to give him a name. Sōseki's cat is intellectually so superior to the humans around him, whose behaviour he scathingly observes, that his inability to remedy this deficiency himself seems particularly unequal. T.S. Eliot's conviction that every domestic feline possesses, in secret, a 'Deep and inscrutable singular Name' is not one he shares. Name-giving is a human prerogative, dependent moreover upon social recognition and accord. Where these are lacking or, as in the case of Aeschylus' Helen in the *Agamemnon*, are abruptly withdrawn, anonymity is a likely consequence. In *Frankenstein*, Mary Shelley's monster can speak to the people he meets, unlike Sōseki's cat, but he too lives and dies without a name, and for the same reason: because no human being will accept or relate to him as an individual. The chief culprit here is Frankenstein himself, whose repudiation of the creature he has brought to life is nowhere clearer than in his refusal to give him a name.

'The name,' Cassirer has written, 'is what first makes man an individual. Where this verbal distinctiveness is not found, there the outlines of his personality tend also to be effaced.'[3] The namelessness of the Atarantes is reductive. Only in rare instances, however, could it be described as a tragic state. Tragedy is drawn to something different: the plight of the individual suddenly stripped, through some misfortune, of a previously existing personal name. This is what happens to Shakespeare's Coriolanus, who becomes 'a kind of nothing, titleless' (v.1.13) in his exile, to Edgar in *King Lear*, forced to shelter under the generic 'Poor Tom' and then under total anonymity because 'Edgar I nothing am' (II.3.21), or to the deposed Richard II who concludes, no longer knowing 'what name to call myself' (IV.1.259), that he must 'nothing be' (IV.1.201). The 'nothing' which overtakes these characters is not to be confused with

154

'Outis,' the cunning alias invented by Odysseus. The strategic concealment of a name, as has already been argued, is usually a winning manoeuvre, even if its temporary replacement is as nugatory as 'Outis.' Although sometimes associated in the post-classical theatre with tragic villains, the ruse is far more often connected with comedy. Enforced namelessness is another matter: a kind of death in life, essentially negative and despairing.

There are intermediate states of surrender, instances where compulsion subtly interweaves itself, at least for a time, with choice. The overwhelming majority of these (as in the cases of Rosalind and Viola, Marina, and Imogen) represent stages on the way to a comic resolution. Far more unusual, but illuminating, is the situation created by Massinger in his Caroline tragedy *Believe as You List* (1631). When Antiochus, King of the Lower Asia, emerges from twenty-three years of concealment to try and reclaim his kingdom, annexed by Rome, he finds himself locked in a mortal struggle with Flaminius, Rome's representative, over his right to possess not just lower Asia but his own personal name. It is the business of Flaminius to persuade other subject nations, and Antiochus' own people, that this man merely 'usurpe[s] the name / Of dead Antiochus,'[4] that he is a pretender – either 'an Apostata Jew' or else 'a cheatinge Greeke calld Pseudolus,' who keeps a whore in Corinth. 'Pseudolus,' a transparently 'speaking' name, was that of the eponymous hero of a comedy by Plautus, one of those clever slaves who assume a false identity in order to trick an old master and benefit his amorous son. Not even Flaminius tries very seriously to foist the title upon a man of such conspicuously noble bearing. He will be content, as he announces, if he can get his captive to confess that he was 'subornde to take on hym the name / Hee still maintaines.'[5] Antiochus is by now starving, friendless, and in chains. Paraded through the streets of Callipolis as an object of mockery, he breaks through his stoic calm only when that name is denied: 'Doe what you please. / I am in your power but still Antiochus / Kinge of the lower Asia.'[6]

The spirit behind that assertion is like the one which impelled Webster's imprisoned heroine to insist, 'I am Duchess of Malfi still,' despite all her brothers were doing to destroy that

155

identity. 'That makes your sleeps so broken,' Bosola had assured her, but the Duchess, unseduced by the dreamless world of the Atarantes, had preferred to retain her nightmares and her name. Massinger's Antiochus arrives in the final scene at a highly individual compromise. Dragged, a slave slowly perishing in the galleys, before Marcellus, Governor of Sicily, and his wife Cornelia, Antiochus is determined to be recognized by these friends of a quarter of a century ago. Doggedly, he confronts them with proof after proof of his identity, culminating in the demonstration that the ring Cornelia wears – a ring he once gave her – has a secret of which she is ignorant. The stone can be slid back to reveal, beneath it, the name 'Antiochus.' This is too much for the governor's wife. Despite the menacing presence of the Roman official, she insists upon kneeling and acknowledging the human wreck before her as the king. Antiochus, however, has obtained what he wants and, as he is grimly aware, the most that he can have. There is no point in destroying his old friends. In producing his proofs of identity, he has ironically claimed to be only what Rome would have him be: an anonymous imposter, a petty magician, the master of juggling tricks. This pretence he maintains to the end: 'For your owne sake bee still incredulous / since your faith cannot save mee.'[7] Emotionally, the scene derives most of its complexity from Antiochus' deep psychological need to have his name confirmed by another person, even if politically it gains him nothing. Like Viola and Imogen, but in a far darker finale, he must regain the designation that is rightfully his. At the same time, his magnanimity in refusing to have it declared publicly as his own invests him with something of the strength of the hero who chooses, of his own free will, to do without a name.

※   ※   ※

Suddenly to encounter (perhaps, merely to hear of) another person with one's own family and given name can be oddly unsettling. The feeling of hostility that often accompanies such a discovery may be irrational. Behind it, however, lurks a very real fear that to have one's name reduplicated amounts to having it stolen, and that the 'theft' imperils one's identity and sense of self. In certain primitive societies, where male children are regularly given the name of a deceased grandfather, or other relative, this invasion of the self by a namesake is regarded as a form of reincarnation, perpetuating the existence within a family of its dead. In an attenuated form, it also governs the practice, in some English (or more often today, American) families, of endowing the eldest son with his living father's Christian name (as with Melville's fictional 'Pierre Glendinning IV,' or Viola's brother 'Sebastian'), or of giving a new-born child the same first name as a deceased elder sibling. The latter habit, common in the Middle Ages and in the Renaissance, had fallen into disfavour by the mid-eighteenth century, probably, as has been argued, because of a growing belief in the uniqueness of the individual child,[8] but also, one may speculate, because parents and offspring alike began to feel uneasy about the ghostly twinning created by the shared name between the living child and the dead.

It is, however, with the discovery of another person possessed not only of one's name, but also of one's physical appearance, life and past that discomfort is likely to turn into nightmare. In the *Cratylus*, Socrates at one point asks his interlocutor if there would

be two things, Cratylus, and the image of Cratylus, if some god should not merely imitate your colour and form, as painters do, but should also make all the inner parts like yours, should reproduce the same flexibility and warmth, should put into them motion, life, and intellect, such as exist in you, and in short, should place beside you a duplicate of all your qualities? Would there be in such an event Cratylus and an image of Cratylus, or two Cratyluses?[9]

In the dialogue, Cratylus concedes, without for a moment thinking himself into the situation emotionally, that in the case outlined by Socrates there would indeed be 'two Cratyluses,' an admission Socrates uses to catch him in a trap. The very idea that there might be two identical Cratyluses – not merely in the manner of physical twins, but down to every detail of inner life, experience, and shared name – is one that Socrates himself regards as nonsense: a ridiculous notion advanced purely for the sake of the argument. The fact that it would be impossible to tell two such men apart interests him only as a way of demonstrating that names and things cannot be identical, because, if they were, all distinction between them would be lost. Reality could not be separated from its imitation and this, for Socrates, is absurd.

It is worth remembering here the story Aelian tells about Socrates' behaviour during Aristophanes' *Clouds*. According to Aelian, the property men made a portrait mask for the actor who played Socrates as much like the original 'as possible.'[10] Socrates was present at the Dionysia of 423 BC when this comedy lampooning him was first performed. There was an admixture of foreigners in the audience and, when they began to enquire loudly who this 'Socrates' might be, Socrates himself rose from his seat and remained standing for the remainder of the performance. It was a characteristically cool, rational, and indeed devastating thing to do. In effect, he challenged the audience to say that his double on the stage really was indistinguishable from the real Socrates, or even a passable imitation. Neither Aristophanes nor his leading actor can have been much pleased.

Stage doubles, impersonations of a real individual by an actor, rarely give pleasure to the original – whether it is Dryden, obliged to watch himself caricatured as 'Mr Bayes' in Buckingham's *The Rehearsal* (1671), or Ben Jonson, who confessed to Drummond in 1618 that the whole scurrilous, untidy Poetomachia that set so many dramatists at each other's throats around 1600 began when Marston 'represented him' on the stage.[11] Unlike Socrates, Jonson's first response was not simply to stand up, trusting the sight of the original to discredit the travesty. He resorted instead to representing Marston in plays of his own. It is difficult to know how convincing the actor who played Crispinus in Jonson's *Poetaster* (1601) was as a simulacrum of Marston, any more than it is possible to estimate now the degree of truth involved in Dekker's portrait of Jonson in *Satiromastix* (1601). There is always, however, something disconcerting about even the best-intentioned stage portrait. As Bergson recognized, caricature tends to render its subject predictable, encrusting something mechanical upon the living, and so attacking the freedom of the individual. If, as seems likely, Jonson appeared on stage in his own person as the 'Author' of the 'Apologetical Dialogue' appended to *Poetaster*, he did resort in the end to the tactics of Socrates: forcing a theatre audience that had been confronted by this time with more than one false Jonson to have a look at the real one and estimate the degree of likeness.

Someone watching a play always knows that there is a rational explanation, however disagreeable, for the appearance on stage of a parody self and, moreover, that it is an imitation and not 'real.' Doubles encountered outside the theatre, in what is supposed to be ordinary life, are altogether more frightening, for reasons analysed both by Freud and, in his essay 'The Double As Immortal Self,' by Otto Rank.[12] The *Amphitryon* of Plautus is the earliest surviving literary text from the ancient world to concern itself, not with twins, but with genuine doubles. It has also been one of the most persistently imitated. When Giraudoux staged his own adaptation in Paris, in 1929, he called it *Amphitryon 38*, in honour of what he calculated to be thirty-seven previous versions. (In fact, he had seriously underestimated the number.) In the *Amphitryon* and its multiple descendants, the hypothetical situation outlined so lightly by Socrates in the *Cratylus* is actually realized, with results that persistently threaten to overstep the bounds of comedy.

Plautus' *Amphitryon* seems, significantly, to have been the first play to make use of the term 'tragi-comedy.' In the Prologue, Mercury threatens the spectators with a tragedy and then, observing their dismay, announces that he will mix things up and call the results 'tragicomoedia.'[13] The Greek original upon which Plautus built is unknown but it must have belonged to the once-popular category of mythological travesty, a form older than New Comedy, of which the *Amphitryon* itself, at a considerable remove, is the only surviving example. The story of Alcmena, the chaste wife who spent a long night of love with Jupiter under the impression that she was embracing her husband Amphitryon, sometimes brought her within an inch of being burned alive as an adulteress, her marriage (and almost her life) irreparably destroyed. Aeschylus, Sophocles, and Euripides all wrote tragedies, now lost, on the subject. On the other hand, it was possible for Amphitryon eventually to accept divine cuckoldom and his wife's essential innocence, as he does in Plautus. Either way, an admixture of comedy and tragedy seems intrinsic to the story, stemming not merely from the presence of gods in the action, but from the mortal/immortal doubling at its centre.

Plautus, it seems likely, invented the below-stairs Sosia/Mercury parallel to the main action involving Jupiter, Amphitryon, and Alcmena. In doing so, he increased the myth's comic component. He also took advantage of the comic dramatist's prerogative when introducing a new (or previously anonymous) subordinate character, to give him or her a name. Yet, in its concentration upon the plight of a man forced to relinquish that name, and with it his entire identity, to a stranger indistinguishable from himself, it was from the start comedy of a disturbing kind. 'Sosia' was a name commonly given to slaves, and occasionally also to free men, in ancient Athens. Aristophanes used it in the *Wasps* for Bdelycleon's retainer. In the *Cratylus* Socrates points out quite accurately (for once) that it means 'saviour.' Greek New Comedy, however, where 'Sosia' formed part of the common stock of slave designations, displays no interest in this derivation nor, despite all the attention he pays to the psychological consequences of its loss, does Plautus. Sosia himself, searching for some way of both continuing to be Sosia and relinquishing his name, as commanded by his ferocious other self, never thinks to explore etymological equivalents. He appeals instead to mimologies: other names hidden within the one at issue, and comes up with 'Socius.' He might be content to be styled Amphitryon's 'associate.'[14] It is a compromise that satisfies neither Mercury, the god in Sosia's likeness, nor Sosia himself. Although a slave name ('Sosiam vocant Thebani'), 'Sosia' is how he identifies himself, and his sense of self is now inextricably bound up with the name.

At the beginning of his ordeal, Sosia flirts with a version of 'Outis,' the 'Nobody' ruse characteristic of comedy. Austin notes that Homer's Cyclops comes as close as Greek will permit to the play on 'Nobody' and 'Somebody' inherent in the English language when he complains, after his encounter with Odysseus, that 'I had always expected it would be a Somebody (*tina phota megan kai kalon*) who would come here, but it turned out to be a little Nobody (*oligos te kai outidanos*) who blinded me after overcoming me with wine.'[15] A similar quibble finds its place in the *Amphitryon*. Terrified by the threats of the unknown doorkeeper who confronts him outside his master's palace, Sosia latches on to Mercury's 'Certe enim hic nescio quis loquitur' ('Yes, of a truth somebody is talking here').[16] If, he comforts himself, it really is *nescioquem* ('somebody' but also, literally, 'I don't know who') to whose prattle in the darkness the doorkeeper objects, he himself is safe, because 'my name is Sosia, I know that for a fact' (*mihi certo nomen Sosiaest*). The certainty quickly dissolves. Although a version of the verbal strategy that saved Odysseus from the Cyclops, it does not work for Sosia, any more than it had for Aristophanes' Philocleon. Some fifty lines later, mercilessly beaten by another and stronger Sosia, informed that he has no right to his own name, Amphitryon's slave descends from comedy's *nescioquem* to the 'Nothing' of tragedy. 'Nemo' is the title he suggests when next asked 'What is your name?'

Nothingness, the enforced condition of being without any name at all is, as usual, intolerable – worse, in some respects, than anything which happens to Sosia's master Amphitryon, whose divine double infuriates him without ever pushing him this far. There is, however, one method, appropriate to tragicomedy, of dealing with it. Sosia can avoid the living death of 'nemo' by consenting to be double, accepting a compound self. Indeed, there may even be certain advantages to such a manœuvre. In Plautus, Sosia invents the formula *ego ille* ('that I') as a way of referring to his doppelgänger. It was an expedient that proved remarkably enduring, becoming the 'he/I' and 'hym/me' of Udall's *Jack Jugeler*, the 'hee mee' and 'I hee' of Heywood's *The Escapes of Jupiter* (1627) the 'autre moi-même' of

Rotrou's *Les Deux Sosies* (1636), 'ce moi' of Molière's *Amphitryon* (1668), and 'other me' of Dryden's *Amphitryon* (1690). It is even possible for Sosia to become proud of this double self which is both courageous and more intelligent than the single identity he has lived with since birth ('brave et genereux moi,' as he puts it in Molière), who can do what he has never managed alone: subdue a tiresome and nagging wife. In Dryden's version, Sosia is almost sorry when his double vanishes at the end, leaving him to cope with Bromia on the old, unequal terms.

Ben Jonson told Drummond that he had once contemplated making his own adaptation of the *Amphitryon*, but left off because he could never find two sets of actors so alike that he 'could persuade the spectators they were one.'[17] This problem Plautus, almost certainly, had been able to bypass through the use of masks. He gives every evidence, indeed, of being more concerned lest the Roman public fail to distinguish between the true Amphitryon and his divine impersonator, the real Sosia and the false, than over any difficulty in crediting the confusion between them. In a theatre without masks, the situation is very different. An audience will always, to a certain extent, be required to imagine that the two pairs of actors look more alike than, in fact, they do. This will particularly affect the Sosia/Mercury part of the play, one which depends, as the Amphitryon/Jupiter imbroglio does not, upon a series of face to face encounters between the doubles. It would be feasible, in Plautus and in most subsequent versions, for the same actor to play both Amphitryon and Jupiter until the final confrontation, when a stand-in would (briefly) be required. With Sosia/Mercury, this is impossible. The fact that, Jonson excepted, dramatists have regularly found this no impediment to adapting the play says a good deal, not only about the extent to which audiences can be made to cooperate in sustaining a theatrical illusion but, more basically, their understanding of how readily a person can be persuaded that he has seen a double, a stranger who is the mirror image of himself.

In *Jacke Jugeler*, the earliest surviving English version of Sosia's predicament, Udall might well have been expected to tone down the passage in Plautus where Sosia claims to see before him exactly what he remembers from stolen glances into a mirror: not only the same attire but 'same leg – foot – height – haircut – eyes – nose – lips – even jaw – chin – beard – neck – everything.'[18] Udall's child actors were not masked. Yet he chose not only to retain this passage, but to make it more extreme:

> I have sene my selfe a thousand times in a glasse
> But soo lyke myselfe as he is, never was.
> He hath in everye poynt my clothing, and my geare,
> My hed, my cape, my shirt, and notted heare;
> And of the same colour my yes, nose, and lypps,
> My chekes, chyne, neake, fyte, leges, and hyppes;
> Of the same stature, and hyght, and age,
> And is in every poynt Maister Boungrace page.[19]

What is remarkable about this in its new context is that Jenkin Careawaye in fact knows Jack Jugeler, the imposter before him, perfectly well. Indeed, the trick Jacke is playing on him constitutes revenge for 'a mattier that fell betwine us a late.'[20] Superficialities of costume put aside, the two are not mirror-images of each other. That Jenkin should be persuaded that they are stems entirely now from the theft of Careawaye's name, a name that indeed comes to seem increasingly inappropriate as its original owner becomes more and more worried and miserable. To this loss he returns compulsively again and again, imagining that unless it is restored, or he can somehow acquire another, he will be compelled 'soo helpe me God, / To runne about the stretes like a maisterlis doge':[21] an anonymous stray whom nobody knows.

Almost half a century later, in the sub-plot of *What You Will* (1601), Marston was making the same assumptions about what his audience would accept when he allowed the merchant Albano, returning to Venice after an absence of three months, and supposed dead, to encounter a double in the form of Francisco Soranza, a perfumer. Soranza, who happens to resemble Albano, has been suborned into impersonating him in order to prevent Albano's 'widow' from remarrying. Treated by everyone as an imposter who merely imitates Albano, the merchant comes to doubt his own existence, to the extent of bidding his double 'use my wife well: good faith, she was a kind soul and an honest woman once, I was her husband and was call'd Albano before I was drown'd, but now after my resurrection I am I know not what.'[22] As usual, the theft of his name is, for Albano, the most excruciating and perplexing part of the entire experience. If only, he reflects, his name were tangible, 'liable to sense, that I could taste or touch / or see or feel it,'[23] he might be able to control the situation. As it is, he is obliged to wait until the plot, in its own good time, restores it to him.

❊   ❊   ❊

To lose one's name is an incipiently tragic situation. To climb out of the abyss of anonymity by acquiring one, although the rarer experience of the two, is quintessentially comic. In Euripides' *Ion*, the temple servant interrogated by Creusa at Delphi, as he goes about his menial tasks at the beginning of the play, confesses sadly that he has neither parents nor a name. He is known merely as 'the slave of the god' (*Loxiou keklēmetha*).[24] It is a common, and unlovely, feature of slave-owning societies both ancient and modern that the master usually controls not only the physical life of his servant but his or her name. In the *Cratylus*, Hermogenes supports his contention that names are merely conventional by alluding to the fact that when a slave's name is changed in this way, the new title is neither more nor less correct than the old. No one in the *Cratylus* points out that the master's arbitrary power to change his slave's name signals, even more than the bondman's shackles, his enforced abandonment of independence. It does just this, of course (hence the principled refusal of many twentieth century women to surrender their own surnames in marriage), and yet it is even more dehumanizing to be forced, as prisoners often are, to answer to a number, or to grow up like Euripides' temple servant, deprived of any name at all.

This slave, however, turns out to be unusually fortunate. In the course of the play, he acquires not only a name but a royal mother, Creusa herself, and two fathers: Apollo, and Creusa's

164

husband Xuthus, ruler of Athens, made to believe that his wife's love-child by the god is the product of a youthful indiscretion of his own. The temple servant is initially reluctant to exchange his humble condition for the splendours but also the perils of Athens. Aliens, he knows, are not welcomed there. The position of Xuthus himself, a foreigner, is wholly dependent upon his marriage to a native princess, of the Erechtheid line. As Xuthus' nameless bastard, he fears he will be called 'Nobody' (*oudenon keklēsomai*), and scorned.[25] About his son's dubious lineage, Xuthus can do nothing. His anonymity, on the other hand, he proceeds to remedy at once. Xuthus decides in the course of their first encounter to call the boy 'Ion' ('going' or, equally, 'coming' forth) because he met him, as the oracle foretold, when leaving the shrine at Delphi. Like Adam in Paradise, or the *onomatourgos* whose art Socrates discusses in the *Cratylus*, Xuthus is an inspired name-giver. 'Ion,' as Hermes has already revealed in the prologue, is the very name chosen by the gods for this individual. They intend, moreover, to stamp it, by way of Ion's descendants, upon a land, a people, and a particular part of the Mediterranean.

Bernard Knox has described the *Ion* as 'a work of genius in which the theatre of Menander, almost a hundred years in the future, stands before us in firm outline.'[26] In its plot structure, its concern for the mundane details of life and the restoration of social normalcy, as well as its frequent excursions into the laughable or ridiculous, Euripides' play is 'the prototype of comedy in the modern sense of the word,' the beginning of a line extending through Menander, Plautus and Terence, Shakespeare, Molière, Etherege and Congreve, Wilde and Eliot, to end (for the moment, at least) with Orton's *What the Butler Saw* (1969). The only work, Knox argues, upon which the *Ion* itself depends, is non-dramatic. The *Iliad* had for long been the archetype for Greek tragedy. With this play, however, a dramatist reached back, apparently for the first time, to the *Odyssey*.

The *Ion* is concerned, to a degree unrivalled by any other surviving Greek tragedy, with naming and the nature of names. Euripides' play can be dated with reasonable certainly at 417 or 418 BC. The date of the *Cratylus* is still a matter of dispute. Although regarded for long as an early dialogue, it tends now to be assigned to Plato's middle period, or even his late.[27] Unlike Aristophanes and the tragic dramatist Agathon, Euripides does not appear as a character in the *Symposium*, although there is no historical reason why he should not have done. The *Ion* was certainly composed considerably before Plato set himself to relate how Cratylus and Hermogenes decided one day to involve Socrates in their disagreement about the nature of names. Yet the play sometimes reads almost like a gloss on the *Cratylus*, an extension at least of that part of it in which Socrates speculates about those far-off, mythic times when cities, tribes, and geographical regions, as well as heroes and kings, received the names by which they are still known.

By the end of the fifth century BC, 'Ion' had become too common a given name, especially among Ionians, to be of much service in identifying a foundling child. (A rhapsode from Ephesus called 'Ion' is the central and eponymous figure in another of Plato's dialogues.) It could say virtually nothing that might interest Cratylus himself about the essential nature of any man who bore it. Euripides' play exploits something different: the interest of its Athenian audience in how the name of a mythological hero, after imprinting itself upon a region and a people, might come full circle: linking individuals who, however different in other respects, at least had racial descent, or a particular geographical area in common. In the *Ion*, a name intricately bound up with the past of Athens itself makes its first appearance on earth. Because it is imposed by the gods, it belongs to that rare class of true names that Socrates praises Homer for distinguishing from the less perfect inventions of men:

SOCRATES
Do you not think [Homer] gives ... great and wonderful information about the correctness of names? For clearly the gods call things by the names that are naturally right? Do you not think so?
HERMOGENES
Of course I know that if they call things, they call them rightly. But what are these instances to which you refer?

SOCRATES

Do you know [w]hat he says about the river in Troyland which had the single combat with Hephaestus, 'whom the gods call Xanthus, but men call Scamander?'

HERMOGENES

Oh yes.

SOCRATES

Well, do you not think this is a grand thing to know, that the name of that river is rightly Xanthus, rather than Scamander?[28]

Socrates declines to comment on why 'Xanthus' (it means 'yellow') should be more 'correct' than 'Scamander' ('limping' or 'winding'), as he does with his next few Homeric examples, pausing only when he reaches 'Astyanax' and 'Scamandrius,' the two names attached, according to Homer, to Hector's young son. In this instance, there has been no divine directive. Socrates reminds Hermogenes, however, that according to Homer the *men* of Troy preferred 'Astyanax.' Men being wiser as a class than women, their choice was more likely to be the right one. 'Astyanax,' moreover, as he goes on to explain, can be supported etymologically. Homer says of Hector that 'he alone defended their city and long walls.' What more appropriate than that his son's name (a compound of 'asty' ['city'] and 'anax' ['lord'])[29] should perpetuate the father's role as 'Lord of the city?'

In Euripides, Xuthus does not know that Apollo has already decided on 'Ion.' He names more wisely than he is aware, as the *onomatourgos* often does. His own explanation for his choice (the meeting as he was 'going/coming forth' from the temple) is only part of the truthfulness of the designation. Ion himself will at the end of the day be 'going forth' from obscurity in Delphi and 'coming' to Athens where he will eventually be a king. His descendants, moreover, will in time 'go forth' from that city to colonize Asia Minor. (In later versions of the legend, Ion himself sometimes leads them out.) The name is cratylically as transparent, and appropriate to its bearer, as 'Astyanax,' or that of Ion's mother 'Creusa,' whose meaning ('ruler,' or 'queen')

167

Ion seizes upon, as Ferdinand does with 'Miranda,' at their first meeting outside the temple, even before he knows what it is: 'High birth is thine, and carriage consonant / Thereto, O lady, whosoe'er thou be.'[30] 'Ion' is unlike 'Creusa' and 'Astyanax' in that it points to a web of actions, rather than to the lineage, position or personal qualities of its bearer. This, under the circumstances, may be one of the rare examples of Apollo's tact. It suggests, however, yet another affinity with comedy, connecting Euripides' central figure not so much with the Menandrian comedy to come as with those contemporary Aristophanic protagonists – Dicaeopolis, Peisetaerus, Lysistrata, and the rest – whose names, belatedly revealed, are also firmly linked to what they do.

It is, as Genette has observed, a matter of some importance that Socrates nowhere in the *Cratylus* harks back to a time when all names were flawlessly expressive of the thing named. That names may be corrupted over the centuries, losing some crucial letter or syllable, acquiring another that obscures the original sense, he never doubts. In the age of myth, when the gods mingled more freely with men, it was only natural that the proportion of correct names should have been higher than in historic times. Socrates never posits, however, any equivalent to the Christian idea of an Adamic world, one in which *res* and *verba* were faithful and invariable mirrors of each other. The *onomatourgos*, in his view, the indispensable name-master, although occasionally (like Xuthus) divinely inspired, was from the start liable to make mistakes. The truth of names, as a result, has always been partial, and will always remain so. Sometimes transparent, sometimes a thing that can be painstakingly recovered or at least made the subject of intelligent speculation, it must be accepted, in many other instances, as non-existent: irremediably flawed.

This is exactly the situation Euripides presents in the *Ion*. Within the action of the play, Apollo, working through Xuthus, ensures that his son by Creusa will be correctly designated. There is no suggestion that whoever named Creusa (presumably her father Erechtheus) received any hint from heaven. He could not have foreseen that this younger daughter would become queen of Athens. Nonetheless, he named her appropriately and well. With Erechtheus himself, however, and with his ancestor Erichthonius, the situation clouds. In alluding to them, Euripides latches on to the chthonic element lodged in the middle of each name. To Erechtheus he attaches the epithet 'earth-swallowed,' to Erichthonius 'earth-born.' These glosses are accurate enough in terms of their life-stories. They are not, however, meanings that can be extracted from their names, the exact significance of which remains as obscure to modern commentators as it apparently was to the dramatist. 'Geleon,' 'Hopletes,' 'Aegicores,' and 'Argades,' the future names of Ion's four sons, although prophesied at the end by Athena herself, are also puzzling. By the time of Euripides, they had come to distinguish the four traditional tribes of Athens and, according to one theory, their original division into nobles, soldiers, farmers, and artisans. Yet only with 'Hopletes' ('armed men') does the derivation seem clear. 'Geleon,' for instance, might relate to *gelein* ('splendid ones'), or to *ge* ('the earth').[31] 'Argades' might be a corrupt form of 'ergades' ('workers'), or of 'Argos,' god of light. 'Aegicores' suggests goats ('aix,' 'aigos') – except that Euripides, at this point, suddenly launches out boldly for himself. He makes Athena announce that this tribe will be 'of my shield named Aegicores.'[32] As an etymology ('aigis'/'shield' and 'kore'/'maiden') this is as fanciful and far-fetched as anything Socrates himself produces in the *Cratylus*. In fact, it is not really an etymology but what Genette calls, in the special context of the *Cratylus*, an *éponymie*: the mimological uncovering (as in Socrates' ingenious linking of *sôma* with *sèma*) of another word or words, hidden within the one at issue, or suggested by it, which can be made to function as a paraphrase, or extension of the original.

Not all names will repay such treatment. Euripides treats 'Xuthus,' for instance, another murky appellation, as strictly hermogenean throughout. 'Athena,' and therefore 'Athens,' presented more of a problem. The name of the goddess, probably pre-Hellenic and notoriously indecipherable, was to spur Socrates into a particularly ingenious flight of mimological imagination.[33] Euripides, however, wanting 'Athens' to speak in the same direct way as 'Ionia,' had to compel it to do so through a cunning sleight of hand. Although 'Athena' is opaque, the goddess's other name, 'Pallas,' is not. It derives (as Socrates explains easily, before Hermogenes lands him with the far more intractable problem of 'Athena') from *pallein* ('shaking' or 'brandishing'), referring to the spear that was her principal attribute.[34] Accordingly, Euripides makes Hermes speak at the beginning of the play of 'a famous city of the Greeks,' named 'of Pallas of the Golden Spear' (*Pallados keklēmēne*).[35] Athena herself, materializing in Delphi at the end, announces that she is 'Pallas,' come from the 'land that bears my name.' Euripides seems to have relied upon his audience (assisted no doubt by their awareness of the great beacon spear wielded by the statue of Athena Promachos in the Parthenon) not to object that their city was called 'Athens,' not 'Pallene.'

It is central to Genette's reading of the *Cratylus* that Socrates' final position with regard to the means of arriving at the truth of names should be pluralist. Etymologies are often revealing. Where they fail, however, or lack imaginative resonance, *éponymies* can almost always be teased out, suggesting why the original name-giver arrived at the designation he did. The one shortcoming of *éponymies*, as Genette points out, for the philosopher of language at least, if not for the poet, is that like a bad dictionary they are infinitely regressive, each word defining itself by means of another word, which then needs, in turn, to be explained by a third, and so on without end. Socrates, he argues, saw the difficulty here, even if his interlocutors did not. Hence his abrupt introduction, midway through the dialogue, of a special class of *prota onomata*, or primary names. Supposedly irreducible, these cannot be broken down into any components other than the bare letters and syllables of which they are formed. Before these essential building blocks of language, etymologies and *éponymies* alike are meant to retreat empty-handed. The kind of analysis they exact is phonic, specifically an investigation into the kind of physical activity involved in articulating certain individual letters of the alphabet. Socrates advances three examples of a primary name, one of them mimetic of restraint, the other two of movement. They are *doun* ('restraint'), *rheon* ('motion'), and by an extraordinary coincidence, *ion*, signifying not merely 'motion' but 'flow.'[36]

As Genette observes, Socrates is by no means on firm ground in this part of his argument. The Greek letter iota, supposedly mimetic of the ability to penetrate and pass through things, does indeed control *ion*. Other words, however, continually present themselves which contain a sound that, according to Socrates' theory, they should not have, or omit one supposedly essential. As Euripides, moreover, makes plain, 'Ion' itself is most certainly a name that invites elaboration and enrichment by way of '*éponymies*.' In the Prologue, immediately after Hermes has communicated Ion's destined name to the audience, but without commenting on its significance, the boy enters. He is certainly 'coming forth,' but Euripides has him do so carrying a bow and arrows. Ion uses his weapons only to frighten birds away from the sacred precincts, but they establish him immediately as a kind of visual equivalent of his father Apollo, whose attributes these were. At this moment, 'ion' melts subtly into 'ios,' the Greek for arrow,[37] uncovering, as it does, between the two words a previously unsuspected – and creative – connection.

❧   ❧   ❧

Character names in the *Ion* are still governed in one important respect by the laws of tragedy. The *Odyssey* had helped to set Western comedy on course not only in its concern with paronomasia and significant names (almost entirely ignored in the *Iliad*) but in its insistence upon finding individual designations for humble or menial characters: the swine-herd Eumaeus, the nurse Eurycleia, even Argus, Odysseus' old dog. Just how alien this practice was to Greek tragedy emerges from the treatment of Cilissa, Orestes' old nurse in the *Choephori* of Aeschylus.[38] She is the exception that proves the rule, not only because she rambles on, with a fine disregard for tragic decorum, about princely babies wetting themselves, but because the Chorus responsible for identifying her by name immediately commits another egregious violation of tragic convention by interfering (through her) in the action. Aristophanes, on the other hand, who found it natural to name 'Xanthias,' slave to the god Dionysus in the

Frogs, and even the plaintiff and defendant dogs of the *Wasps*, was used to finding room, and names, as a matter of course for figures like Cilissa. Plautus, in the *Amphitryon*, had both Homer and Old Comedy behind him when he ranged 'Sosia,' the serving maid 'Bromia,' and 'Blepharo' the pilot, alongside such dignitaries as Jupiter, Mercury, and Amphitryon, king of Thebes. Euripides, however, while anticipating New Comedy in so many other ways, steadfastly declines in this play, just as he does with the Phyrgian slave of the *Orestes*, or the Farmer in *Electra*, to invent names. He accepts those of the myth. Where the story is silent about a designation, as it is with respect to the old family tutor who accompanies Creusa to Delphi, and almost wrecks the divine plan, so is the dramatist. Only symbolically – in Xuthus' provision of a name for the lowly temple servant who will, one day, rule Athens in his place – can the *Ion* be seen to reach out in the direction of comedy's most traditional and unwavering prerogative.

There is something singularly appropriate about the way Plato's *Cratylus*, that primal investigation of the truthful or accidental nature of names, and Euripides' *Ion*, the prototype of what was to become the great tradition of stage comedy in the West, persistently speak to each other. Never again would a particular play and Plato's dialogue come so close. Yet for thousands of years, comedy in England and Europe has continued to glance over its shoulder in the direction of the *Cratylus*, inclining sometimes towards the position of Hermogenes, sometimes towards that of Cratylus himself, according to the nature of particular theatres, dramatists and plays. New Comedy itself was to prove both adaptable and remarkably enduring:

At Melania, every time you enter the square, you find yourself caught in a dialogue: the braggart soldier and the parasite coming from a door meet the young wastrel and the prostitute; or else the miserly father from his threshold utters his final warnings to the amorous daughter and is interrupted by the foolish servant who is taking a note to the procuress. You return to Melania after years and you find the same dialogue still going on; in the meanwhile the parasite has died, and so have the procuress and the miserly father; but the braggart soldier, the amorous daughter, the foolish servant have taken their places, being replaced in their turn by the hypocrite, the confidante, the astrologer.[39]

The foundations of Melania, Italo Calvino's 'invisible city' of Comedy, are Hellenistic. The city itself, perpetually changing and renewing itself, yet always recognizably the same, is both Roman and medieval, renaissance, eighteenth century, and persistently contemporary. There are places beyond it, but it is from Melania's harbour (just off-stage, on the opposite side from her market-place) that travellers to these foreign localities have traditionally embarked. Some of them went a long way. Even Shakespeare, however, kept returning to Melania's central square. He has been followed by innumerable later dramatists, many of them less persuaded than their admirers that their comic form (as opposed to what they did with it) ought to be regarded as genuinely innovatory and new. 'My stories,' as Shaw explained in his preface to *Three Plays for Puritans*, 'are the old stories; my characters are the familiar harlequin and columbine, clown and pantaloon': the immemorial *commedia dell'arte* cast.[40]

It is one of the characteristics of the dialogue in Melania, as imagined by Calvino, that the participants have no names. To discover these is the business of the dramatist. And he has usually insisted that names are linked somehow with human personality and action. They do not need to speak cratylically in order to fulfil that function, although in practice most of them have been at the least mimologically true. This is partly because comedy, that most urban and social of literary forms, is naturally drawn to and nourished by particularities. Folk and fairy tales are another matter. Anonymity, a phenomenon common to them, contributes to their timelessness and universality, allowing them to flow with little alteration across the boundaries of different nations, languages, and historical periods. Comic dramatists, on the other hand, travellers to Calvino's invisible city of Melania, have almost always found as they stand in the public square listening to the dialogue, that to understand these people and exactly what they are saying on this particular occasion, is also to divine what they ought to be called, and to single them out by those names.

EPILOGUE

In 1694, Lawrence Echard prefaced his edition of *Terence's Comedies: Made English* with some observations on the deficiencies of English comedy generally in comparison with that of the ancient world. One 'great Fault,' he remarked,

common to many of our Plays is, that an Actor's name, Quality or Business is scarce ever known till a good while after his appearance; which must needs make the Audience at a great Loss, and the Play hard to be understood, forcing 'em to carry Books with 'em to the Play-house to know who comes in, and who goes out.

The Ancients were guilty of none of these Absurdities, and more especially our Author.[1]

Echard conveniently forgets about the Old Comedy of Athens in making this claim. Spectators in the theatre of Aristophanes had often had to wait a long time before learning the name of a major character. Nor were they able to 'carry Books with 'em' in order to identify Dicaeopolis or Peisetaerus – and, given the absence of speech prefixes in early dramatic texts, would have been little enlightened if they had. It is just possible that, on occasion, they complained. A tantalizing fragment from the parabasis of a lost comedy by Cratinus, one of Aristophanes' contemporaries, seems to allude to some episode in which a member of the audience interrupted the performance to ask 'Who are you?,' forcing the character concerned into a witty, impromptu reply: 'I'm out for the quip and the tag, a Euripidaristophaniser am I.'[2] Both Terence and Plautus, on the other hand, do habitually name characters within one line of their first entry, a practice they inherited, along with so much else, from their Greek New Comedy originals. It has been calculated that of the two hundred and forty-two named parts in Plautus and Terence, only twenty-one fail to be identified within one hundred lines of appearing. None of the twenty-one is a cratylic name.[3]

Midway through the eighteenth century, the desire of theatre audiences to be apprised in advance of the names, not only of performers but of the characters they played, preferably in order of appearance, began to be gratified in the form of bills posted outside the theatre. Even new, unpublished plays were forced now to give up their names as a matter of course before a single line had been spoken. The next step, taken in the latter half of the nineteenth century, was to make available inside the auditorium itself those cast-lists which, in our own theatre, playgoers can be seen scanning intently in the last moments before the house lights dim. Not even Shaw could dispossess audiences of what they had come by his time to regard as their right. It was only in the printed texts of his comedies that he had complete control over the release of names. This he exercised by refusing to include lists of dramatis personae, as well as by his frequent use of generic designations in speech prefixes and stage directions up to the point – often very late in the play – at which the name of a character is actually introduced in the dialogue:

TALLBOYS
What is your name?
THE RIDER
Meek, sir,
TALLBOYS
[with disgust] What!
THE RIDER
Meek sir. M, double e, k.
The colonel looks at him with loathing, and tears open the letter. There is a painful silence while he puzzles over it.
TALLBOYS
In dialect. Send the interpreter to me.

It's of no consequence, sir. It was only to impress the headman.[4]

The printed text, paradoxically, has become the last refuge of what, for centuries, was a performance phenomenon usually obliterated or obscured in the play as read.

It was one of the boasts of the editors of the Beaumont and Fletcher Second Folio (1679) that they had not only added seventeen plays to the thirty-eight in the First Folio of 1647, but that 'whereas in several of the Plays there were wanting the Names of the Persons presented therein, in this Edition you have them all prefixed, with their Qualities, which will be a great ease to the Reader.' In fact, five plays in the collection lack any list of 'the Persons Represented,' and by no means all the lists that do appear are annotated. About half the plays, however, append underneath 'The Persons Represented' the names of those 'principal actors' (usually between six and eight) among the King's Men who had performed in them before the Restoration. No attempt is made in the Second Folio to combine the two lists, matching actors' names to particular parts. Such detailed information was probably, at this date, almost impossible to reconstruct. Cast-lists and, as a result, records for individual roles, had been extremely rare in play texts before the Restoration. In 1629, three quartos issuing from three different printing houses (Massinger's *The Roman Actor*, Shirley's *The Wedding*, and Carlell's *The Deserving Favourite*) had offered the reader cast-lists – possibly, as G. E. Bentley has speculated, as the result of some kind of agreement among the dramatists concerned.[5] Not, however, until the Restoration did the habit become widespread. By 1679, cast-lists were a common feature of contemporary play texts, a reflection of the interest taken now in the personalities and lives of particular actors and (more especially) actresses, and in lines of parts.

'Books' of this latter kind were probably among those carried to the playhouse by theatre-goers concerned to spare themselves the effort of registering names as they were spoken. There must, however, have been less demand for help with recent comedies, especially if these happened to be set (as the best of them were) in contemporary London, than for revivals of those by Shakespeare or Fletcher. There are exceptions. Etherege, largely for plot reasons, does not allow the woman addressed almost obsessively as 'Widow' in *The Comical Revenge* (1664) to emerge as 'Mrs Rich' until Act v. Wycherley, in *The Plain-Dealer* (1676), rather more subtly, refuses to reveal either in his prologue ('spoken by the Plain-Dealer'), or in the dialogue, that the protagonist's name is 'Manly' until line 574 of Act II. The name, when finally released, compounds that ambiguity of response to the plain-dealer which the play has encouraged from the beginning, an ambiguity which, as Peter Holland has demonstrated, Wycherley augmented by casting Hart in the title role: an actor associated in his line of parts both with heroic virtue and the savage libertinism of Horner in *The Country Wife* (1675).[6] For the most part, however, dramatists writing in the second half of the seventeenth century were more rather than less punctilious than their predecessors about identifying characters before or shortly after their first appearance. They did not, moreover – as both Middleton and Fletcher frequently had in earlier London comedies – leave major figures unnamed.

Restoration comedy (understood here, rather liberally, as embracing all those plays written between 1660 and Farquhar's *The Beaux' Stratagem* of 1707) was like that of the preceding century and a half in England in gravitating towards hermogenean names (usually single) if the action was supposed to be taking place 'abroad,' cratylic if it unfolded in, or near, the London of its audience. (Dryden, the only major comic dramatist of the period who regularly employed both native and foreign settings, exemplifies this division clearly.) It also adopted many of its names for young, unmarried men about town from pre-Restoration (usually Caroline) comedy: 'Manly,' 'Mirabell,' 'Careless,' 'Constant,' 'Loveless,' 'Valentine,' 'Bellmour,' or the various compounds based on 'Heart' or 'Wild.' Restoration dramatists, while greatly extending this list of libertine names, seem not to have worried about their duplication, either in the past or in other, contemporary comedies. Almost invariably, such designations functioned now as surnames, as 'Mirabell' does, for instance, in Congreve's *The Way of the World* (1700), although originally, in Fletcher's *The Wild-Goose Chase* (1621), it had been the protagonist's Christian name. Even 'Valentine,' that old Elizabethan and Jacobean stand-by, could shift into surname position, as it does in Wycherley's *Love in a Wood* (1672), and Otway's *Friendship in Fashion* (1678). Young rakes are frequently supplied with Christian names as well. The principal function of these, however, in a meticulously observed social world, is to mark degrees of intimacy between individuals. Such intimacy may be merely wishful, as with the ageing Sir Oliver Cockwood's over-use of 'Frank' and 'Ned' when addressing the young blades he struggles to imitate, in Etherege's *She Would if She Could* (1668), or (as with Frank Freeman and Ned Courtall themselves, who make a more sparing use of each other's praenomen) genuine. It is not by accident that the Christian name of Mr Dorimant (both 'golden' and 'gold' lover), Etherege's aloof and secretive libertine in *The Man of Mode* (1676), is never disclosed.

In so far as Restoration comedy possess a repertory of names, more cratylic than that of Hellenistic comedy (or, for that matter, the *commedia dell'arte* nomenclature employed by the French theatre at this time) but functioning in a similar way – to alert audiences to certain basic facts about the age, quality, and general disposition of a recurring type of character – it is with these witty, young, unmarried men that it is lodged. This group of related names is all the more striking by comparison with the palpably grotesque, usually one-off designations invented for their imitators: mere pretenders to wit and fashion whose inadequacies are exposed from the start by names like 'Sparkish,' 'Brisk,' 'Flutter,' 'Tattle,' 'Foppington,' 'Witwoud,' or 'Nice.' Equally distinctive, in a quite different sense, is the nomenclature reserved for the truewits' complements in this comedy: those spirited girls whose business it is to manoeuvre the rake into wedlock despite opposition from relatives or guardians, as well as the rake's own reluctance to be tied down. To these women is assigned, in the dialogue as well as in speech prefixes, and the list of dramatis personae, a wide variety of mildly suggestive Christian names – 'Harriet,' 'Bellinda,' 'Camilla,' 'Gatty,' 'Ariana,' 'Alithea,' 'Emilia,' 'Hippolita,' or 'Sylvia' – and, usually, no surnames at all. A state of affairs normal in Shake-spearean, and indeed much earlier English comedy, these single names call attention to themselves here because they set the young women apart from everyone else in the play. Dramatists often seem to go to considerable lengths to repress, or at least minimize, the family names of their heroines. The two sisters Ariana and Gatty in *She Would if She Could* are described as 'kinswomen' of Sir Joslin Jolly and Lady Cockwood, under whose dubious surveillance they are enjoying a visit to town, but we are no wiser about their own surname than we are with Lady Brute's niece Bellinda in Vanbrugh's *The Provok'd Wife* (1697), those other Bellindas in *The Man of Mode* and Congreve's *The Old Batchelor* (1693), Foresight's niece Angelica in *Love for Love* (1695), Millamant, Lady Wishfort's niece in *The Way of the World*, and innumerable others.

Most of these heroines are active in their pursuit of the rake. Their view of marriage, however, even as they reach out for some of its advantages, is quite as disabused as his own, if kept more discreetly under wraps. That dramatists should be reluctant to give these self-possessed and intelligent young women surnames at this stage of their lives stems not from any feeling that this is an essential attribute they must owe to a husband's 'generosity' (as Ian Watt once put it, when writing about the focus on heroines' Christian names in the eighteenth century novel),[7] but rather from attitudes towards both marriage and middle age characteristic of this drama. It is axiomatic in Restoration comedy that matrimony is not a happy state, and that it is extremely difficult to grow old with grace. The cynicism of the young wits, the fears of the heroines, are amply justified by the pre-existing marriages they see around them, and by the hypocrisy and folly of almost all their elders. Surnames among the older generation, attached both to men and women, tend to be savagely cratylic: 'Wishfort,' 'Loveit,' 'Cockwood,' 'Squeamish,' 'Pinchwife,' 'Plyant,' or 'Froth.' To tarnish with names like these young people devoid as yet of such humours would be inappropriate, and possibly misleading. The rakes in these plays can, and usually do, operate without visible fathers or mothers. Young, unattached women, on the other

179

hand, require, if they are respectable, some form of family protection in London. By placing them wherever possible in the care of aunts, uncles, or vaguely defined 'kin,' rather than with their own parents, dramatists freed themselves to name chaperones as outrageously as they liked without adverse reflection on their charges. Where this is not convenient, they have to hope either that the implied 'humour' surname goes unnoticed (Alithea *Pinchwife*, in *The Country Wife*, Hippolyta *Formal* in *The Gentleman Dancing Master* [1672]) or, as with Cynthia *Plyant* in *The Double Dealer* (1693), find a way of making it carry an independent and less pejorative shade of meaning. When, from the late seventies onwards, dramatists began to turn their attention to the plight of sympathetic women (the witty heroines of the early Restoration) trapped by their own or their relatives' fault in demeaning unions, they encountered a further difficulty: that of devising surnames ('Fainall,' 'Friendall,' 'Goodvile,' 'Loveless,' 'Dunce,' or 'Brute') that both pilloried the husband and said something relevant about the woman – often deprived of a Christian name – upon whom the sour designation had, through marriage, been imposed.

❁ ❁ ❁

The moral and emotional reaction against Restoration comedy that manifested itself around the turn of the century, in the polemics of Blackmore, Jeremy Collier, and (somewhat later) Steele, brought about a radical readjustment, in the new 'sentimental' drama, of this onomastic system. Cibber's *The Lady's Last Stake* (1707), with its tearful conversion to virtue at the end of the peccant Lord and Lady 'Wronglove,' through the agency of one 'Sir Friendly Moral,' comes close to suggesting Bunyan in its nomenclature – or a return to morality drama. Certainly it raises once again the old problem of the damning cratylic name that its bearer's reform renders inapposite, a problem that had not troubled Restoration comedy because it was too tough-minded to entertain the idea of overnight transformation of personality, as opposed to the gradual deterioration of wit and self-awareness with time. The latter it had handled through the simple expedient of giving characters names appropriate to them at the time of the action, and declining to imagine them at an earlier (or later) stage.

The nomenclature of *The Lady's Last Stake* is not, however, really typical of sentimental comedy. More often, plays of this kind relegated those speaking names they chose to employ to minor characters, on the fringes of the action, reserving for their principals dignified but neutral designations designed to attract audience sympathy. Surnames, in the case of young people of both sexes, are habitually stressed – as might be expected in a drama much concerned with family (and especially paternal) power, and in no sense inclined to mock the older generation. Lack of respect for their elders was one of the qualities Steele found most repellent in the young men and women of Restoration comedy.[8] In his own play, *The Conscious Lovers* (1722), the lovers of the title can be imagined as acquiescing in paternal assumptions that Congreve, in *Love for Love*, had presented as comically outrageous: 'May'nt I do what I please? Are not you my Slave? Did not I beget you?'[9] Steele's list of characters establishes the centrality of tight, middle-class family groups dominated by the father: 'Sir John Bevil,' his son and namesake 'John Bevil Junior,' 'Mr Sealand,' his wife 'Mrs Sealand,' his unmarried sister 'Isabella,' and daughters 'Indiana' and 'Lucinda.' Indiana, Sealand's lost child by an earlier marriage, initially experiences some difficulty in recognizing the parent for whom she has been searching, owing to his change of name ('for reasons too tedious now to mention')[10] when misfortune drove him to the West Indies years before. A fortunate fit of hysterics, however, leading her to tear off a bracelet that Sealand immediately recognizes as the last token he gave his dead wife, reunites father and daughter. The situation itself, like the Standish/Lady Lurewell recognition in Farquhar's *The Constant Couple* (1699), harks back directly to classical comedy, but Steele (unlike Farquhar) has insisted, as many eighteenth-century writers in England and on the continent now did, both in theory and practice, in sentimentalizing Roman comedy, reading into a selected group of plays by Plautus and Terence the emotional qualities of their own quite alien drama of sensibility.[11]

181

In general, eighteenth-century comedy saw a shift away from cratylic in the direction of hermogenean naming. Significantly, those dramatists who, from time to time, tried to resurrect 'laughing,' as opposed to 'sentimental,' comedy along broadly Restoration lines, also tended to favour speaking names for some, at least, of their central characters – as Goldsmith does with the 'Hardcastle' family, 'Charles Marlow,' and 'Tony Lumpkin' in *She Stoops to Conquer* (1773), or Sheridan with his 'Lydia Languish,' 'Captain Absolute,' 'Mrs Malaprop,' 'Joseph Surface,' or 'Lady Sneerwell.' In *A Trip to Scarborough* (1777), his attempt to render a bowdlerized version of *The Relapse* (1696) acceptable to audiences at Drury Lane, Sheridan retained Vanbrugh's original 'Foppington,' 'Fashion,' 'Clumsy,' 'Hoyden,' and 'Loveless,' while nervously jettisoning 'Worthy' in favour of 'Townly' for a character who (while no longer allowed to 'ravish' Berinthia) could even contemplate adultery with Amanda.

Sentimentalism, however, with its need to establish rapport with stage characters, was not the only factor governing the new hermogenean bias. Farce, an increasingly popular form in the eighteenth century, was naturally drawn towards cratylic names, some of them derived distantly from the Restoration, many ludicrous in the manner perpetuated by Groucho Marx's 'Otis P. Driftwood.' This was also true of pantomime, another eighteenth-century phenomenon, which succeeded as well in popularizing some of the *commedia dell'arte* names long employed by comedy in France: 'Harlequin,' 'Columbine,' and 'Pantaloon.' It became desirable for comedy proper to distinguish itself onomastically from its rivals, especially if, as was increasingly the case, it was obliged to compete in the same program with rollicking 'after-pieces,' and other diversions of a 'low-comedy' kind. It was a competition that became more and more unequal. By the early nineteenth century, melodrama had largely displaced both comedy and tragedy on the English stage, and it was only beginning its reign. In the Victorian theatre, few new comedies were written, and not many old ones revived.[12]

When, towards the end of the nineteenth century, plays began to appear that set out with fresh determination to provoke and

disturb audiences, upsetting moral as well as emotional compla-
cencies and questioning what had become the enshrined values
of English domestic life, it was not immediately obvious, even to
their authors, that 'comedy' was the term by which they ought
to be described. Shaw, while insisting that his work generally
should be seen as an extension of the central comic tradition in
the West, nonetheless wrote only two 'comedies' (the first part
of *Man and Superman* [1901–3] and *On the Rocks* [1933]) according to his own designation, among over fifty dramas variously
labelled 'Plays' (whether 'for Puritans,' 'Pleasant,' 'Unpleasant,'
or 'Disquisitory'), 'Melodrama,' 'Fantasia,' 'Chronicle history,'
'Romance,' 'Farce,' or 'An Almost Historical Comedietta.' He
also produced a single 'Tragedy': *The Doctor's Dilemma* (1906).
On the whole, 'Play,' or no description at all (also a Shavian
practice), has come over the last hundred years to replace the
two, long-established genre terms. The disintegration and blur-
ring of old forms in the nineteenth century is partly responsible
for this. Where 'tragedy' has persisted, it has usually done so,
as in the case of Arthur Miller, as part of a conscious effort to
redefine its territory and meaning. 'Comedy' was used in a similarly defiant way by Chekhov, as a description of *The Sea-Gull*
(1896). It seems to be synonymous today, at least as far as new
work is concerned, with television sagas about the rough and
tumble of family life, or West End trivialities distantly derived
from those 'society' plays, themselves emasculated versions of
Restoration comedy, that were popular towards the end of the
nineteenth century.

The virtual disappearance of tragedy dealing with historical
or mythological subjects has meant that the giving of names is
no longer comedy's special prerogative. Nor can names that
once would have been virtual synonyms for the comic any
longer be relied upon to confine themselves to that sphere, as
Arthur Miller demonstrated when he bestowed the cratylic title 'Willy Loman' upon the protagonist in *Death of a Salesman*
(1949). As a deliberate flouting of tradition, it could be balanced,
later, by Tom Stoppard's *Rosencrantz and Guildenstern Are Dead*
(1967), a comedy of sorts wrested out of the radical readjustment of Shakespeare's tragic perspective in *Hamlet*, in which

only one name (that of 'Alfred,' the victimized players' boy) is not to be found in the original. Yet the old onomastic strategies and options remain the special province of the comedic, if not 'comedy' as it was once formally defined. In general, the prevailing bias over the last one hundred years has continued to be hermogenean. In his only comedy and best play, *The Importance of Being Earnest* (1904), Wilde transformed the position of Cratylus into a glorious joke, in the form of Gwendolen's and Cecily's conviction that happiness depends upon marriage to a man named 'Ernest.' (*Gwendolen.* 'The only really safe name is Ernest.' *Cecily.* 'I pity any poor married woman whose husband is not called Ernest.')[13] Old Mr Cardew emerges as an *onomatourgos* who got it half-right when he stumbled on the near-equivalent 'Worthing' (a form of the Restoration's 'Worthy') as the surname for a lost baby already christened 'Ernest.' On the other hand, the fact that 'Ernest' is not only the name the foundling is subsequently led to invent for himself in his role of feckless London prodigal, but misleading as a comment on his genuine character, suggests the triumph of Hermogenes. Significantly, apart from Chasuble and Miss Prism, all the other characters in Wilde's comedy have mimologically sensitive but neutral names, just as they do in T.S. Eliot's *The Confidential Clerk* (1949), although that play is a reworking of Euripides' *Ion*, and in *What the Butler Saw*, Orton's brilliant parody of a similar New Comedy formula.

Among twentieth-century dramatists, Samuel Beckett stands out both for his interest in names and for pursuing the implications of namelessness in the theatre to an extreme beyond which it would seem impossible to go. The manuscripts of his earlier plays, when he was still allowing his characters proper names, reveal a tentativeness, a need to experiment with designations in the course of writing, akin to Shakespeare's. (Estragon, for instance, in *Waiting for Godot*, seems to have begun life in Beckett's imagination as 'Lévy,' Hamm and Clov in *Endgame* [1957] as 'Guillaume' and 'James' in the dialogue, indeterminate 'A' and 'B' in speech prefixes.) Once found, however, Beckett's names have tended to attract attention to an almost unparalleled extent. *Waiting for Godot* (1955), his first completed play, immediately embroiled its London audience and reviewers in what turned out to be an irresolvable controversy over the referent of that 'Godot' who requires two acts never to appear: French bicyclist, a character in Balzac, 'godinot' (a deformed man), 'godillet' (a large shoe), or a pejorative version of 'God'? Only after a time did it become apparent that the names of the play's actual characters, 'Vladimir' and 'Estragon' (and their diminutive forms 'Didi' and 'Gogo,' with one single exception in each case the names used in the dialogue) as well as 'Pozzo' and 'Lucky,' were just as tantalizing: deliberately riddling titles taken individually, virtually inexhaustible in their mimological ramifications and overlap when combined.[14]

The play's roots in *commedia dell'arte* and exploitation of wordless, immemorial clown routines have always been as obvious as its bleakness. Beckett's extraordinarily detailed directions throughout, for the entrances and exits of Lucky and Pozzo, or the stage business involving shoes, trousers and hats, maintain authorial control over the play in performance, while also being mandatory for its realization on the page. Both the reader and, by way of the cast-list, the theatre audience are in possession of the names 'Vladimir' and 'Estragon,' 'Pozzo' and 'Lucky' from the start. Yet Beckett handles their release in the dialogue as though he were writing for a much earlier theatre, using them as a commentary on the pairing of his characters and their grasp of self. Both Vladimir and Pozzo declare their own names, with a measure of confidence, on their first appearance. The subordinate pair, Lucky and Estragon, whose sense of identity is more tenuous, never speak theirs. Pozzo is finally responsible for identifying Lucky, after the appalling inappropriateness of the designation has had ample time to become clear. Estragon, asked by Pozzo for his name, puts him off with 'Catullus' (in variant texts with 'Adam' or 'Magregor') either because he can't or doesn't want to speak it, or more probably, because he himself no longer remembers what it is. It is Vladimir, near the very end, who suddenly introduces 'Estragon,' in place of the usual, childish 'Gogo,' as he imagines the possibility of saying something significant about the day now ending: 'That with Estragon, my friend, at this place, until the fall of night, I waited for Godot.'[15]

However exiguous their hold on life, Vladimir, Pozzo, Hamm, Winnie in *Happy Days* (1961), and the solitary, eponymous figure in *Krapp's Last Tape* (1958) are all still able to name themselves and others, and to deploy the personal pronoun 'I.' In Beckett's later dramatic work (shadowing the progress of his novels through such titles as *Murphy*, *Watt*, or *Malone Dies*, to *The Unnameable*), the 'A' and 'B' of the earlier play drafts have tended to perpetuate themselves, moving forward into the finished version, where they can be varied to 'W' and 'M,' 'V' and 'F,' 'Opener,' 'Speaker,' or 'Mouth.' Beckett has, with time, increasingly refused to endow his characters with the individuality and integrated self that has always, in some sense, been implied by a name. In extreme cases, such as *Not I* (1972), even the first person singular becomes an impossibility. It seems extraordinary that Beckett at the end of the twentieth century should (in effect) be reinventing, from a position of extreme sophistication, the primitive name taboo. He is also, of course, resurrecting that 'A' and 'B' to which Medwall had nervously resorted in *Fulgens and Lucres* (1497), the first surviving English secular comedy, written at a time when the dramatist's right to name characters not present in his source was still uncertain. Beckett's uncertainty, metaphysical rather than artistic, an end (as it is likely to seem) rather than a beginning, is very different from Medwall's. What it reveals, however, across the gap of some four hundred years, is how fundamental within the entire Western comic tradition, from Aristophanes onwards, the dramatist's role as name-giver has been, and how drastic the decision, for someone as onomastically sensitive and aware as Beckett, that in his case it is a function no longer possible to fulfil.

NOTES

Introduction (pp 3–15)

In the following notes Loeb refers to the volumes of the Loeb Classical Library, EETS to the Early English Text Society.

1 'The Naming of Cats' *Old Possum's Book of Practical Cats* (London 1939) 1–2

2 Richard Cavendish *The Black Arts* (London 1967) 44. I am indebted to Mr C.L. Whitby, whose MA dissertation 'Character Names in the Comedies of Shakespeare' (The Shakespeare Institute, Birmingham University 1975) originally drew my attention to this passage.

3 Alfred Einstein *Mozart: His Character, His Work* trans Arthur Mendel and Nathan Bruder (London 1971) 96

4 Anthony G. Petti 'Beasts and Politics in Elizabethan Literature' *Essays and Studies* (1963) 68–90 at 77–8

5 *Tristes Tropiques* trans John and Doreen Weightman (London 1973) 278–9, 296–7

6 Jacques Derrida *De la Grammatologie* (Paris 1967) 161–78

7 *Cratylus* 397d, 402e, ed and trans H.N. Fowler, in Loeb *Plato* vol 4 (London 1927) 53, 71

8 Ibid 401e, 411b, 399, 396d, trans Fowler 67, 97, 59, 49

9 Ibid 408, 408b, trans Fowler 85, 87

10 For an account of some of these attempts, in particular the compromise worked out by Ammonius, see M.A. Screech *Rabelais* (London 1979) 377–97, and R. Howard Bloch *Etymologies and Genealogies: A Literary Anthropology of the French Middle Ages* (Chicago 1983) 1–63. Bloch, whose book appeared in the same year as my Alexander

Lectures, also uses Lévi-Strauss and Derrida as a starting point, but for a different purpose.

11 Ernst Robert Curtius *European Literature and the Latin Middle Ages* trans Willard R. Trask (London 1953) 496

12 *Isidore de Séville, Étymologies, Livre XII: Des Animaux* chap 2, ed and trans Jacques André (Paris 1986) 120–1

13 Among recent studies, see especially: Norman Kretzmann 'Plato on the Correctness of Names' *American Philosophical Quarterly* 8 (1971) 126–38; Gail Fine 'Plato on Naming' *The Philosophical Quarterly* 27 (1977) 289–301; Julia Annas 'Knowledge and Language: The *Theatetus* and the *Cratylus*' and Bernard Williams 'Cratylus' Theory of Names and Its Refutation,' both in *Language and Logos: Studies in Ancient Greek Philosophy Presented to G.E.L. Owen* ed Malcolm Schofield and Martha C. Nussbaum (Cambridge 1982) 95–114 and 83–95; Mary Mackenzie 'Putting the *Cratylus* in Its Place' *Classical Quarterly* 36 (1986) 124–50.

14 *The Concept of a Person and Other Essays* (London 1963) 133

15 *Mimologiques: Voyage en Cratylie* (Paris 1976) 374

16 Ibid 426

Chapter One (pp 16–34)

1 *Symposium* 223, ed and trans W.R.M. Lamb, Loeb *Plato* vol 3 (London 1925) 245

2 Antiphanes 'Poesis' (fr 191K), quoted by Athenaeus, in *The Deipnosophists* 222b, ed and trans Charles Burton Gulick, Loeb *Athenaeus* vol 3 (London 1929) 2–5

3 Charles Segal *Tragedy and Civilization: An Interpretation of Sophocles* Martin Classical Lectures 26 (Cambridge, Mass 1981) 207–48

4 *Agamemnon* ll 681–8, ed and trans Herbert Weir Smyth, Loeb *Aeschylus* vol 2 (London 1983) 59–61. Hugh Lloyd-Jones, in the commentary to his translation of the play (London 1970) 54, notes that 'the name "Helen" is treated here as though the first part were connected with the root "hele," meaning "kill," or "destroy."' See Simon Goldhill *Reading Greek Tragedy* (Cambridge 1986) 29.

5 This point is made by Alan H. Sommerstein in the commentary to his edition of *Peace* (Warminster 1985) 136. I am in general much indebted to Sommerstein's collected edition of Aristophanes (still

at this date in progress) for enlightenment about proper names in the comedies.

6 The *Birds* ll 65, 68, ed and trans Alan H. Sommerstein (Warminster 1987) 23

7 *Ibid* ll 280–4, trans Sommerstein 47

8 The *Acharnians* l 1071, ed and trans Alan H. Sommerstein (Warminster 1980) 141

9 Lowell Edmunds 'Aristophanes' *Acharnians*,' in *Aristophanes: Essays in Interpretation* ed Jeffrey Henderson, Yale Classical Studies vol 26 (Cambridge 1980) 1–36, at 20

10 Satyrus 'Life of Euripides' *Oxyrhyncus Papyri* 9 (London 1912) n 1176

11 For Menandrian naming, see the invaluable work of A.W. Gomme and F.H. Sandbach *Menander: A Commentary* (Oxford 1973), and T.B.L. Webster *An Introduction to Menander* (Manchester 1974) 94–9

12 *Poetics* 1451b, ed and trans W. Hamilton Fyfe, Loeb *Aristotle* vol 23 (London 1926) 34–5

13 A.S. Gratwick 'Drama,' in *Latin Literature* ed E.J. Kenney and W.V. Clausen, The Cambridge History of Classical Literature 2 (Cambridge 1982) 104

14 E.W. Handley *Menander and Plautus: A Study in Comparison* (London 1968) 9

15 *The Persian* ll 706–8, ed and trans Paul Nixon, Loeb *Plautus* vol 3 (London 1933) 502

16 B.J. Ullman 'Proper Names in Plautus, Terence and Menander' *Classical Philology* 11 (1916) 62–3

Chapter Two (pp 35–59)

1 *Ludus Coventriae* ll 102–8, ed K.S. Block, EETS extra series 120 (London 1922 [for 1917]; rpt 1960), 19. These plays, no longer believed to have been associated with Coventry, are now generally known as the 'N-Town' cycle.

2 See for instance: 'Lucifer' ll 101, 144–5, in *The Chester Mystery Cycle* ed R.M. Lumiansky and David Mills, EETS supplementary series 3 (Oxford 1974) 5, 7; 'The Creation' ll 82–4, in *The Towneley Plays* ed George England and Alfred W. Pollard, EETS extra series 71 (Oxford 1897; rpt 1952) 3; 'The Fall of Lucifer' ll 77–8, in *Ludus Coventriae* ed

Block 19; 'The Fall of the Angels' ll 50–2, 82–4, in *The York Plays* ed Richard Beadle, York Medieval Texts, second series (London 1982) 50, 51.

3 'Lucifer' ll 126–7, in *The Chester Mystery Cycle* ed Lumiansky and Mills 6; 'The Fall of the Angels' ll 100–1, *The York Plays* ed Beadle 52

4 'The Salutation and Conception' ll 219–20, in *Ludus Coventriae* ed Block 104

5 'Dream of Pilate's Wife' ll 13–16, in *The York Plays* 254

6 *The Creacion of the World* ll 400–12, in *The Creacion of the World: A Critical Edition and Translation* ed Paula Neuss, Garland Medieval Texts 3 (New York and London 1983) 32–5

7 'Adam' ll 149–52, 269–72, in *The Chester Plays* ed Lumiansky and Mills 19, 24

8 'Abraham and Isaac' ll 25–8, in *The York Plays* ed Beadle 91

9 See Weldon A. Niva *Significant Character Names in English Drama to 1603* (PH D dissertation, University of Pennsylvania 1959). He points out that 'Mak' is Gaelic for 'son.'

10 Richard McKinley *Norfolk and Suffolk Surnames in the Middle Ages* English Surnames Series 2 (London 1975) 14

11 'Buffeting' l 379, in *The Towneley Plays* 240. For 'Froward' as a nickname that became a recorded surname, see Richard McKinley *The Surnames of Oxfordshire* English Surnames Series 3 (London 1977) 201.

12 'The Trial of Joseph and Mary' l 3, in *Ludus Coventriae* ed Block 124

13 Ibid ll 9–32, ed Block 123

14 Joseph Allen Bryant Jr 'The Function of *Ludus Coventriae* 14' *Journal of English and Germanic Philology* 52 (1953) 340–5

15 See J.C. Holt *What's in a Name? Family Nomenclature and the Norman Conquest* The Stenton Lecture, University of Reading (Reading 1982).

16 Charles Wareing Bardsley *Curiosities of Puritan Nomenclature* (London 1880) 4–5. Bardsley cites, among others, the surprisingly late entry, in a parish register for 1550, indicating that one 'John Barker' had three surviving sons all named 'John Barker,' and two daughters named 'Margaret Barker.'

17 See P.H. Reaney *A Dictionary of British Surnames* (London 1958; rpt 1961); Bo Seltén *Early East-Anglian Nicknames: 'Shakespeare' Names* Scripta Minora, Regiae Societatis Litterarum Lundensis (Lund 1969)

3–27, and Jan Jonsjo *Studies on Middle English Nicknames* Lund Studies in English 55 (Lund 1979).

18 P.H. Reaney *The Origin of English Surnames* (London 1967) 171–2, and his *Dictionary of British Surnames*

19 *New Custom,* in *A Select Collection of Old English Plays* ed R. Dodsley (1744); 4th ed rev W. Carew Hazlitt (London 1874–6) 3:48

20 *Like Will to Like* ll 289–90, in *Tudor Interludes* ed Peter Happé (Harmondsworth 1972) 331–2

21 *Hick Scorner* ll 558–60, in *Two Tudor Interludes* ed Ian Lancashire, The Revels Plays (Manchester 1980) 204

22 *Mankind* ll 111, 114, in *The Macro Plays* ed Mark Eccles, EETS 262 (Oxford 1969) 157. An entire leaf is missing in the manuscript between the entrance of Myscheff (l 71) and of New Gyse, Nowadays, and Nought. Thus, the lines in which Mercy unwittingly invoked them do not appear in the text as it has survived. The dialogue, however, together with Nought's insistence that they were explicitly summoned ('Yf ye say þat I lye, I xall make yow to slyther') makes the situation plain.

23 *Like Will to Like* ll 695–700, ed Happé 345

24 *The Marriage between Wit and Wisdom* ll 300–39, prepared by Trevor N.S. Lennam, Malone Society Reprints (Oxford 1966 [1971]) 13–14. My punctuation. Speech prefixes have been moved to the left of the page and some minor alterations made in lineation and spelling for ease of reading.

25 *Mankind* ll 33–4, ed Eccles 164

26 *Jacke Jugeler* ll 26, 61, in *Three Tudor Classical Interludes* ed Marie Axton, Tudor Interludes (Woodbridge 1982) 65, 66

27 *Play of the Weather* ll 135–40, prepared by T.N.S. Lennam, Malone Society Reprints (Oxford 1971 [1977]). My punctuation

28 *Mankind* ll 505–17, ed Eccles 170

29 For the identities and occupations of the people named, see the note at Eccles 222 and W.K. Smart 'Some Notes on "Mankind" ' *Modern Philology* 14 (1916–17) 48–55.

30 *Like Will to Like* ll 641–4, ed Happé 344

31 Reaney *The Origin of English Surnames* 287

32 Reaney *A Dictionary of British Surnames* xii

33 Bardsley *Curiosities of Puritan Nomenclature* 117–212

34 *Occupacioun and Ydelness,* in *Non-Cycle Plays and the Winchester Dia-*

logues ed N. Davis, Leeds Texts and Monographs, Medieval Drama Facsimiles 5 (Leeds 1979). I am grateful to Dr Richard Beadle for providing me with a transcript of this as yet unedited play.

35 *Hick Scorner* ll 159–60, ed Lancashire 170
36 William Wager *The Longer Thou Livest the More Fool Thou Art* ll 263–74, in *'The Longer Thou Livest the More Fool Thou Art' and 'Enough is as Good as a Feast'* ed R. Mark Benbow, Regents Renaissance Drama Series (London 1967) 14
37 Germain Marc'hadour 'A Name for All Seasons,' in *Essential Articles for the Study of Thomas More* ed R.S. Sylvester and G.P. Marc'hadour (Hamden, Connecticut 1977) 539–62
38 *Mucedorus* ll 68–70, 78–88, in *The Shakespeare Apocrypha* ed C.F. Tucker Brooke (Oxford 1908; rpt 1967) 109

Chapter Three (pp 60–82)

1 Henry Medwall *Fulgens and Lucres* ll 24, 195, 344–54, in *The Plays of Henry Medwall* ed Alan H. Nelson, Tudor Interludes (Woodbridge 1980) 32, 11, 75
2 Nicholas Udall *Royster Doyster* l 25, in *Tudor Plays: An Anthology of Early English Drama* ed Edmund Creeth (New York 1966) 232
3 Ibid ll 5–8, ed Creeth 313
4 Ibid ll 74–7, ed Creeth 284
5 Mr S. *Gammer Gurtons Needle* l 67, in *Tudor Plays* ed Creeth 360. I am indebted to Alison Hennegan for pointing out to me the existence of a classical beast fable involving a cat, a cock, and a mouse (*Motif-Index of Folk Literature* ed Stith-Thompson J132 6.5). A cat, a cock, and a rat are later the subject of one of La Fontaine's *Fables*.
6 I have treated the naming of characters in Jonson's plays at much greater length in *Ben Jonson, Dramatist* (Cambridge 1984).
7 *The Menaechmi of Plautus* trans William Warner (1595), in *Narrative and Dramatic Sources of Shakespeare* ed Geoffrey Bullough vol 1 (London 1975) 17
8 A.S. Gratwick 'Drama,' in *Latin Literature* ed E.J. Kenney and W.L. Clausen, The Cambridge History of Classical Literature 2 (London 1982) 104
9 Murray J. Levith *What's in Shakespeare's Names* (London 1978) 68–9

10 Ibid

11 Gratwick 'Drama' 113

12 For the first derivation, see Charles Wareing Bardsley's *Our English Surnames: Their Sources and Significations* (London nd) 124. For the second: P.H. Reaney *A Dictionary of British Surnames* (London 1958; rept 1961) 295

13 'Ode to Sir William Sidney on His Birthday,' in *Ben Jonson: Poems* ed Ian Donaldson (Oxford 1975) 116

14 'On Lucy, Countess of Bedford,' in *Ben Jonson: Poems* 40–1

15 Lord Herbert of Cherbury 'Elegy for Doctor Donne,' in *Minor Poems of the Seventeenth Century* ed R.G. Howarth (1931; rev ed, London 1953) 41

16 'To the Immortal Memory and Friendship of That Noble Pair, Sir Lucius Cary and Sir H. Morison,' in *Ben Jonson: Poems* 238

17 'The Most Noble William, Earl of Pembroke ...' Dedication to *Epigrams*, in *Ben Jonson: Poems* 5–6

18 *Love's Triumph through Callipolis* ll 192–6, in *Ben Jonson: The Complete Masques* ed Stephen Orgel, the Yale Ben Jonson (New Haven 1969) 461

19 *The Haddington Masque* ll 20–1, in *Ben Jonson: The Complete Masques* 108

20 D.J. Gordon '*Hymenaei*: Ben Jonson's Masque of Union' *Journal of the Warburg and Courtauld Institutes* 8 (1945) 107–45

21 'To Sir Robert Wroth,' in *Ben Jonson: Poems* 91–2

22 See Orgel's 'Note on the Identity of the Gypsies' (with its reference to material in the earlier Herford and Simpson edition of Jonson masques), in *Ben Jonson: The Complete Masques* 495.

23 *The Gypsies Metamorphosed* l 318, in *Ben Jonson: The Complete Masques* 330

24 George E. Duckworth 'The Unnamed Characters in the Plays of Plautus' *Classical Philology* 33 (1938) 267–282

25 William Power 'Middleton's Way with Names' *Notes and Queries* 205 (1960) 26–9, 56–60

26 *The Phoenix*, in *The Works of Thomas Middleton* ed A.H. Bullen, vol 1 (London 1885) 184

27 I am grateful to Dr Roger Holdsworth for allowing me to read part of the section on names from his work on Middleton in progress.

Chapter Four (83–105)

1 Gary Taylor 'The Fortunes of Oldcastle' *Shakespeare Survey* 38 (1985) 93–9. I cannot, however, agree with Dr Taylor that Shakespeare himself may have deliberately set out to lampoon Oldcastle.

2 'The Scene Interloping' 1 2, *A Tale of a Tub* in *Ben Jonson* ed C.H. Herford and Percy and Evelyn Simpson vol 3 (Oxford 1927) 63

3 C.L. Whitby 'Character-Names in the Comedies of Shakespeare' (MA dissertation, The Shakespeare Institute, Birmingham University 1975) 47

4 See Stanley Wells and Gary Taylor *William Shakespeare: A Textual Companion* (Oxford 1987) 271.

5 W.W. Greg *The Shakespeare First Folio: Its Bibliographical and Textual History* (Oxford 1955) 354–5. Greg cites Dr Johnson on the 'Peter'/'Thomas' confusion, and also points to the number of names, but mute characters who appear or are mentioned in this play: 'Flavius,' 'Valencius,' 'Rowland,' 'Crassus,' and 'gentle Varrius.'

6 See the facsimile of this portion of the manuscript in Wells and Taylor *William Shakespeare: A Textual Companion* 11, and the complete transcript 463–7.

7 Edith Wharton *A Backward Glance* (1934; rpt London 1972) 249

8 *The Complete Notebooks of Henry James* ed Leon Edel and Lyall H. Powers (New York and Oxford 1987) 74

9 Ibid 76

10 *Autobiography: The Middle Years* ed F.W. Dupee (London 1956) 578–9

11 Harry Stone *Dickens' Working Notes for His Novels* (Chicago 1987) xx–xxii

12 George Bernard Shaw, from a letter to *The New York Times* of 2 June 1912, quoted in Charles E. Berst *Bernard Shaw and the Art of Drama* (Chicago 1973) xv

13 Wells and Taylor *William Shakespeare: A Textual Companion* 501–2

14 *The Dramatic Works in the Beaumont and Fletcher Canon* gen ed Fredson Bowers, vol 3 (Cambridge 1976) 119–20

15 For a discussion of 'Viola,' see chapter 6 pp 137–9. The belated release by Menenius, at v.4.52, of 'Volumnia,' in a play much concerned with namelessness and naming, marks the triumphal return to Rome of a woman who has finally put the interests of the whole city before her loyalty to her son, and her own patrician

class. 'Mother,' 'madam,' and 'noble lady,' the earlier, generic titles identifying her with family and class, give way startlingly at the end to an individual designation. Her son Caius Martius, no longer able to use the sur-addition 'Coriolanus,' and so in his own eyes 'titleless,' tries to forge himself a new 'name a' th' fire / Of burning Rome' (v.1.14–5), and fails. To his mother, paradoxically, the play awards a personal name only as she enters the city she has saved from destruction at his hands.

16 'Astrophil and Stella' sonnet 50, in *The Poems of Sir Philip Sidney* ed William A. Ringler, Jr (Oxford 1962) 190

Chapter Five (pp 106–30)

1 'Of Glory,' in *Montaigne: Essays* trans John Florio, ed L.C. Harmer, Everyman's Library, 3 vols (London 1965; rpt 1980) 2:340

2 'Of Names' trans Florio 1:312. See Claude Blum 'Les *Essais* de Montaigne: Les signes, la politique, la religion,' in *Columbia Montaigne Conference Papers* ed Donald L. Frame and Mary B. McKinley (Lexington, Kentucky 1981) 10–17; Ian Maclean ' "Le pais au dela": Montaigne and Philosophical Speculation,' in *Montaigne: Essays in Memory of Richard Sayce* ed I.D. McFarlane and Ian Maclean (Oxford 1982) 106–7, 121. I am indebted to Warren Boutcher for directing me to this material.

3 'Of Names' trans Florio 1:316

4 'What's in a Name?,' in *The Sovereign Flower* (London 1958) 172. Also see the essay by Harry Levin, 'Shakespeare's Nomenclature,' in *Essays on Shakespeare* ed Gerald W. Chapman (Princeton 1965) 59–90.

5 Falstaff's monopolization of 'Hal' has been pointed out by Warren J. Macisaac, in a brief and somewhat inaccurate contribution, ' "A Commodity of Good Names" in the *Henry IV* Plays' *Shakespeare Quarterly* 29 (1978) 417–19, at 417. More generally, see Joseph Candido 'The Name of King: Hal's "Titles" in the "Henriad," ' in *Texas Studies in Language and Literature* 26 (1984) 61–73.

6 Arthur Brooke 'The Tragicall Historye of Romeus and Juliet,' in *Narrative and Dramatic Sources of Shakespeare* 1, 288

7 Textual Notes to *Romeo and Juliet*, in *The Riverside Shakespeare* gen ed G. Blakemore Evans (Boston 1974) 1098

8 Giovanni Battista Giraldi Cinthio, *Gli Hecatommithi* excerpt from the 1566 edition, trans Bullough, in *Narrative and Dramatic Sources of Shakespeare* ed Geoffrey Bullough, vol 7 (London 1973) 252

Chapter Six (pp 131–52)

1 'Rumpelstiltzkin,' in *The Blue Fairy Book* ed Andrew Lang (circa 1889; rpt New York 1965) 99

2 As Segal, for instance, does; see *Tragedy and Civilization: An Interpretation of Sophocles* Martin Classical Lectures 26 (Cambridge, Mass 1981) 212.

3 Norman Austin 'Name Magic in the *Odyssey' California Studies in Classical Antiquity* 5 (1972) 1–19, at 15

4 *The Odyssey* 9. 502–5, ed and trans A.T. Murray, Loeb *Homer* (London 1919) 1:338–9

5 Calvin S. Brown 'Odysseus and Polyphemus: The Name and the Curse' *Comparative Literature* 18 (1966) 194

6 *Cyclops* ll 689–90, ed and trans Arthur S. Way, Loeb *Euripides* vol 2 (London 1922) 508–9

7 *The Fortunate Isles* l 54, in *Ben Jonson: The Complete Masques* ed Stephen Orgel, The Yale Ben Jonson (New Haven 1969) 435

8 *Nobody and Somebody* ed John S. Farmer, Tudor Facsimile Texts (London 1911) sig B

9 *Wasps* ll 182–5, ed and trans Alan H. Sommerstein (Warminster 1983) 20–21

10 *Thesmophoriazusae* ll 619–20, ed and trans B.B. Rogers, Loeb *Aristophanes* vol 3 (London 1955) 184–5

11 *The Revenger's Tragedy* l 168, ed R.A. Foakes, The Revels Plays (London 1966) 76

12 *Iphigeneia in Taurica* l 502, ed and trans Arthur S. Way, Loeb *Euripides* vol 2 (London 1922) 318–19

13 Ibid l 779, trans Way 344–5

14 *Helen* ll 490–9, ed and trans Arthur S. Way, Loeb *Euripides* vol 1 (London 1912) 508–9

15 Ibid ll 10–15, trans Way 466–7

16 *The Lady of Andros* ll 934, 942, ed and trans John Sargeaunt, Loeb *Terence* vol 1 (London 1908) 102–3

17 See the conjectural reconstruction of the plot of this fragmentary

Menandrian comedy by A.W. Gomme and F.H. Sandbach *Menander: A Commentary* (Oxford 1973) 438–42.

18 David Konstan has a note on 'Daemones' as a name probably invented by Plautus in *Roman Comedy* (Ithaca 1983) 85.

19 A.S. Gratwick 'Drama,' in *Latin Literature* ed E.J. Kenney and W.V. Clausen, The Cambridge History of Classical Literature 2 (London 1982) 98–103

20 *Poenulus* ll 1139–40, ed and trans Paul Nixon, Loeb *Plautus* vol 4 (London 1932; rpt 1980) 112–13

21 *Clyomon and Clamydes* B1^v, prepared by W.W. Greg, Malone Society Reprints (Oxford 1913) l 191

22 Ibid D4^v, ed Greg ll 978–80

23 Ibid H4, ed Greg ll 2071–2

24 Ibid I1^v, ed Greg l 2201

25 *The Thracian Wonder*, in *The Dramatic Works of John Webster* ed William Hazlitt (London 1857) 136. This explanation is offered by the Chorus at the end of Act I.

26 Ibid 210

27 *The Foure Prentises of London*, in *The Dramatic Works of John Heywood* vol 2 (London 1874; rpt 1964) 238

28 The resemblance between the scene in which Imogen mistakes Cloten's headless body for that of Posthumus, and one in *Clyomon and Clamydes* is noted by J.C. Maxwell in his introduction to the play in the The Cambridge Shakespeare, gen ed John Dover Wilson (London 1960) xxiv–vi and by Stanley Wells in his introduction to *Cymbeline*, in *William Shakespeare: The Complete Works* (Oxford 1986) 1275. For Shakespeare's knowledge of *The Thracian Wonder*, see my edition of *Cymbeline* in The Oxford Shakespeare (forthcoming).

29 Holinshed, from *The First Volume of Chronicles* (1587), in *Narrative and Dramatic Sources of Shakespeare* ed Geoffrey Bullough vol 8 (London 1975) 44

Chapter Seven (pp 153–73)

1 *The Histories* bk 4, trans Aubrey de Selincourt, Penguin Classics (Harmondsworth 1954) 304

2 William Camden *Remains concerning Britain* ed Leslie Dunkling (Wakefield 1974) 52

3 Ernst Cassirer *Language and Myth* trans Suzanne Langer (New York 1946) 51

4 *Believe as You List* ll 99–100, 207, 208, in *The Plays and Poems of Philip Massinger* ed Philip Edwards and Colin Gibson, 5 vols (Oxford 1976) 3:331, 334, 335

5 Ibid ll 72–3, ed Edwards and Gibson 3:360

6 Ibid ll 65–7, ed Edwards and Gibson 3:374

7 Ibid ll 138–9, ed Edwards and Gibson 3:385

8 Michael Ragussis *Acts of Naming: The Family Plot in Fiction* (Oxford 1986) 6. Ragussis quotes, in this context, Lawrence Stone *The Family, Sex and Marriage in England, 1500–1800* (London 1977) 409.

9 *Cratylus* 432 b–c, ed H.N. Fowler, in Loeb *Plato* vol 4 (London 1927) 163

10 K.J. Dover 'Portrait Masks in Aristophanes,' in *Komoidotragemata: Studia Aristophanea Viri Aristophanei W.J.W. Koster in Honorem* (Amsterdam 1967) 16–28, at 27–8

11 Jonson 'Conversations with Drummond,' in *Ben Jonson* ed C.H. Herford and Percy and Evelyn Simpson vol 1 (Oxford 1925) 141

12 *Beyond Psychology* (New York 1941) 62–101

13 *Amphitryon* l 59, ed and trans Paul Nixon, Loeb *Plautus* vol 1 (London 1916; rpt 1921) 10–11

14 Ibid l 384, trans Nixon 40–1

15 Norman Austin 'Name Magic in the *Odyssey*' *California Studies in Classical Antiquity* 5 (1972) 1–19 at 16

16 *Amphitryon* ll 331–2, 383, trans Nixon 34–5, 40–1

17 'Conversations with Drummond' in *Ben Jonson* ed Herford and Simpson 144

18 *Amphritryon* ll 445–6, trans Nixon 46–7

19 *Jacke Jugeler* ll 572–9, in *Three Tudor Classical Interludes* ed Marie Axton, Tudor Interludes (Woodbridge 1982) 80

20 Ibid l 119, ed Axton 68

21 Ibid l 479, ed Axton 77

22 *What You Will* ll 1716–19, ed M.R. Woodhead, Nottingham Drama Texts (Nottingham 1980) 56

23 Ibid ll 1259–61, ed Woodhead 42

24 *Ion* l 311, ed and trans Arthur S. Way, Loeb *Euripides* vol 4 (London 1912; rpt 1980) 32

25 Ibid l 594, trans Way 64–5

26 *Word and Action: Essays on the Ancient Theater* (Baltimore 1979) 257

27 See Mary Margaret Mackenzie 'Putting the *Cratylus* in Its Place' *Classical Quarterly* 36 (1986) 124–50 for a summary of the arguments for an early or middle-period date and her own reasons for believing that the dialogue belongs, in fact, to the same late period as the *Laws*.

28 *Cratylus* 391e–392, trans Fowler 34–5

29 Ibid 392 b–e, trans Fowler 36–7

30 *Ion* ll 237–8, trans Way 24–5

31 See 'Appendix on the Names of the Tribes' in A.S. Owen's edition of the *Ion* (Bristol 1939; rpt 1987) 194–6.

32 *Ion* l 1581, trans Way 150–1. Owen 180 remarks on this etymology in the commentary to his edition.

33 *Cratylus* 406e–407c, trans Fowler 82–3

34 Ibid

35 *Ion* ll 8–9; 1054–5, trans Way 6–7, 148–9

36 *Cratylus* 421c, trans Fowler 128–9

37 This point is made by Anne Pippin Burnett, in a note to line 82 of her translation of the *Ion* Prentice-Hall Greek Drama Series (Englewood Cliffs 1970) 30.

38 There are three traditional names for Orestes' nurse: 'Laodamia' in Stesichorus and Pherecydes, 'Arsinoe' in Pindar, and Aeschylus' 'Cilissa,' indicating geographical origin. Her possession of a name of some kind is clearly pre-Aeschylean, but it is uncertain whether, in the manner of comic dramatists, he invented 'Cilissa.' See the commentary on ll 730–82 in A.F. Garvie's edition of the *Choephori* (Oxford 1986) 243–51. Also D. Bain *Masters, Servants and Orders in Greek Tragedy: A Study of Some Aspects of Dramatic Technique and Convention* (Manchester 1981) 46 n 7

39 Italo Calvino *Invisible Cities* trans William Weaver (London 1974) 64–5

40 *The Bodley Head Bernard Shaw Collected Plays with Their Prefaces* vol 2 (London 1971) 46

Epilogue (pp 174–86)

1 *Prefaces to Terence's Comedies and Plautus's Comedies* intro John Barnard, The Augustan Reprint Society 129 (Los Angeles 1968) xiii

2 *The Fragments of Attic Comedy* fr 307, ed and trans John Maxwell Edmonds (Leiden 1957) 1:129

3 David Martin Key *The Introduction of Characters by Name in Greek and Roman Comedy* (Chicago 1921)

4 *Too True to Be Good*, in Bernard Shaw *Three Plays* (London 1934) 50–1 I am indebted to Peter Holland for drawing my attention to Shaw's practice, and to Nicholas Grene for establishing that Shaw did not adopt it until the publication of *Plays Pleasant and Unpleasant* in 1898. In the earlier text of *Widowers' Houses* (1893), he had used the conventional stage directions and prefixes of the time.

5 *The Jacobean and Caroline Stage* 7 vols (Oxford 1941–68) 5:1165

6 *The Ornament of Action: Text and Performance in Restoration Comedy* (Cambridge 1979) 185–6

7 'The Naming of Characters in Defoe, Richardson and Fielding' *The Review of English Studies* 25 (1949) 322–38, at 332

8 *The Spectator* no 65, Tuesday, 15 May 1711, in *'The Spectator,' by Joseph Addison, Richard Steele and Others* ed C. Gregory Smith, with an introduction by Peter Smithers, Everyman's Library, 4 vols (1907; rpt London 1961) 1:201–2

9 *Love for Love* II. 1.323–4, in *The Complete Plays of William Congreve* ed Herbert Davis, Curtain Playwrights (Chicago 1967) 244

10 *The Conscious Lovers*, in *British Dramatists From Dryden to Sheridan* ed George H. Nettleton and Arthur R. Case (Boston 1939) 470

11 Ernest Bernbaum *The Drama of Sensibility: A Sketch of the History of English Sentimental Comedy and Domestic Tragedy 1696–1780* Harvard Studies in English 3 (Gloucester, Mass 1958) 11–26

12 George Rowell *The Victorian Theatre: 1792–1914* 2nd ed (Cambridge 1978) 63

13 *The Importance of Being Earnest* ed Russell Jackson, The New Mermaids (London 1980) 24, 64

14 For a book-length study of the onomastics of the play, see Frederick Busi's *The Transformations of Godot* (Kentucky 1980).

15 *Waiting for Godot*, in *Samuel Beckett: The Complete Dramatic Works* (London 1986) 83

GENERAL INDEX

INDEX OF NAMES

210

211

212

217

The Alexander Lectures

The Alexander lectureship was founded in honour of Professor W.J. Alexander, who held the Chair of English at University College, University of Toronto, from 1889 to 1926. The Lectureship brings to the university a distinguished scholar or critic to give a course of lectures on a subject related to English literature.

1928–9
L.F. Cazamian (Sorbonne): 'Parallelism in the Recent Development of English and French Literature.' Included in *Criticism in the Making* (Macmillan 1929).

1929–30
H.W. Garrod (Oxford): 'The Study of Poetry.' Published as *The Study of Poetry* (Clarendon 1936).

1930–1
Irving Babbit (Harvard): 'Wordsworth and Modern Poetry.' Included in 'The Primitivism of Wordsworth' in *On Being Creative* (Houghton 1932).

1931–2
W.A. Craigie (Chicago): 'The Northern Element in English Literature.' Published as *The Northern Element in English Literature* (University of Toronto Press 1933).

1932–3
H.J.C. Grierson (Edinburgh): 'Sir Walter Scott.' Included in *Sir Walter Scott, Bart* (Constable 1938).

1933–4
G.G. Sedgewick (British Columbia): 'Of Irony, Especially in Drama.' Published as *Of Irony, Especially in Drama* (University of Toronto Press 1934).

1934–5
E.F. Stoll (Minnesota): 'Shakespeare's Yonge Lovers.' Published as
Shakespeare's Young Lovers (Oxford 1937).

1935–6
Franklin B. Snyder (Northwestern): 'Robert Burns.' Included in *Robert Burns,
His Reputation, and His Art* (University of Toronto Press 1936).

1936–7
D. Nichol Smith (Oxford): 'Some Observations on Eighteenth-Century
Poetry.' Published as *Some Observations on Eighteenth-Century Poetry*
(University of Toronto Press 1937).

1937–8
Carleton W. Stanley (Dalhousie): 'Matthew Arnold.' Published as *Matthew
Arnold* (University of Toronto Press 1938).

1938–9
Douglas Bush (Harvard): 'The Renaissance and English Humanism.'
Published as *The Renaissance and English Humanism* (University of Toronto
Press 1939).

1939–41
C. Cestre (Paris): 'The Visage of France.' Lectures postponed because of the
war and then cancelled.

1941–2
H.J. Davis (Smith): 'Swift and Stella.' Published as *Stella, A Gentlewoman of
the Eighteenth Century* (Macmillan 1942).

1942–3
H. Granville-Barker (New York City): 'Coriolanus.' Included in *Prefaces to
Shakespeare* volume II (Princeton 1947).

1943–4
F.P. Wilson (Smith): 'Elizabethan and Jacobean.' Published as *Elizabethan and
Jacobean* (Clarendon 1945).

1944–5
F.O. Matthiessen (Harvard): 'Henry James: The Final Phase.' Published as
Henry James, The Major Phase (Oxford 1944).

1945–6
Samuel C. Chew (Bryn Mawr): 'The Virtues Reconciled: A Comparison of Visual and Verbal Imagery.' Published as *The Virtues Reconciled, an Iconographical Study* (University of Toronto Press 1947).

1946–7
Marjorie Hope Nicholson (Columbia): 'Voyages to the Moon.' Published as *Voyages to the Moon* (Macmillan 1948).

1947–8
G.B. Harrison (Queen's): 'Shakespearean Tragedy.' Included in *Shakespeare's Tragedies* (Routledge and Kegan Paul 1951).

E.M.W. Tillyard (Cambridge): 'Shakespeare's Problem Plays.' Published as *Shakespeare's Problem Plays* (University of Toronto Press 1949).

1949–50
E.K. Brown (Chicago): 'Rhythm in the Novel.' Published as *Rhythm in the Novel* (University of Toronto Press 1950).

1950–1
Malcolm W. Wallace (Toronto): 'English Character and the English Literary Tradition.' Published as *English Character and the English Literary Tradition* (University of Toronto Press 1952).

1951–2
R.S. Crane (Chicago): 'The Languages of Criticism and the Structure of Poetry.' Published as *The Languages of Criticism and the Structure of Poetry* (University of Toronto Press 1953).

1952–3
V.S. Pritchett. Lectures not given.

1953–4
F.M. Salter (Alberta): 'Mediaeval Drama in Chester.' Published as *Mediaeval Drama in Chester* (University of Toronto Press 1955).

1954–5
Alfred Harbage (Harvard): 'Theatre for Shakespeare.' Published as *Theatre for Shakespeare* (University of Toronto Press 1955).

1955–6
Leon Edel (New York): 'Literary Biography.' Published as *Literary Biography* (University of Toronto Press 1957).

1956–7
James Sutherland (London): 'On English Prose.' Published as *On English Prose* (University of Toronto Press 1957).

1957–8
Harry Levin (Harvard): 'The Question of Hamlet.' Published as *The Question of Hamlet* (Oxford 1959).

1958–9
Bertrand H. Bronson (California): 'In Search of Chaucer.' Published as *In Search of Chaucer* (University of Toronto Press 1960).

1959–60
Geoffrey Bullough (London): 'Mirror of Minds: Changing Psychological Assumptions as Reflected in English Poetry.' Published as *Mirror of Minds: Changing Psychological Beliefs in English Poetry* (University of Toronto Press 1962).

1960–1
Cecil Bald (Chicago): 'The Poetry of John Donne.' Included in *John Donne: A Life* (Oxford 1970).

1961–2
Helen Gardner (Oxford): 'Paradise Lost.' Published as *A Reading of Paradise Lost* (Oxford 1965).

1962–3
Maynard Mack (Yale): 'The Garden and the City: The Theme of Retirement in Pope.' Published as *The Garden and the City* (University of Toronto Press 1969).

1963–4
M.H. Abrams (Cornell): 'Natural Supernaturalism: Idea and Design in Romantic Poetry.' Published as *Natural Supernaturalism* (W.H. Norton 1971).

1964–5
Herschel Baker (Harvard): 'The Race of Time: Three Lectures on Renaissance Historiography.' Published as *The Race of Time* (University of Toronto Press 1967).

1965–6
Northrop Frye (Toronto): 'Fools of Time: Studies in Shakespearean Tragedy.'
Published as *Fools of Time* (University of Toronto Press 1967).

1966–7
Frank Kermode (Bristol): 'Criticism and English Studies.'

1967–8
Francis E. Mineka (Cornell): 'The Uses of Literature, 1750–1850.'

1968–9
H.D.F. Kitto (Bristol): 'What is Distinctively Hellenic in Greek Literature?'

1969–70
W.J. Bate (Harvard): 'The Burden of the Past and the English Poet
(1660–1840).'

1970–1
J.A.W. Bennett (Cambridge): 'Chaucer at Oxford and at Cambridge.'
Published as *Chaucer at Oxford and at Cambridge* (University of Toronto Press
1974).

1971–2
Roy Daniels (British Columbia): 'Mannerism: An Inclusive Art Form.'

1972–3
Hugh Kenner (California): 'The Meaning of Rhyme.'

1973–4
Ian Watt (Stanford): 'Four Western Myths.'

1974–5
Richard Ellmann (Oxford): 'The Consciousness of Joyce.' Published as *The
Consciousness of Joyce* (Oxford 1977).

1975–6
Henry Nash Smith (Berkeley): 'Other Dimensions: Hawthorne, Melville, and
Twain.' Included in *Democracy and the Novel: Popular Resistance to Classic
American Writers* (Oxford 1978).

1976-7
Kathleen Coburn (Toronto): 'Some Perspectives on Coleridge.' Published as *Experience into Thought: Perspectives in the Coleridge Notebooks* (University of Toronto Press 1979).

1977-8
E.P. Thompson (Worcester): 'Wiiliam Blake: Tradition and Revolution 1789-93.'

1978-9
Ronald Paulson (Yale): 'The Representation of Revolution 1789-1820.' Published as *The Representation of Revolution (1789-1820)* (Yale 1983).

1979-80
David Daiches (Edinburgh): 'Literature and Gentility in Scotland.' Published as *Literature and Gentility in Scotland* (Edinburgh 1982).

1980-1
Walter J. Ong, SJ (St Louis): 'Hopkins, the Self, and God.' Published as *Hopkins, the Self, and God* (University of Toronto Press 1986).

1982
Robertson Davies (Toronto): 'The Mirror of Nature.' Published as *The Mirror of Nature* (University of Toronto Press 1983).

1983
Anne Barton (Cambridge): 'Comedy and the Naming of Parts.' Published as *The Names of Comedy* (University of Toronto Press 1990).

1984
Guy Davenport (Kentucky): 'Objects on a Table: Still Life in Literature and Painting.'

1985
Richard Altick (Ohio): 'The Victorian Sense of the Present.' To be published as *The Presence of the Present: Topical Realism in the Victorian Novel* (Ohio State University Press).

1986
Jerome J. McGann (Virginia): 'Adverse Wheels: The Truth Functions of Poetic Discourse.' Published as *Social Values and Poetic Acts* (Harvard University Press 1988).

1987
Inga-Stina Ewbank (Leeds): 'The Word and the Theatre: Strindberg, Ibsen and Shakespeare.'

1988
Christopher Ricks (Boston): 'Allusion and Inheritance 1784–1824.'

1989
John Burrow (Bristol): 'Langland's *Piers Plowman*: The Uses of Fiction.'